Popular Mechanics Complete Car Repair Manual

Simplified auto repair for the Saturday mechanic

Book Division, The Hearst Corporation,
New York, N.Y. 10019

Printed in the United States of America
ISBN 0–910990–57–3

Contents

Your engine

Chapter 1

Fighting pollution and fuel loss with a full-scale engine tune-up

Quick and half-hearted adjustments are out of the question if we are to prevent pollution, conserve fuel, and drive automobiles that give top-notch performance. A skillful fine-tuning of the engine is necessary.

THE MODERN AUTOMOBILE ENGINE is a complex machine. One system or part affects the performance of other systems and parts.

You cannot, therefore, separate the maintenance and repair of emissions-control systems from the engine tune-up. Without one, the other suffers.

Furthermore, engine tune-up, and to some extent the servicing of emissions-control systems, have a direct effect on an engine's overall fuel economy and performance. A tune-up if performed as defined in earlier days ("changing plugs, points and condenser") may fail to correct a considerable loss in fuel economy and engine power.

Engine tune-up means the fine-tune adjustment of the *entire* engine!

Since tune-up is an undertaking that involves many different tasks, we discuss it here in the order in which we feel it should be performed. You may want to devise your own procedure, which is okay as long as you do each task.

Automobile manufacturers generally suggest that an engine tune-up be performed once every 12,000 miles. We feel that conscientious auto buffs who do their own work may want to shorten this period, especially if they notice a reduction in performance and fuel economy.

Before we discuss what's involved in engine tune-up, a discussion of what you will encounter in the area of emissions-control systems is necessary. Why? Because every car has fuel and ignition systems, a battery, and all other systems and parts that are adjusted, tested or replaced during tune-up. But not every car has the same kind of

Your modern auto engine won't settle for an old-fashioned tune-up; it won't do the job

emissions-control systems. Recognizing what your car possesses will make your work easier.

Notice the use of the plural

IN REFERRING TO the systems that keep pollution under control, we've used the terms emissions-control systems. The reason for the use of the double plural is that there is more than one kind of pollutant given off by the internal-combustion automobile engine, and a car could have more than one system to control emissions.

Emissions given off by cars are hydrocarbons (HC), carbon monoxide (CO), oxides of nitrogen (NOx), and particulates. HC, CO and NOx are gases. Particulates are tiny particles of lead that are discarded from the exhaust system as the engine consumes leaded gasoline.

Pollutants that cause the most concern are HC, CO, and NOx. Systems have been developed to control them.

There is no system to control particulates. They are being reduced by reducing the amount of lead in gasoline.

By 1979, the average lead content per gallon of gas is expected to be only 0.5 gram as compared to the 2.5 grams per gallon of fully leaded fuel.

Where emissions come from

EMISSIONS COME FROM four different areas: the crankcase, gas tank, carburetor, and exhaust pipe.

Hydrocarbons are emitted from the crankcase, gas tank and carburetor. Hydrocarbons, carbon monoxide, and oxides of nitrogen are emitted from the exhaust.

At the time this book was being prepared, three systems were in common use to fight pollutants. One system controls the crankcase, another system keeps emissions from the carburetor and gas tank in check, and a third system holds down emissions from the exhaust.

All about the crankcase emission control system

POLLUTION FROM THE CRANKCASE in the form of hydrocarbon emissions has ceased to be a problem, thanks to the perfection of the crankcase-emission control system. On cars made by U.S. manufacturers, this control system takes the form (with few exceptions) of the so-called positive crankcase ventilation (PCV) system. As you'll see below, manufacturers of imported cars use different methods.

Hydrocarbons are actually vapors of unburned fuel which are pushed past piston rings into the crankcase during the combustion process. You may have heard the term "blowby." That's another name for it. Blowby gets worse as an engine gets older and rings wear.

These vapors have to have some way of escaping from the crankcase; otherwise they would condense, mix with oil and form sludge that would foul parts and ruin the engine. Before crankcase-emission controls were developed, vapors were allowed to escape through an open tube that extended from inside the crankcase to the atmosphere. These vapors were a prime contributor to the serious air-pollution problems that existed during the 1950's and 1960's.

The first positive crankcase ventilation system was introduced in California on 1961 model cars sold in that state. Because of its critical smog conditions, California has served as a testing ground for emissions-control equipment of all kinds, leading the rest of the nation by a year or two in requiring controls on new cars. Limited nationwide installation of PCV began with the 1963 models.

In 1968, it became mandatory for every new car sold in the U.S. to be equipped with a crankcase emission-control system. Since then, crankcase pollution has been declining, and today it no longer poses a threat.

How the PCV system works

THE PCV SYSTEM that has been put on new cars since 1968 is a closed system, which means that no blowby vapors can escape unless the system is damaged (Figure 1). The system draws in fresh air through the carburetor air cleaner. Air is passed down through a filter and hose to the crankcase through a cap that covers the opening in the valve cover.

In the crankcase, the fresh air mixes with and dilutes blowby gases. The diluted gases surge up through a hose, partly by means of the force of the air and partly because of engine vacuum. They pass through a vacuum-spring control device called the PCV valve, and then into the intake manifold.

In the intake manifold, blowby mixes with the incoming fuel mixture and is burned in the combustion process. Remember: blowby is hydrocarbon, which is unburned fuel vapor.

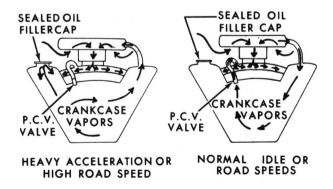

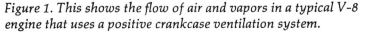

Figure 1. This shows the flow of air and vapors in a typical V-8 engine that uses a positive crankcase ventilation system.

If an excessive amount of pressure builds up in the crankcase, perhaps because of a clogged outlet hose or an inoperative PCV valve, vapors reverse their flow; they back up into the carburetor air cleaner through the cap over the valve cover and hose.

The vapors then enter the manifold through the carburetor, which disrupts the normal air:fuel ratio, resulting in rough engine performance, especially at idle. In no way could vapors escape into the atmosphere, however.

PCV systems installed on most new cars from 1961 to 1968 were open systems. Fresh air is taken in through the oil filler cap and directed to the crankcase. If pressure builds up in the crankcase, causing a reverse flow of blowby, vapors escape into the air through the oil filler cap.

The PCV valve is an important part of the system. It not only controls of the flow of diluted vapors into the intake manifold, but also acts as a safety device.

If the engine backfires, the PCV valve springs shut, which contains the flashback in the intake manifold where it does no harm. But if the valve fails and backfire occurs, unburned blowby vapors in the crankcase might ignite. There could be a crankcase explosion, which could rip the crankcase apart.

As you might imagine, periodic maintenance of the PCV system is important if good engine performance and the safety feature provided by the PCV valve are to be maintained. This maintenance should be done as part of engine tune-up.

Crankcase emission controls used on imports

MANY FOREIGN-MADE CARS use the PCV system, including Datsun, Toyota, Capri, Opel and Fiat. Others use either an *orifice* (metering) system or a *diaphragm-valve* system which is referred to as a *gulp* valve or *Smith* valve.

Imported cars employing a metering system include Cricket, Colt, Subaru and Volkswagen. Each differs a bit from the others.

For example, Cricket employs a flame trap on the valve rocker arm cover that is connected by hose to the air cleaner. Crankcase blowby passes through the flame trap and is drawn through the hose into the air cleaner where it mixes with air and enters the carburetor through the air filter.

The flame trap performs a function similar to the PCV valve, if the engine backfires, by trapping flame to prevent a crankcase explosion.

If you own a Cricket, service this crankcase-emission control system when doing an engine tune-up. Remove and wash the flame trap in solvent, and make sure that the metal pipe on the valve rocker arm cover and the hose are free of sludge.

The metering crankcase-emission control system used by Colt employs two routes from the crankcase to the cylinders. Blowby is fed by a breather hose from the front of the rocker arm cover to the intake manifold. There is also a ventilation hose from the rear of the rocker arm cover to the intake manifold.

When the engine is operating with little or no load on it, blowby is drawn from the rear of the rocker arm cover through the ventilation hose to the intake manifold. Under high-load conditions, gases from both the rear and front rocker arm covers are drawn into the intake manifold.

Service this system by checking hoses for damage, and by cleaning the steel filter located in the air-cleaner breather hose.

The sealed crankcase-emission control system used by Subaru consists of a baffle plate that's mounted on the valve rocker arm cover. Its job is to block oil mist from the combustion process. A hose brings blowby vapors to a narrow pipe in the air cleaner cover where they mix with air and enter the combustion chambers through the carburetor.

When doing an engine tune-up, service this system by inspecting the hose for damage, and by making sure that the narrow pipe at the air cleaner cover isn't clogged.

Blowby from the crankcase of a Volkswagen is drawn from the filler neck through the air cleaner into the carburetor. Make sure that the air cleaner, hose, oil filler, and rubber drain valve are kept clean.

The heart of Volvo's crankcase-emission control metering system is a fitting at the intake manifold through which blowby enters the manifold for burning. Make sure this fitting is kept clear.

Those cars that use the gulp valve include Austin Marina, BMW, Citroen, Fiat and MG. The valve is a diaphragm-equipped device that is controlled by engine vacuum to permit blowby to enter the combustion process.

All three types of crankcase emission controls need servicing at tune-up time

The valve must be serviced when engine tune-up is performed. Remove the diaphragm and spring, and inspect them for integrity. Clean out deposits clogging the orifice, and check all hoses.

Figure 2. A typical sealed fuel-evaporation emission-control system.

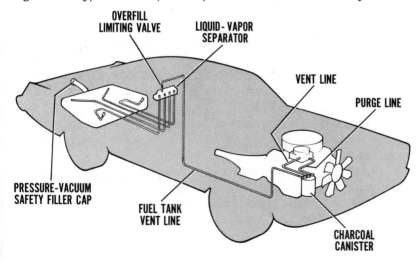

What uses which

TO GIVE YOU AN IDEA of the crankcase-emission control system your imported car possesses, we offer the following table. Keep in mind that this list is a limited one. From one model year to the next, the method employed by any one manufacturer may change.

	PCV	Metering System	Gulp Valve
Alfa Romeo		x	
Audi		x	
Austin Marina			x
BMW			x
Capri	x		
Citroen			x
Colt		x	
Cricket		x	
Datsun	x		
Fiat			x
Jaguar			x
Mazda	x		
Mercedes-Benz		x	
MG			x
Opel	x		
Peugeot	x		
Porsche		x	
Renault	x		
Saab		x	
Subaru		x	
Toyota	x		
Triumph	x		
Volkswagen		x	
Volvo		x	

Stopping hydrocarbons from fuel tank and carburetor

EVERY MODEL CAR before 1971 (1970 in California) allowed raw gasoline fumes (HC) to escape into the atmosphere from open vents in the carburetor and the gas-tank cap or gas tank. These vapors must have a means of relief—otherwise they would cause an over-rich fuel mixture in the carburetor, which would affect engine starting and performance. Vapors would also cause fuel-tank damage.

No car produced since 1971 has these open vents. Vapors are allowed to relieve themselves through closed lines to a charcoal-filled canister in the engine compartment (on some imported models, the canister is in the luggage compartment). No vapors can escape and pollute the air (Figure 2).

When the engine is started, fresh air is pulled into the canister by vacuum. Air cleanses charcoal of vapors. The diluted vapors are drawn through a purge line to the engine for burning with the fuel mixture.

Other features have been developed to eliminate the possibility of HC pollution from the fuel system. Fuel tanks have been redesigned so they can't be overfilled and spill gas. Fuel-tank caps have been sealed and form a fail-safe lock with filler necks when tightened.

The internally vented system is called different names by car manufacturers. American Motors terms it the Fuel Tank Vapor Emission Control System; Chrysler's name is Vapor Saver Evaporation Control System; Ford, Evaporation Control System; and General Motors' name is either Evaporation Control System or Evaporation Emission Control System.

Automobiles made in this country use a charcoal canister with a filter in its base. This filter should be removed when an engine tune-up is performed, and replaced if dirty.

Hoses coming to the canister from the fuel tank and carburetor, and the purge hose going from the canister to the manifold, should be examined. If clogged they should be cleaned, and if damaged they should be replaced.

Some imported cars use canisters with filters; others use canisters without filters. The same maintenance steps apply as above if your vehicle has a canister with a filter. If it uses the other type, the entire canister should be discarded, usually after 50,000 miles of service, and replaced with a new one.

Exhaust emissions hang tough

SEVERAL DIFFERENT METHODS have been developed to reduce emissions from the exhaust. Compared to this, solving the problem of pollution from the crankcase and fuel system was child's play.

What makes combatting exhaust emissions so difficult is the involvement of three separate gases that act differently. Hydrocarbons and carbon monoxide can be controlled by increasing combustion temperature. But a rise in temperature causes oxygen and nitrogen to ignite, which produces oxides of nitrogen.

NOx in the air is the main element causing photochemical or "Los Angeles" smog—an irritating, noxious gas.

Fortunately, progress has been made in the fight against exhaust emissions by drawing a delicate balance between excessive HC and CO, and excessive NOx. The first cars to possess exhaust-emissions controls were the 1968 models (1966 for cars sold in California).

Although some developments are internal so you aren't required to do anything to them during engine tune-up, it is interesting to know what they are:

• Camshafts which provide increased valve overlapping. Valve overlap is the interval when both intake and exhaust valves are open at the same time. During this period, the incoming fuel charge is diluted slightly by exhaust gases being discharged from the cylinders. This helps to control peak combustion temperatures at which NOx is produced.

• Combustion chambers which eliminate the pockets and narrow clearance spaces which cause the combustion flame to quench. Confined areas cause the flame to go out before all the fuel mixture has burned. The redesigned combustion chambers provide increased "quench" height so that the fuel mixture is burned more completely. Hence, the amount of HC is reduced.

• Intake manifolds that provide more rapid fuel vaporization during engine warm-up. More rapid vaporization permits the use of leaner fuel mixtures. This, in turn, lessens the output of carbon monoxide.

• Redesigned piston heads that reduce compression ratios so engines can operate satisfactorily on low-lead or no-lead gasoline, which has a lower octane rating. This reduces the emission of lead particulates.

In addition to these internal engine modifications, various components have been placed on the outside of engines to help control HC, CO and NOx emissions from the exhaust. Generally, two different systems to help control HC and CO have evolved. These are the air-injection system and the controlled-combustion system.

Air injection and controlled combustion have no role in the fight against NOx. NOx control devices will be discussed following our examination of HC and CO control devices.

Before examining the differences between air injection and controlled combustion, it is necessary to discuss an anti-HC and CO component now employed in almost every car. This is the thermostatically controlled air cleaner.

An air cleaner that provides cleaner starts

AMERICAN MOTORS, FORD and General Motors have used thermostatically controlled air cleaners since 1968. Chrysler adopted the device in 1971. Many imported cars also possess it.

This air cleaner obtains warm air to help a cold engine burn a lean mixture

The thermostatically controlled air cleaner reduces HC and CO levels by maintaining the minimum temperature of air entering the carburetor and mixing with gasoline at 100°F. Having the temperature of the air at this point as soon as a cold engine is started, even on the coldest day, permits calibration of the carburetor for the leanest possible fuel mixture consistent with proper engine performance. The hot air assures that a lean fuel mixture will burn.

Obviously, a lean fuel mixture (one that has less gasoline) produces less waste products (HC and CO).

For comparison, consider older engines that don't have thermostatically controlled air cleaners. The air coming into the carburetor when a cold engine is started is about the same temperature as the atmosphere. Given a lean fuel mixture using cold air, a cold engine would be difficult to start, and when it does start would stall. Less gasoline mixed with cold air has a tough time burning. That is why carburetors of cars without thermostatically controlled air cleaners are calibrated to provide richer fuel mixtures.

The thermostatically controlled air cleaner at work

LOOK INTO THE SNORKEL of the air cleaner on your car. If you see a flapper valve (it may be in the "up" position), your engine uses a thermostatically controlled air cleaner (Figure 3).

This valve is the heart of the system. Check its functioning periodically—for example, when the engine is being tuned up. Checking is a matter of observation.

The valve is controlled by a thermostat (some manufacturers call it a "sensor"). When a cold engine is started with air around the air cleaner at a temperature that is less than 100°F, the thermostat causes the flapper valve to close down. This seals off the snorkel, blocking air intake to the carburetor.

Have you checked the flapper valve in your snorkel lately? It's the heart of the system

Air needed for the fuel mixture is diverted to the carburetor from the exhaust manifold through a "shroud." As soon as the engine starts, gases entering the exhaust manifold are heated to at least 100°F. This is done by another valve—the manifold heat control valve— sealing off the exhaust manifold to prevent combustion gases from escaping. It is this hot gas that is diverted to the carburetor.

Figure 3. Air from hot exhaust manifold passes through hose, enters flange "C". Butterfly valve "A" closes off snorkel tube; preheated air goes directly to carburetor. When engine warms up, butterfly valve opens to admit outside air. Cover "B" closes off hot air from manifold.

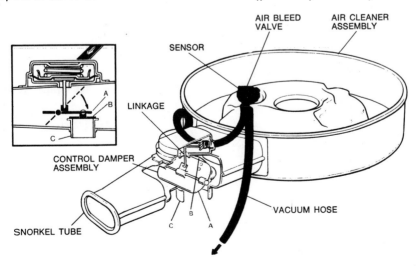

Now, as the engine warms up and the temperature around the air cleaner gets hotter, heat acts on the thermostat. It "relaxes" and pressure on the flapper valve is released.

Springs pull the valve open when the temperature around the snorkel reaches about 100°F. At the same time, the manifold heat-control valve opens to allow hot exhaust gases to escape. If this did not happen, excessive heat would result, causing (for one thing) pre-ignition. Pre-ignition is premature ignition of the fuel mixture. It can ruin an engine.

Although it is not part of the thermostatically controlled air cleaner, the manifold heat control valve works hand in hand with it. If the valve sticks so exhaust gases escape when a cold engine is started, the temperature of the air going to the carburetor is not at 100°F. Rough engine performance results.

Check and lubricate the manifold heat control valve as described in Chapter 10, pages 149–150.

With introduction of the thermostatically controlled air cleaner, it was possible for automobile manufactures to seal idle-mixture adjusting screws on carburetors to assure that engines would continue to run on leaner fuel mixtures. The law dictates that the idle-mixture

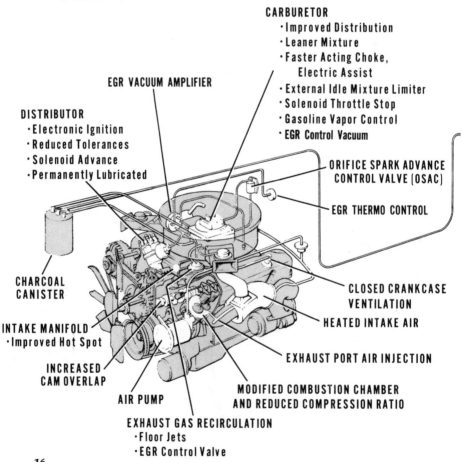

CARBURETOR
· Improved Distribution
· Leaner Mixture
· Faster Acting Choke, Electric Assist
· External Idle Mixture Limiter
· Solenoid Throttle Stop
· Gasoline Vapor Control
· EGR Control Vacuum

EGR VACUUM AMPLIFIER

DISTRIBUTOR
· Electronic Ignition
· Reduced Tolerances
· Solenoid Advance
· Permanently Lubricated

ORIFICE SPARK ADVANCE CONTROL VALVE (OSAC)

EGR THERMO CONTROL

CHARCOAL CANISTER

CLOSED CRANKCASE VENTILATION

INTAKE MANIFOLD
· Improved Hot Spot

HEATED INTAKE AIR

INCREASED CAM OVERLAP

EXHAUST PORT AIR INJECTION

AIR PUMP

MODIFIED COMBUSTION CHAMBER AND REDUCED COMPRESSION RATIO

EXHAUST GAS RECIRCULATION
· Floor Jets
· EGR Control Valve

screw locking caps be kept in place at all times, to prevent enriching of the fuel mixture.

It is a violation for anyone other than an authorized mechanic doing carburetor repairs to remove caps. Once repairs are made, caps must be replaced. Failure to observe the law can result in a fine.

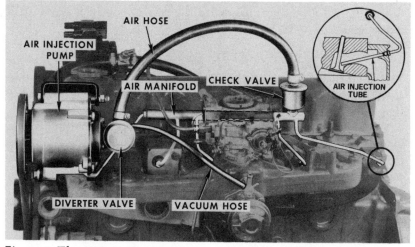

Figure 4. The air injection system uses an air pump that injects air into the exhaust manifold for more complete burning of exhaust gases.

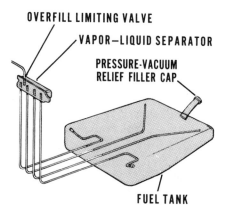

Figure 5. Drawing on this and opposite page provides an idea of the extent of devices and methods used by auto manufacturers to control emissions. This is a composite of the 1973 anti-emissions system employed by Chrysler.

How the air-injection system functions

THE WAY TO TELL if your car possesses an air-injection system is to look for a belt-driven air pump. This pump injects air directly into the exhaust port of each cylinder.

When air meets hot exhaust gases, more complete oxidation (burning) of the gases takes place in the exhaust manifold before gases enter the exhaust pipe for expulsion. More complete burning of the exhaust reduces the amounts of HC and CO discharged through the exhaust into the atmosphere.

Critical parts of the air-injection system (also referred to as the AIR system—"R" standing for reactor) that should be inspected during engine tune-up are the drive belt, hoses and fittings, a check valve that prevents hot gases from backing up into hoses and air pump, and a diverter valve that reduces the flow of air to exhaust ports during deceleration so backfire won't occur (Figure 4).

See tune-up procedures below for the way in which to service AIR components.

What you should know about controlled combustion

THE CONTROLLED COMBUSTION system is more complex than air injection. It uses several different components to achieve a reduction in HC and CO. Not every engine uses the same devices.

Controlled combustion provides for a more thorough burning of fuel by means of higher engine temperature, special carburetor calibrations, more sophisticated ignition adjustments, and spark controls that more closely relate ignition (and, hence, combustion) to driving speed (Figure 5).

American Motors refers to the controlled combustion system it uses as MOD; Chrysler calls its system the Cleaner Air System (CAS); Ford calls its system Improved Combustion (IMCO); and General Motors refers to its as Controlled Combustion. All are similar.

Some of the components you may find in the controlled combustion system of your car:

• Higher-temperature (190°–220°) cooling-system thermostats that permit the engine to reach a higher temperature quickly. Engine heat that can be applied as fast as possible provides more complete combustion during the warm-up period.

• Electric-assist choke mechanisms that also help reduce emissions as the engine warms up. Choke plates not outfitted with electric assists stay closed longer. A closed choke plate provides cylinders with a richer fuel mixture, which raises the level of emissions.

The electric-assist choke is an ordinary automatic choke that is equipped with an electric coil. The coil is activated by current when the temperature that activates the choke thermostat reaches about 60°. This causes the choke plate to open at once.

• A vacuum switch that keeps the engine from overheating when idling. Engines with controlled-combustion systems operate at more retarded timing settings.

Retarded timing is timing that delivers the ignition spark when the piston reaches a higher point in the compression stroke. Greater compression of fuel assures more thorough burning once spark occurs.

For example, in cars without exhaust-emissions controls, it was not uncommon to have ignition timing set at 6° to 12° before the piston reached full extension in the compression stroke. (The more technical term for full extension is "top dead center.")

In cars with exhaust-emissions controls, the spark is usually set to occur when the piston is at top dead center.

More complete burning of fuel creates higher internal temperatures. The vacuum switch is a device that senses temperature and causes manifold vacuum to operate the spark-advance mechanism when it gets too high. This creates an increase in engine speed, which circulates more cool air inside the engine.

Whether an engine is equipped with air injection or controlled combustion, it is subject to dieseling. Here's what I mean:

The idling speed of an engine equipped with either emissions control system is set higher than engines without systems. One reason for this is to keep the engine from stalling, because it is required to burn a leaner fuel mixture.

A higher idling speed means that a certain amount of the fuel mixture is going to be delivered past the carburetor throttle valve to the cylinders after the ignition is turned off. There is a delay before the throttle valve can close completely to seal off the flow of fuel. When excess fuel mixture gets into hot cylinders, it starts burning. This allows the engine to run (chug) with the ignition turned off for several seconds.

No harm can come to the engine, but it is frightening. To prevent dieseling, most carburetors of engines with exhaust-emissions controls are equipped with a so-called idle-stop solenoid. This is an electrically operated device that causes the throttle valve to close shut immediately on ignition shut-off.

How NOx is being fought

THE FIGHT AGAINST oxides of nitrogen began in 1973 with the addition to most engines of a control device called the exhaust-gas recirculating (EGR) system. The EGR sends metered amounts of exhaust gas into the intake manifold to dilute the air:fuel mixture. This helps reduce peak combustion-chamber temperatures at which oxygen and nitrogen combine to form NOx (Figure 6).

Figure 6. Exhaust-gas recirculation system reduces nitrogen oxides.

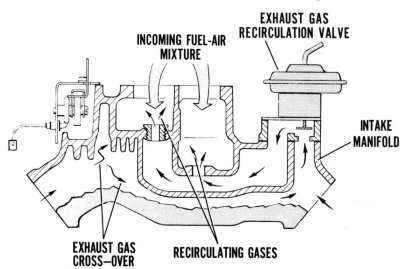

INCOMING FUEL-AIR MIXTURE

EXHAUST GAS RECIRCULATION VALVE

INTAKE MANIFOLD

EXHAUST GAS CROSS—OVER

RECIRCULATING GASES

The amount of exhaust gas allowed to enter the intake manifold at any one time is controlled by the EGR valve. This device, which is subject to fouling by carbon, must be serviced during engine tune-up.

A rundown of tune-up services

THE FOLLOWING LIST will help you guide yourself. It is a rundown of those services that should be performed during engine tune-up in the order in which we recommend they be done, but this order is not hard-and-fast—revise it to suit yourself:

You may want to copy this list and hang it up on the garage wall

1. Service the battery
2. Service the crankcase-emission control system
3. Service and test the carburetor air cleaner, and lubricate the manifold heat control valve
4. Service drive belts
5. Test compression
6. Service spark plugs
7. Service the distributor and coil
8. Service spark-plug cables
9. Set dwell and ignition timing
10. Replace the fuel filter
11. Service the automatic choke
12. Make carburetor adjustments
13. Service the fuel-evaporation emission control system
14. Service the A.I.R. system if the car has one
15. Service the EGR system if the car has one
16. Road-test the vehicle

Start by servicing the battery

TOOLS AND MATERIAL you need for servicing the battery prior to tuning the engine are the following:
- Distilled water (possibly)
- Battery hydrometer
- Battery-cable puller
- Battery-post and terminal-cleaning tool
- Baking soda or ammonia and a pail of clean water
- Petroleum jelly (Vaseline)
- Scrub brush
- Hose

The battery is the source of energy for the electrical circuits. If the battery is weak, an erroneous judgment might be made concerning a component that depends for its functioning on the battery.

Steps that should be done in servicing a battery prior to tuning the engine are these:

1. Check battery water. Add distilled water, if necessary, but be sure to drive the car so fresh water will be mixed with electrolyte.

Never take a hydrometer (specific gravity) reading after adding fresh water without driving the car. The result you get will be wrong.

2. Test specific gravity—as discussed in Chapter 3 (on reviving a faltering battery). Charge the battery if necessary.

3. Remove battery cables from the battery. To avoid creating sparks that could ignite hydrogen gas given off by the battery, disconnect the ground cable first. The ground cable in all American-made and most foreign vehicles is the negative cable, but to be certain trace the cable to see if it is connected to the engine or frame. A cable that is connected to the engine or frame is the ground cable. The other cable—the "hot" cable—goes to the starter motor. Use a battery-cable puller to disconnect cables to avoid damaging the battery. Never loosen a cable by prying beneath its terminal with a screwdriver, using the battery for leverage. When cables have been removed, take the battery from the car.

4. Clean corrosion from battery-cable terminals and battery posts with the post- and terminal-cleaning tool.

5. Wash the battery with a mixture of baking soda or ammonia and water as described in Chapter 3 (on reviving a faltering battery).

6. Reinstall the battery and attach cables firmly. The ground cable should be connected last.

7. Coat cables with a light film of petroleum jelly.

Giving crankcase-emission control systems the once-over

NO SPECIAL TOOLS are necessary.

Service a positive crankcase ventilation (PCV) system in the following manner:

1. After 12,000 miles of use, the PCV valve should be replaced.

2. If you do an engine tune-up more frequently, test the functioning of the valve. Start the engine. Find the location of the PCV valve (consult your owner's manual or a service manual). Pull the valve from its seat (Figure 7). You should hear a hissing noise. Cover the end of the valve with your finger. You should feel a strong vacuum (pull) (Figure 8). If not, the valve probably has to be replaced, but first clean the hose and test again.

The vacuum test tells if the PCV valve is working as it should

3. Check the hose extending from the PCV valve to the intake manifold. Check the hose extending from the carburetor air cleaner to the cap over the rocker-arm cover. Both should be free of cracks and kinks. If a hose is deteriorating, replace it with a new PCV hose that is oil-resistant.

4. Remove hoses, if possible. Clean deposits from inside them as you would clean a rifle. Cut rag patches and ram them through the hose using a metal rod (an ordinary metal clothes hanger that you straighten will serve) (Figure 9). Reinstall the clean hoses.

5. Remove the carburetor air-cleaner cover and take out the small air-filter element—on the other side of which is the PCV hose that extends to the rocker arm cover (Figure 10). Not every PCV system

Figure 7. The PCV valve is located in a different spot on different engines. Hunt yours down.

Figure 8 (left). Check PCV valve by feeling suction as engine runs.
Figure 9. Drive rag patch through crankcase emission control hoses.

Figure 10 (left). Hose ends in emission control system air filter.
Figure 11. The filter may be just a wad of mesh jammed in opening.

employs this filter.) Tap the filter lightly on a surface. If dust falls from it, replace the filter.

Some filters are simply a mesh material stuffed into a hole in the side of the air cleaner (Figure 11). Other filters are cotton types that are held in a small housing attached to the air-cleaner cover (Figure 12). The entire housing comes off.

Servicing a crankcase-emission control system that employs a gulp valve or metering orifice is also easy. Check and clean hoses first.

Open the gulp valve (it has a spring clip over it) and remove and check the diaphragm for pinholes. Replace a damaged diaphragm. Clean carbon from the valve's housing and make sure that the small metering hole isn't clogged. If it is, ream it out with a piece of narrow-diameter wire. Clean out a clogged metering orifice in the same way.

Servicing and testing the air cleaner

SINCE YOU HAVE removed the lid to service the crankcase-emission control system filter, you might as well service the air cleaner. No special tools are needed.

Figure 12 (left). Some crankcase emission control system filters are elements contained in holders. Replace the entire assembly.
Figure 13 (below). It's important to keep the air cleaner clean.

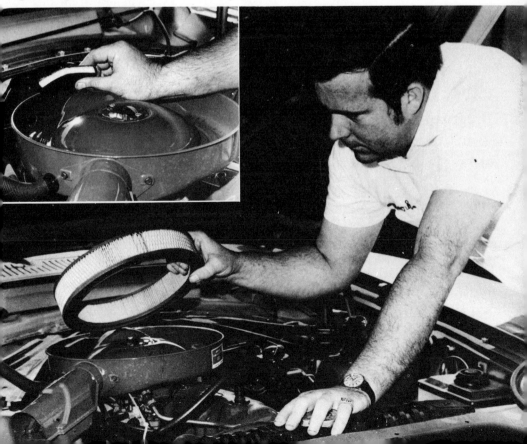

Remove the filter. Hold a drop light or lamp inside the filter and peer through the element with the light on. If the filter is clogged, replace it. If dirt buildup is negligible, tap the filter against a hard surface to remove whatever dust you can.

Also see to it that the filter is not damaged. If the element is ripped or otherwise impaired, replace the filter.

Take off the air-cleaner housing and wipe it clean of dirt and grease. Put it back on the carburetor, install the filter element, and replace the lid (Figure 13).

Caution: The wing nut or bolt holding the lid in place must *not* be be overtightened. Too much pressure can damage the carburetor housing. Tighten the nut until it is finger-snug.

If your car possesses one of those rare oil-bath air cleaners, dump old oil, wash out the housing and replenish the air cleaner with fresh oil of the type specified on the housing or in your owner's manual.

Check a thermostatically controlled air cleaner when the engine is cold. The valve in the snorkel should be closed down over the snorkel (Figure 14).

Start the engine. As it warms up, the valve should open freely until it is fully opened. If the valve *doesn't* operate this way, proceed as follows:

Here's the way to repair a malfunctioning air cleaner

1. Let the engine get cold again. Lubricate the valve pivots with SAE 20-20W engine oil to make sure that the valve itself isn't binding.

2. Disconnect the diaphragm-assembly vacuum hose at the thermostat (sensor) and pull in on the hose by mouth. This creates a vacuum. The valve in the snorkel should close (Figure 15).

3. Bend the hose, trapping the vacuum. Hold it this way for about a minute. The valve should stay closed. If it doesn't, a leak exists in the hose or in the diaphragm assembly. Check the hose. If it's okay, replace the diaphragm assembly.

4. If the valve responds properly during the mouth-vacuum test, failure to respond as the engine was warming up means that the thermostat has gone bad (Figure 16). Replace it.

The manifold heat control valve plays an important role in the controlling of exhaust emissions in cars possessing thermostatically controlled air cleaners. For this reason, when doing an engine tune-up, make sure that the valve is operating freely and that it is lubricated with manifold heat control valve lubricant or graphite (see Chapter 10 for details).

Caution: Do not lubricate the manifold heat control valve with oil, which contains deposits that will cause the valve to stick.

Drive belts don't last forever

EXAMINE THE DRIVE BELT or belts. All cars have one belt that turns the fan, alternator and water pump off the crankshaft pulley. Some cars have two or more belts to operate other components, in-

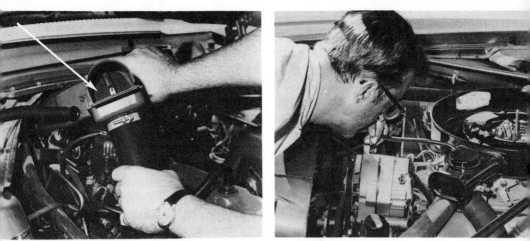

Figure 14 (left). *Arrow points to air-cleaner snorkel valve.*
Figure 15 (right). *Mouth suction on hose should close snorkel valve.*

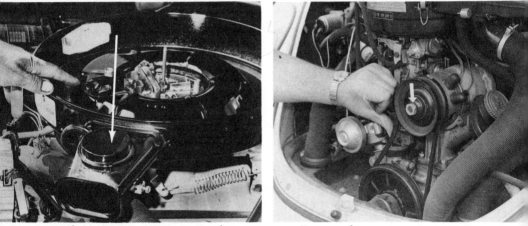

Figure 16 (left). *Finger points to air-cleaner sensor. Remove by opening retainer clips. Bump on snorkel (arrow) is the control motor.*
Figure 17 (right). *A hand test of drive-belt tension of a Volkswagen. Adjust it by adding or removing shims behind pulley (arrow).*

cluding the power-steering pump, air-conditioner compressor, or air-injection pump of an A.I.R. exhaust-emission control system.

Drive belts are sturdy components that retain their integrity for many thousands of miles, but in time they begin cracking, loosening, or building up glaze that causes them to slip on pulleys. A weakened belt can't do its job, and the efficiency of the components it drives is therefore hampered.

Furthermore, a damaged belt is one that can give way on the road, presenting you with an emergency. If a belt snaps, electrical energy to the engine is cut off at once. So is cooling. The car will stop dead.

Examine belts for cracking and fraying. Look for a slick glaze. Test each belt for tension by pushing down on it midway between two pulleys with your thumb (Figure 17). A belt should "give" about ½-inch.

How to replace and tighten drive belts

NO SPECIAL TOOLS are needed.

The one belt that needs replacement most often is the belt serving the alternator, fan and water pump. The steps below outline how to replace and tighten this belt. If another belt needs servicing, it is done in a similar manner:

1. Loosen the alternator by turning the adjusting arm bracket bolt.

Caution: If the adjusting arm bracket bolt is "frozen," apply several drops of penetrating solvent carefully. Do not allow this solvent to drop into the cooling fins of the alternator. It may damage the alternator.

2. Push the alternator in toward the fan and crankshaft pulleys until the belt slackens. Remove the old belt.

3. Worm the new belt over the fan and crankshaft pulleys, and around the alternator pulley. Pull the alternator back toward you as far as it can go by hand.

A little caution will prevent damage when you're tightening the drive belt

4. Place a pry bar (the wheel-nut tightening [lug] wrench will serve) between the alternator housing and engine, and pull back against the alternator until the belt it taut.

Caution: Place the bar and pry against the thick center of the alternator housing. Placing pressure on the thinner end plates may crack them.

5. When the belt is tense, test for tension. If tension is satisfactory (remember: ½ inch), tighten the alternator adjusting arm bracket bolt.

6. Check tension again. If the alternator moved so the belt loosened, undo the adjusting arm bracket bolt again and retighten.

Engine pep must be tops for successful tune-up

THE MOST PRECISE engine tune-up cannot compensate for inefficient performance resulting from low or uneven compression. Compression refers to the reduction of volume within a cylinder by the piston and, therefore, to the resulting pressure brought to bear on the fuel mixture within the cylinder prior to ignition.

If an engine is idling roughly or lacks power at cruising speed because of a malfunction that is causing low compression, a tune-up will not correct the condition. For this reason, a compression test becomes an integral part of the tune-up procedure. There is no sense in taking the time or spending the money to do a tune-up without first repairing the cause of a compression loss.

To make a compression test, you need a compression gauge. Two types are available: one allows you to screw the gauge's hose into the cylinder hole, while the other requires you to hold the hose adapter in the cylinder. The screw-in type reduces the possibility of compression loss around the adapter as the engine is cranked for the test. Besides, it gives you the use of both hands.

Another tool you might want to consider purchasing is a remote starter. Make sure you can get to the starter solenoid, though. Some are difficult to reach with the remote starter connection. If a remote starter is not used, have an assistant crank the engine for you from behind the wheel.

Getting ready to do the compression test

TOOLS AND EQUIPMENT you need are:
- Masking tape
- Felt marking instrument
- Spark-plug socket (be sure you get the correct size—plugs are generally $1\frac{3}{16}$- or $\frac{5}{8}$-inch)
- Socket wrench
- Wrench extension if needed to reach plugs

Drive the engine if it isn't already warmed up. Park on level ground.

Spark plugs must be removed before you can test compression. It is necessary to identify spark-plug cables as you remove them from plugs so they can be reattached to the correct cylinders.

As you remove each cable from the plugs of a six-cylinder in-line engine, simply attach a strip of masking tape on which is written a number from one to six, depending upon the position of the cylinder looking from front to rear, as follows:

1	2	3	4	5	6
0	0	0	0	0	0

Careful marking of cables and distributor-cap towers will save you embarrassment later on

For a V8 engine, number strips of masking tape L1, L2, L3 and L4; and R1, R2, R3 and R4. "L" means left; "R" means right.

Remember: The left side of the engine is the driver's side—the right side is the passenger side.

Use the following diagram to determine how to attach strips of tape to spark-plug cables of a V8 engine:

R1	R2	R3	R4
•	•	•	•

•	•	•	•
L1	L2	L3	L4

Also place strips of masking tape with the corresponding numbers on the distributor cap towers. Cables must be placed in their proper tower to maintain correct firing and avoid serious engine damage.

Removing spark-plug cables from spark plugs must be done carefully to avoid damaging the cables (Figure 18). Grasp the insulator boot—never the cable itself. Twist the boot with a pulling motion until the boot pops from the plug (Figures 19 & 20).

Pulling on the cable can tear wires apart. You can't see what is happening inside the insulation, so damage goes undetected and won't show up until the engine is started and run. Then, you are left wondering why you have an engine miss.

As you remove each cable, wipe it clean of dirt and grease with a dry rag.

Caution: To grasp cables, you may be reaching down near hot engine parts. Use care.

Although you will test the cables after reinstalling spark plugs, now is as good a time as any to examine insulator boots. They may be dried out and cracked. If so, flashover, which results in loss of engine power, may be occurring.

Electricity takes the path of least resistance. Instead of running along the cable to the spark-plug terminal and onto the spark-plug electrodes, electricity can leak out through a cracked boot. This produces spark between the boot and outside of the spark-plug insulator (flashover). There may be no spark at the plug electrodes.

Replace cracked, dried-out boots.

Time to remove the spark plugs

BLOW DIRT PARTICLES from around each spark plug. Use an ear syringe or an ordinary soda straw. Particles must not fall inside cylinders as plugs are removed. They will damage pistons and cylinder walls.

Figure 18 (left). Never pull on an ignition cable. You will destroy it.
Figure 19 (right). Remove a cable by grasping boot. Twist and pull.

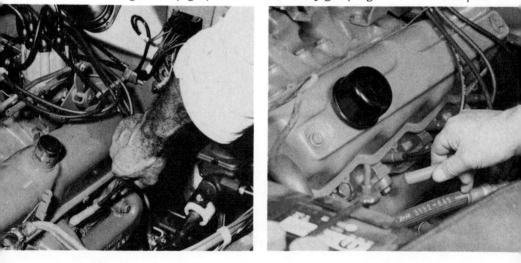

Turn each spark plug counterclockwise to remove it (Figure 21). If plugs are equipped with metal gaskets, do not lose these. They will be needed if spark plugs are reused.

As you take each plug from its port, write its number on the insulator with the felt marking instrument. Numbers should coincide with the cable serving the particular plug—that is, R1, R3, L2, L4, etc.

Another way of identifying plugs is to place them in a tray in which holes are cut and marked to coincide with each plug's position in the engine. This method has the advantage of providing a holder for the plugs so they will be protected from dropping. Once a plug is dropped and its insulator cracks, the plug must be discarded.

If a spark plug is difficult to remove, let the engine cool down. This may solve the problem.

However, if the plug is still overly tight, apply a few drops of penetrating oil around its base and place a socket over the plug. Apply steady pressure until the plug breaks loose.

Look for carbon or other deposits on the threaded area of the spark-plug port. This may have been the reason for overtightness.

You might as well clean off deposits now if you find them. Carefully brush them out with a small wire brush. If deposits are hardened, use a thread chaser which you can buy in an auto-parts supply store. A thread chaser is screwed onto the threads, and cuts and picks off deposits.

Now make the compression test

MAKE SURE THE choke butterfly plate is open. Move the throttle lever so the throttle plate is wide open. Carefully insert a screwdriver into the carburetor so it goes past the choke plate and throttle plate

Figure 20. Better yet, buy a pair of spark-plug cable pliers, to provide leverage and a firmer grip.

(Figure 22). This is done to keep the throttle plate wide open for the compression test if you use a remote starter.

If you have someone crank the engine for you, be sure the choke plate is open. Your assistant can keep the throttle plate open from inside the car by holding the accelerator pedal right on the floor.

Find the distributor. Extending from the side of the distributor to the ignition coil is the coil-to-distributor primary wire. Disconnect it at the coil. The other thin wire leading from the coil goes to the ignition switch. The coil-to-distributor primary wire is disconnected to break the circuit and prevent unnecessary strain on ignition points.

If you are using a remote starter switch, connect one of its leads to the starter solenoid's solenoid terminal (marked S) and attach its other lead to the battery's "hot" terminal.

Caution: Be sure that you now turn on the ignition switch and leave the ignition switch on during the compression test.

Screw or hold the compression gauge into one of the cylinder openings and crank the engine until the gauge's needle records its highest reading. This takes several strokes of the piston. Be sure that no compression leaks from around the gauge's adapter. You may hear hissing if it does.

Take readings at each spark-plug port. Jot down each reading, referencing it to the cylinder from which it is taken.

Make sure that the gauge is held tightly in the cylinder opening

If someone is helping you make this test (that is, if a remote starter switch is not being used), have him hold the accelerator pedal right to the floor and keep it there as he cranks the engine. Be sure the engine is cranked through sufficient compression strokes to get the highest compression reading from each cylinder.

Figure 21. A spark-plug socket wrench of the right size is needed to remove the plugs.

Figure 22. Carefully insert a screwdriver through the carburetor to keep throttle and choke plates open for the compression test.

What compression readings tell you

TO CORRECTLY INTERPRET compression readings, you must have the engine's standard and minimum compression specifications. Specifications are given in the car's service manual and in general automobile reference manuals, many of which are available in local public libraries. You may be able to get specifications, too, by calling the service department of a dealer who sells your make of car.

Specifications are important if you are to avoid condemning a good engine that shows low compression. Suppose, for example, that most of the cylinders in your car show a reading of 170 pounds per square inch (psi), while one or two show a compression of 120 psi. If you use general rules of thumb given in many auto-repair books, you would conclude that there is a breakdown in the low-reading cylinders. However, with the modern engine, such may not be the case.

It's easy to make a wrong diagnosis if you just follow general rules about compression readings

High-performance engines have long valve overlaps. Valve overlap refers to the period of time during which both exhaust and intake valves are open. You might just hit a cylinder with your compression gauge at the "wrong" time. Manufacturer specifications make allowance for this.

Once allowances for valve overlap are made, if applicable, some conclusions can be reached regarding your compression readings. A cylinder which shows a reading that is 80 percent lower than the highest-reading cylinder may have a sticking or burned valve. A cylinder that shows less than the minimum allowable compression is one in which piston rings are probably worn. This is pretty much confirmed if the engine has been using an excessive amount of oil.

Virtue of the cylinder-leak test

THE CYLINDER-LEAK TEST is a more accurate way than compression testing of determining engine condition. However, you need compressed air and a leakage tester.

With pistons at top dead center, 60 to 70 psi of compressed air is injected into each cylinder in turn through an adapter that is screwed into the spark-plug port. If the tester shows more than 20 percent loss of air, there is a malfunction in the cylinder tested.

By continuing to apply compressed air, you can quickly determine the area of malfunction, as follows:

• If you hear air escaping from the tailpipe, an exhaust valve is leaking.

• If you hear air coming into the carburetor, an intake valve is leaking.

• If you hear air by listening at the oil filler port, air is entering the crankcase through worn piston rings or cylinder walls.

• If you see bubbles in the radiator coolant, suspect a leak in the head gasket, or a crack in the block or head.

Spark-plug service: the heart of engine tune-up

IF THE COMPRESSION or cylinder-leakage test informs you that the engine is in good condition, proceed with tune-up by considering the spark plugs. New spark plugs should be installed at every 12,000 mile tune-up. If you do a tune-up every 5,000–6,000 miles, plugs may be cleaned and regapped if they are still usable.

We recommend replacing spark plugs every 12,000 miles, because spark plugs normally give trouble-free service only for that mileage. Therefore, they may appear usable, but can break down at any time. The life of a spark plug under normal use is 12,000 miles.

Worn-out spark plugs waste gas. In a series of fuel-economy tests, Champion Spark Plug Company found that approximately two-thirds of the total fuel-economy improvement gained from engine tune-up was attributed to new spark plugs. These tests revealed that new plugs save about one gallon of gasoline per 18 to 20 gallons.

Spark plugs must conduct high-ignition voltage to the combustion chambers to ignite the fuel mixture (Figure 23). They must do this in all kinds of weather and under all sorts of driving conditions. If a spark plug fails to deliver high voltage, fuel in the particular cylinder will not be burned. It will be expelled from the exhaust. This wastes fuel and leads to engine misfire—a mechanical malfunction that disrupts engine performance.

After 12,000 miles, spark-plug electrodes wear to a point where the distance that the spark must jump is excessive. Misfire occurs, resulting in loss of power (as much as 24 percent) and loss of fuel. In addition, a strain is put on the rest of the ignition system.

Select the right spark plug for your engine

THE SPARK PLUG recommended by the manufacturer of your car in the owner's manual may not be the one your engine needs. Recommended plugs are designed to meet normal driving conditions—that is, more or less equal amounts of idling, slow-speed and high-speed operation.

If spark plugs recommended by the manufacturer are forced to function under unusual conditions, they may not meet the thermal conditions which are present most often inside the cylinder head. The plugs will either overheat or undercool. In any case, serious problems may result.

If spark plugs cannot get rid of heat fast enough, they begin to glow and could ignite the fuel mixture before spark actually occurs. This condition is called "preignition," and it can have disastrous consequences. Preigniton can blow holes in pistons.

Conversely, if spark plugs do not heat up to a temperature that is sufficient to burn off combustion deposits which form on the plugs' tips, deposits can build up between electrodes. When deposits meet, "fusing" the two electrodes together, the plug short-circuits. Misfire occurs, and misfire is a condition that wastes gasoline and robs an engine of power.

Figure 23. Spark plugs that are in good condition ignite the fuel mixture on time so the mixture burns smoothly and fully.

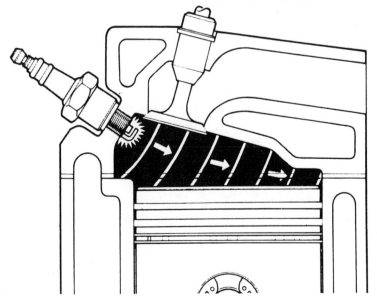

To determine which spark plug your engine actually needs, install the plug which is recommended by the manufacturer in your owner's manual. Run the car for several days. Then remove a few plugs from the engine for inspection.

If the insulator tips are gray or light tan, and are covered with a light chalky deposit, the particular spark plug is suitable. If the insulator tips are sooty or oily, you should switch to a hotter spark plug. If the insulator tips are ghostly white, switch to a colder spark plug.

In making the switch to hotter or colder, move up or down the heat-range scale one notch at a time. Use the new plugs in the engine for a few days; then inspect them. Maybe a still colder or hotter plug is needed (Figure 24).

How to buy spark plugs

YOU MUST USE the proper spark-plug code, which denotes the heat range and size. Correct size refers to the thread and reach which match the dimensional requirements of the cylinder head.

Start with the plug designated in the owner's manual. Suppose it is a Champion UJ-12Y. This means that your engine requires spark plugs having a 14-mm. thread and a ⅜-inch reach.

This is always true! Even if you switch to a hotter or colder spark plug, you will need one having a 14-mm. thread and a ⅜-inch reach.

The important thing to keep in mind when ordering spark plugs from an automotive-parts supply dealer is the designation of the plug recommended by the car's manufacturer. If you have to switch to a different heat-range plug, tell him, "I need the next colder (or hotter) plug from thus-and-so (for example, from UJ-12Y)." He will refer to a chart that tells him which plug to give you.

What spark plugs can tell you about your engine

SPARK PLUGS MAKE good engine analyzers. When all plugs have been removed from the engine and identified, examine the lower insulators (Figure 25). Conditions you may find and what they mean are these:

1. Insulators have light tan or brown deposits, and electrodes are worn, but not excessively. This is normal spark-plug wear.

2. Insulators are coated with black, dry, fluffy carbon. If only a few plugs are this way, check for a bad high-tension (spark plug) cable, faulty distributor breaker points, weak condenser, weak coil, or a burned or sticky valve. If all plugs are coated with carbon, check for a lean fuel mixture, dirty carburetor air-cleaner element, stuck manifold heat control valve, or spark plugs that are too cold for the stop-go driving you do.

3. Insulators are coated with oil. If the engine is not new or has not

recently been overhauled, it probably possesses worn rings, worn cylinders, or worn valve guides. New or rebuilt engines may oil-foul spark plugs before piston rings seat.

4. Insulators are coated with dark gray, black, yellow, or tan cindery deposits, or a shiny glaze. This condition signifies an accumulation of the byproducts of combustion brought about by high speed or heavy-load operation. If you do much of this type of driving, you should switch to a colder spark plug.

5. Insulators have a ghostly white appearance, and there is excessive electrode erosion. You are either using spark plugs of the wrong heat range, or ignition timing is overadvanced, the fuel mixture is too lean, or the cooling system is partially clogged.

How to service spark plugs that will be reused

TOOLS YOU WILL NEED are:
- An old hacksaw that has been ground to a ⅛-inch-wide taper at one end
- Small ignition file
- Small "dust" brush (a small, new paintbrush will suffice)
- Spark-plug feeler gauge

If the spark-plug heat range is correct and no engine malfunction exists, the spark plugs should be serviced at 5,000 miles and put back into service. The way to do this is as follows:

1. Using the bending tool that should be part of your spark-plug feeler gauge (buy a gauge that has a bending tool), carefully open the plug electrode gap by bending the ground (side) electrode.

Figure 24 (left). A cold plug loses heat more rapidly than hot plug.
Figure 25 (right). Spark plugs can tip you off to a problem. This oil-fouled plug was removed from an engine that needed new rings.

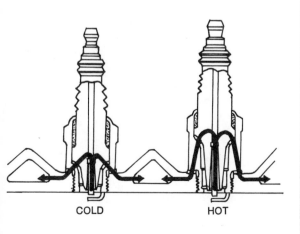

COLD   HOT

Caution: Never use any other tool, such as pliers, to manipulate the spark-plug electrode. You will ruin the plug. Do not bend the center electrode. If this electrode is damaged, the plug is ruined.

2. Using the modified hacksaw blade, scrape deposits from the lower insulator. Scrape hard. No harm will be done.

3. Blow particles away by mouth. Use the "dust" brush to assure complete cleanliness.

4. Using the ignition file, file electrodes to obtain square, bright edges (Figure 26). Again, use the "dust" brush to get rid of particles.

5. Set electrode gap to the specification given in the owner's manual (Figure 27). This specification is also provided on the "tune-up specification" decal that is mounted somewhere under the hood of most late-model cars.

In setting the gap, bend the side electrode only. Insert the correct size of feeler gauge. Proper gap is attained when you can move the feeler gauge between the electrodes and feel a slight resistance.

Important: The electrode gap of *new* spark plugs must be set before spark plugs are placed in the engine.

Install spark plugs carefully and correctly

A TOOL YOU SHOULD have is a pound-foot torque wrench. Although you can install spark plugs without one, it is best to use one to attain properly seated plugs. Anyway, if you are going to do automotive work, you will need a torque wrench for other tasks.

Proper installation of spark plugs is important. If the plugs are not tight enough, compression is lost. If the plugs are too tight, damage may be done to plugs or engine.

Follow these steps when installing spark plugs:

1. Remove identification marks from each spark plug as you install it.

Figure 26 (left). File electrodes clean and square. Use dust brush.
Figure 27 (right). To gap a plug, bend the side electrode only and use the correct-size gauge. Decal under hood lists the specification.

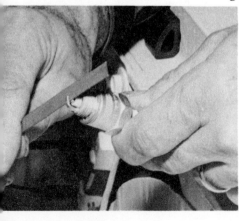
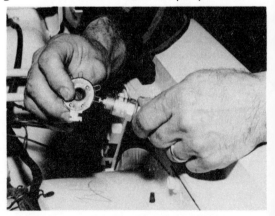

2. Dab several drops of engine oil on the threads to make installation easier. If the engine has an aluminum cylinder head, apply anti-seizing compound to threads if the engine is warm.

3. Screw plugs into ports by hand until they are finger-tight. If a plug starts binding, do not force it. Remove the plug and start it into the port again.

4. Finish tightening plugs with a torque (or socket) wrench to the following specification:

	CAST-IRON HEAD		ALUMINUM HEAD	
SPARK-PLUG THREAD SIZE	Torque Wrench	Socket Wrench	Torque Wrench	Socket Wrench
Gasket Type:				
10 mm.	8–12 lb. ft.	¼ turn	8–12 lb. ft.	¼ turn
12 mm.	10–18 lb. ft.	¼ turn	10–18 lb. ft.	¼ turn
14 mm.	26–30 lb. ft.	¼-⅜ turn	18–22 lb. ft.*	¼ turn
18 mm.	32–38 lb. ft.	¼ turn	28–34 lb. ft.	¼ turn
Tapered Seat: *(no gasket)*				
14 mm.	10–20 lb. ft.	¹⁄₁₆ turn (snug)	10–20 lb. ft.	¹⁄₁₆ turn (snug)
18 mm.	15–20 lb. ft.	¹⁄₁₆ turn (snug)	15–20 lb. ft.	¹⁄₁₆ turn (snug)

* Tighten Mazda's plug 8–13 lb. ft. (¹⁄₁₆-¼ turn)

Notes before you tackle the distributor and coil

THE DISTRIBUTOR IS the most complicated component you handle when doing an engine tune-up. It consists of the distributor cap, advance mechanisms, rotor, breaker points, and condenser (Figure 28). Each part must be in good condition if the spark plugs are to receive the electricity they need to ignite the fuel mixture.

Some cars possess electronic ignition systems. The distributors of these do not possess breaker points or condenser (Figure 29). However, they do have rotors, caps and other mechanisms, so the information below which deals with conventional distributors is applicable.

If a problem arises with an electronic ignition system, consult a professional mechanic. He must test the unit with a special instrument. Purchasing this instrument is not a worthwhile investment.

Tools and equipment you will need to service the distributor of a conventional ignition system are as follows:
- Distributor tower cleaning tool
- Fine-cut ignition point file
- Feeler gauges
- Distributor wrench
- Dwell/tachometer
- Stroboscopic timing light

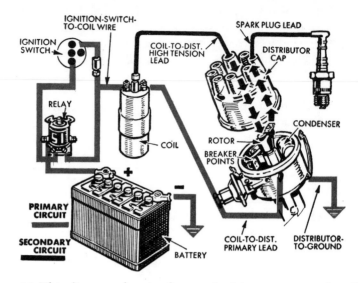

Figure 28. *This diagram showing how an ignition system works will acquaint you with the various components.*

Figure 29. *These are the major parts of an electronic ignition system. Note absence of points and condenser inside the distributor.*

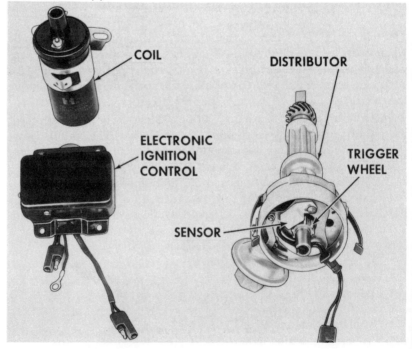

Distributor-coil service by the numbers

THE FOLLOWING is a logical, orderly way to proceed with coil and distributor service:

1. Clean the coil off with rags or paper towels and examine it closely. Replace the coil if it is cracked or if the tower is eroded.

To replace a coil, detach the wires, unseat the old unit from its bracket, and install the new coil. Reattach wires. Be sure to buy the coil your car needs.

If the old coil looks okay, clean deposits from the inside of its tower with the distributor-tower cleaning tool.

2. Remove the distributor cap. Some caps are held by spring clips. Insert the tip of a screwdriver behind each clip and twist. The clip will snap off.

Some caps are held by L-shaped latches that have screwdriver grooves in their heads. Insert a screwdriver and open the latch.

Lift the cap from the distributor and wipe it clean with a rag or paper towels (Figure 30).

3. Examine the cap closely. Look for cracks, chips, broken towers, worn or burned contacts, burned terminals in towers, and carbon tracks. Replace the cap if it shows any sign of damage. However, if terminals are only slightly black or corroded, clean out towers with the distributor-tower cleaning tool and keep the cap in service.

Figure 30. Wipe the distributor cap clean and inspect it. Look for cracks, chips, broken towers, damaged contacts or terminals.

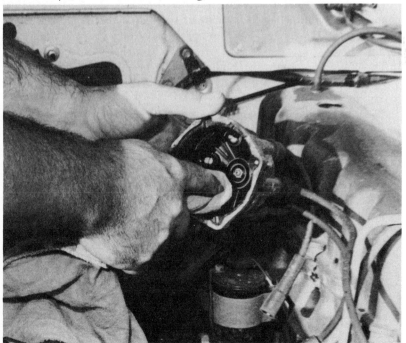

4. Remove the rotor from the top of the distributor shaft. Some can be lifted off. Others are held by two screws.

Wipe the rotor clean, and examine it for cracks and corrosion. Check the metal terminal for damage. If the rotor shows any damage at all, buy a new one of the exact type.

5. Some distributors have radio-frequency interference shields covering the inside of the housing. This covering does what its name implies—it prevents electrical impulses from interfering with radio reception. Unscrew the shield and lay it aside.

6. Test the operation of the centrifugal advance mechanism, which consists of two counterweights that are joined by springs. The job of the centrifugal advance mechanism is to control the timing of the spark in respect to engine speed, so that fuel has time to ignite and burn completely before a new supply of fuel and another spark are introduced.

You may be able to see the centrifugal advance mechanism—you may not. Some are covered. In either event, turn the distributor shaft about five degrees in the direction of rotation.

You can determine the direction of rotation by having someone in the car crank the engine momentarily as you watch to see how the shaft turns.

Release your hold on the shaft. The shaft (centrifugal advance counterweights) should snap back at once and with authority.

If the mechanism sticks or is sluggish, the distributor should be overhauled. Button everything up and consult a professional at an automobile-ignition repair shop.

7. Test the vacuum advance mechanism. This is the bell-shaped chamber that's attached to the side of the distributor housing (Figure 32). Its job is to control ignition spark according to the load placed on the engine.

The chamber contains a diaphragm that permits ignition timing to vary automatically according to vacuum (load) changes taking place inside the engine.

To test the vacuum advance, press against the breaker-point assembly in a direction that is opposite that of distributor-shaft rotation. This causes the distributor base plate to move.

Release pressure on the points. The base plate should swivel immediately and with authority back to position.

If this fails to occur, replace the distributor vacuum advance mechanism, but first check the vacuum line leading from the chamber to the vacuum source to make sure it's not cracked or loose, leaking vacuum (Figure 33).

To replace the vacuum advance mechanism, the distributor usually must come off the engine. Note the position of the rotor. When the distributor is put back into the engine, the rotor must be in this exact position.

Here's a way to make it easy on yourself: Lay a pen or a sharp pointed instrument, such as an awl, along the rotor and scribe a line

Figure 31. The centrifugal advance mechanism controls the spark in relation to engine speed.

SPARK ADVANCE
VACUUM CHAMBER

VACUUM LINE
TO CARBURETOR

Figure 32. The vacuum advance unit is found on the distributor.

Figure 33 (right). Replace a damaged vacuum hose. This hose leads from the bell-shaped vacuum advance mechanism to a vacuum source in the engine.

on a suitable adjacent surface (Figure 34). When the distributor is reinstalled, just make sure the rotor and line lineup.

Unbolt the distributor with a distributor wrench (usually one bolt holds the distributor to the engine) (Figure 35). Lift the distributor out (Figure 36).

Now, find the fasteners that hold the vacuum advance to the distributor housing. One bolt is usually used to attach the distributor ground wire to the link between the advance unit and breaker plate. Another bolt is normally employed to attach the link to the breaker plate (Figure 37).

Remove these bolts and slide the vacuum advance unit away from the distributor. Replace the faulty chamber with one of the exact model. Reassembly is done in the opposite manner of disassembly.

8. Continue tune-up of the distributor by examining the distributor breaker points (Figure 38). A thorough examination can only be done by removing the points from the distributor. You won't be able to look between them if you don't.

To take the points from the distributor, loosen the terminal screw holding the coil-to-distributor primary wire. Also loosen the terminal screw holding the condenser pigtail. Do not drop or lose these screws.

Lift the two wires out of the way, but note where they attach so reassembly will be easier.

Advice: It is often wise to make a rough sketch of things as you proceed with disassembly. It will make reassembly easier.

Now, remove the screw or screws holding the breaker-point assembly to the breaker base plate and lift the points from the unit.

9. Spread the points apart carefully. If they are coated with light gray deposits and are only slightly burned or pitted, they can be kept in use.

Clean off scale by passing a clean fine-cut ignition-point file between them once or twice, but that's all. Don't attempt to clean points to bare metal. You'll rub away too much.

Caution: Never use emery cloth or sandpaper to clean points. The residue these abrasives leave will cause the points to burn.

10. Points that are badly burned or pitted should be replaced. If points seem to fail frequently, find out why (Figures 39 & 40).

Causes of rapid point failure include an improperly adjusted or inoperative voltage regulator or ballast resistor; a defective condenser (always replace the condenser when you replace points, and this problem shouldn't arise); oil or crankcase vapors that work their way into the distributor because of a clogged breather; a distributor cam that is overlubricated—the cam tosses off lubricant and it winds up on the points; a weak contact-point spring; and points that are not gapped properly.

11. Before reinstalling points, wipe the breaker plate clean and apply a drop of distributor-cam lubricant to the cam if the distributor is not equipped with a wick-type cam lubricator. The size of the drop

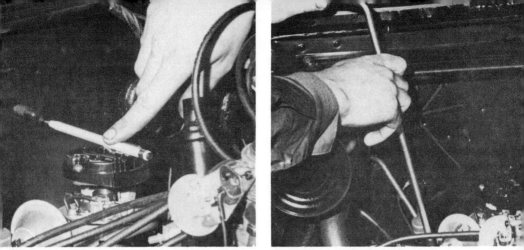

Figure 34 (left). Make a reference mark using the rotor as a guide.
Figure 35 (right). Unbolt the distributor with a distributor wrench.

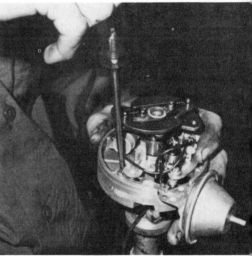

Figure 36 (left). With the bolt off, remove the distributor.
Figure 37 (right). Remove bolts holding the vacuum advance chamber.

Figure 38 (left). Examine breaker points for excessive wear, damage.
Figure 39 (right). Replace the points that are damaged.

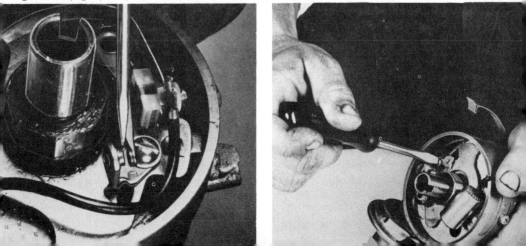

of lubricant should be equal to the head of a match—no larger. Apply lubricant to *one* cam lobe only (Figure 41).

If the distributor is equipped with a wick-type cam lubricator, replace it with a new one (Figure 42).

12. Install the point assembly and a new condenser if new points are being installed. Reconnect primary and condenser wires, but make sure their clips are not touching the breaker plate. Tuck wires back into their original positions.

13. Gap points to specification (consult the owner's or service manual, or the tune-up specification decal in the engine compartment) (Figure 43).

To gap points the right way, set the rubbing block of the assembly on one of the cam lobes. If the cam has to be turned so one of its lobes comes beneath the rubbing block, have someone in the car crank the engine in short spurts until the rubbing block rests on the high point of the cam. A remote starter may also be used if you have one.

Select a feeler gauge of the same thickness as the specified gap setting. Insert the gauge between the points, if you can, holding the gauge straight. Don't twist it; you will spread the points.

Slide the gauge back and forth. You should feel slight friction. If friction is heavy (or the gauge couldn't be inserted) or no friction exists, the points have to be adjusted. This is done in one of two ways, depending on the setup:

If the points have a notch or slot near the mounting screw, loosen the mounting screw slightly. Insert a screwdriver in the notch or slot, and twist the tip until the points open or close, as the situation warrants.

As a final touch, clean residue from breaker points with lighter fluid and a card

Keep the gauge in place and keep testing until the proper gap is attained. Then, tighten the mounting screw, and check the gap one last time.

Some distributor points have an adjustment screw that you turn with an Allen wrench. Install the wrench and turn the screw with the feeler gauge in place until the correct gap is attained.

14. After the breaker point gap is set, squirt a little lighter fluid on a clean card or tag that's about as thick as a business card and pass it through the points to remove residue.

If the rotor is the type that simply lifts off the shaft, apply two drops of engine oil directly into the shaft, but make sure oil goes inside the shaft, and not into the distributor. Install the rotor.

Now, replace the distributor cap. See that it is firmly latched.

Install ignition cables. At this point, the cables should be examined.

Faulty cables cause engine misfire, which is failure of a spark plug to spark and ignite the fuel mixture in a cylinder. Misfire robs an engine of power and wastes gasoline.

All you need to know about ignition cables

TOOLS YOU WILL NEED are:
- Jumper wire with an alligator clip fastened to each end
- Ohmmeter

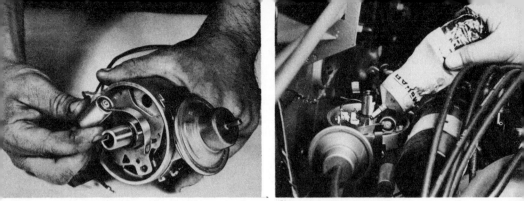

Figure 40 (left). *Replace the condensor when you replace the points.*
Figure 41 (right). *If the distributor doesn't have a self-lubricator, add a drop of distributor cam lube.*

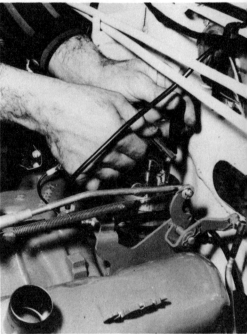

Figure 42 (above). *Replace a wick-type cam lubricator by snapping it from place.*
Figure 43 (right). *Gap points to specification shown in owner's manual and on tune-up specification decal in engine compartment of newer cars.*

A four-cylinder engine has five high-tension cables—one for each spark plug and one between the coil and center tower of the distributor (Figure 44). A six-cylinder engine has seven cables, and an eight-cylinder engine has nine.

Electricity flowing to spark plugs takes the path of least resistance. In a sound ignition system, the path of least resistance is across spark-plug electrodes.

However, if a high-tension cable is damaged, the path of least resistance is often through the cable insulation to ground. In other words, if a cable is leaking electricity, current doesn't reach the spark plug to ignite the fuel mixture.

Before you reinstall cables, therefore, clean each off by rubbing it down with a rag that has been moistened in kerosene. Then, wipe the cable dry with a clean cloth.

Bend the cable over its entire length. Discard the cable if tiny cracks appear, if insulation is brittle, or if the insulation is chafed.

Check spark-plug boots, too, if you haven't already done so. If they are cracked or brittle, replace the cable.

Examine terminals on each end (Figure 45). If a terminal is eroded because of burning, replace the cable, and let this serve as a reminder to firmly seat terminals. Burning is a sign that arcing has taken place. Arcing refers to electricity that has to jump the gap between two terminals, because the two are not firmly seated.

Caution: Boots covering the spark-plug end of cables are usually molded on. Do not attempt to break the bond to examine the terminal. Peer inside to see if corrosion is present.

If the cables pass the examination, install them. Be sure each goes to its respective spark plug and distributor-tower position.

Figure 44 (left). This Fiat 124 Spider with 1756 cc. four-cylinder engine has five high-tension cables (arrow).
Figure 45 (right). Examine terminals for signs of arcing.

Figure 46 (left). Squeeze boot to release air when installing cables.
Figure 47 (right). Check cables for high resistance with ohmmeter.

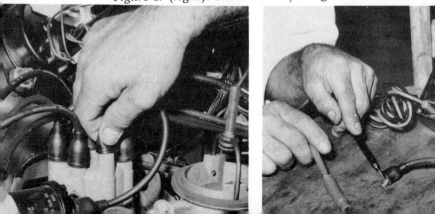

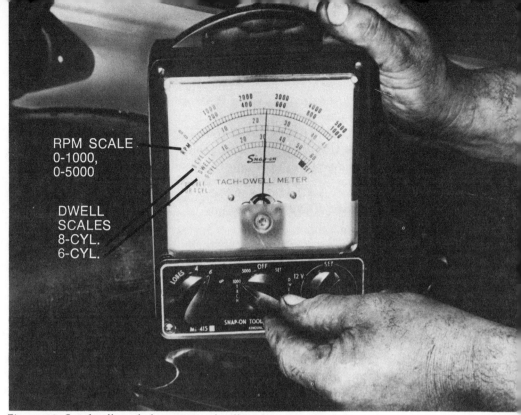

RPM SCALE
0-1000,
0-5000

DWELL
SCALES
8-CYL.
6-CYL.

*Figure 48. Set dwell angle by using a dwell/tachometer. Note that
it has settings for four, six and eight-cylinder engines.*

Install a cable at the distributor by entering its terminal into the tower with light pressure. As the terminal enters the tower, pinch the large-diameter part of the boot to release air that can get trapped between the boot and tower (Figure 46). Continue pushing until the cable is firmly seated.

Before seating the cables on the spark plugs, wipe off the insulators. Be sure that felt-marker identification markings are cleaned off, or (if you used masking tape) that tape strips are removed. Use mineral spirits to remove adhesive.

Be sure connections between cables and spark plugs are secure to prevent arcing.

Inspecting for electrical leaks

WHEN ALL CABLES have been reconnected, strip off masking-tape identification markings. Now, conduct the leak test. This is done to reveal punctures and damage in cables not uncovered by visual examination.

Fasten one alligator clip of the jumper wire to a clean ground on the engine. Attach the other alligator clip to the shank of a screwdriver.

Start the engine and allow it to idle. Remove one cable from a spark plug. Position the boot end so it doesn't point to ground.

Probe all around the cable and boot with the tip of the screwdriver.

If a defect is present, a spark will jump from the defective area to the probe. Discard the cable.

To test the high-tension cable from the center tower of the distributor to the coil, keep that cable connected. However, disconnect one spark-plug cable.

Now is a good time to test the output of the coil. Shut off the engine. Make sure that all high-tension cables are connected at spark plugs, and remove the coil-to-distributor cap cable at the distributor cap.

Attach a clip-type wooden clothespin to the cable just above the boot. Hold the cable by the clothespin and position the cable's end about one-quarter of an inch from a clean ground. Have someone in the car crank the engine briefly.

You should get a thick blue spark jumping from the end of the cable to ground. If the spark is thin and yellow, recheck to see that the distributor point gap is to specification and that all connections are tight. Failing this, have a mechanic check ignition-coil output. You might need a new coil.

Cables which are damaged internally may look sound and pass the leak test. Internal damage is caused by manhandling. Pulling on cables causes the inner core to break. This increases resistance, and reduces the current going to spark plugs. Misfire results.

You need an ohmmeter to check cable integrity. Test one cable at a time. The ohmmeter test assumes that your car is equipped with electronic suppression cable, as practically all cars have been since the early 1960's. Electronic suppression cable is identified by markings on the insulation.

Figure 50 (left). The timing light is connected as pointed out here.
Figure 51 (right). The vacuum advance unit hose should be disconnected and plugged. If any vacuum leaks from hose, timing will be affected.

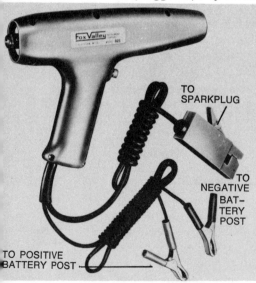

TO
SPARKPLUG

TO
NEGATIVE
BAT-
TERY
POST

TO POSITIVE
BATTERY POST

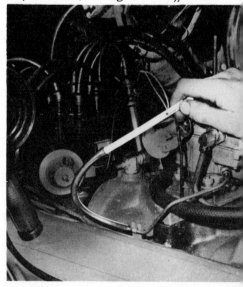

Figure 49 (above). Aim the timing light straight and true at timing mark.

SPRING

Figure 52 (left). Remove an internal fuel filter from carburetor inlet.

To make an ohmmeter test—

1. Remove the distributor cap. Keep the cables connected in cap towers.

2. Disconnect one cable at a spark plug for testing.

3. Insert the ohmmeter probe into the spark-plug end of the cable so it contacts the terminal. Hold the other ohmmeter probe to the corresponding electrode inside the distributor cap of the cable you are testing. Make sure the probes make sound contact.

4. Check the meter. If resistance is more than 30,000 ohms for cables 25 inches in length or smaller, and 50,000 ohms for cables longer than 25 inches, remove the cable and check resistance without the cap. Replace cables that fail to meet the 30,000-ohm or 50,000-ohm specification (Figure 47).

However, if the disconnected cable does meet specification, then a problem exists in the distributor cap. Clean it out with the distributor-cap cleaning tool and test again. If resistance is too high, replace the cap.

5. To test the cable between coil and distributor cap, connect the ohmmeter between the center contact in the cap and either primary terminal at the coil. Combined resistance should not exceed 25,000 ohms. If it does, remove the cable at the coil and test resistance. If it is now more than 15,000 ohms, replace the cable. If resistance is less than 15,000 ohms, check for loose connections and/or a weak coil.

Next: Set the distributor-point dwell

Here's why the distributor-point dwell angle is so critical

WITH ALL CABLES in good shape and connected properly, you must now set the distributor-point dwell angle. This refers to the distance, in degrees, that the distributor cam rotates while the distributor breaker points are closed.

If the points stay closed for too short or too long a period, not enough current reaches the spark plugs, and engine performance suffers.

Dwell angle is set by using a dwellmeter, which is usually combined with a tachometer in one instrument (Figure 48). If you don't have this instrument and don't wish to purchase one (one that will do a good job sells for about $25), you should have a mechanic set dwell for you—it is that important.

Here is how to set dwell:

1. Connect the dwell/tachometer as outlined in the instruction manual that comes with the meter. In most cases, the ground lead is attached to a clean metal part of the engine (ground), and the red-colored lead is attached to the distributor primary wire at the coil. This is the "thin" wire that extends from the coil to the distributor. Attach the dwellmeter lead's clip to the small bolt holding the wire in place.

2. Set the switches of the meter properly for the type of engine (four-, six- or eight-cylinder) you are working on. Have the function switch set initially to "Tach" mode.

3. Specifications you must have are the dwell angle for your distributor and the recommended slow (curb) idle speed of the engine. These are given in the car's service manual, in some owner's manuals, and on the tune-up specification decal in the engine compartment.

4. Start the engine and let it idle in Neutral. Read the tachometer scale, which tells at what speed the engine is running. If the engine is not running at the recommended slow-idle specification, adjust idle.

This is done differently for different engines. With some, idle is set by turning an idle-speed screw. With others, the lug of an idle-stop solenoid is turned. An idle-stop solenoid is used on most of today's cars to prevent an engine from dieseling (see Chapter 8 on how to stop a car that won't stop).

To increase idle speed, turn the idle-speed screw or solenoid clockwise. To reduce idle speed, turn the idle-speed screw or solenoid counter-clockwise. Turn until the tachometer shows the specified idle speed.

5. Switch the instrument to "Dwell" mode. If the meter doesn't record the specified dwell, set the dwell.

If your distributor has a sliding door, let the engine idle, lift the door, and insert an Allen wrench into the screw of the distributor breaker points. Turn slowly until dwell on the meter reaches the specified setting.

Caution: Be sure the sliding door is closed all the way. If it isn't, dirt may enter the distributor and cause damage.

Don't be surprised if you fail to set the dwell angle exactly right the first time

If there is no sliding door, shut off the engine, remove the distributor cap and rotor, and reset distributor breaker points. If the dwell angle was too small, move the points closer together. If the angle was excessive, move the points further apart.

Close up the distributor and test dwell once more. You may have to repeat the procedure a couple of times until dwell is set to specification.

How to set ignition timing

TIMING REFERS TO the instant that sparks are delivered to the cylinder to ignite the fuel mixture. To set timing, you must be equipped with a stroboscopic timing light and have the timing specification for your ignition system, which is given in the owner's and service manual, and on the tune-up-specification decal in the engine compartment.

Note that the specification is given in degrees. This refers to the position of the crankshaft when spark should occur. For example, if the timing specification for your engine calls for a setting of 5° BTDC (Before Top Dead Center), it means that spark should occur when the crankshaft has five degrees to turn before the piston reaches top dead center in the cylinder.

The timing light is aimed at timing marks on the crankshaft pulley, engine block, or flywheel (Figure 49).

Advice: Your task can be made simple if you identify the correct timing mark beforehand by consulting a service manual or asking a mechanic to point it out. Dab some white paint on the mark to make it stand out.

The timing light "freezes" the timing mark in relation to an adjacent pointer. If the mark wavers, the timing is not correct and has to be readjusted.

Timing is set by loosening the distributor and turning it one way or the other until the timing mark is brought into proper range with the pointer and does not waver. You only have to time one cylinder—No. 1 is the one usually selected, because it is easiest to get at. Timing one cylinder automatically sets the others.

Here is a step-by-step way to time the ignition system of your car:

1. Warm up the engine, connect a tachometer and make sure the engine idle speed is to specification. Timing is always tested with the engine idling at its specified curb idle speed.

2. Connect the timing light to No. 1 spark plug circuit. Make sure there is contact between the timing light and spark plug (Figure 50). If necessary, use an adapter.

An adapter is a long length of cable with exposed connectors that is hooked between the spark plug and its cable. Use of an adapter makes it easier to connect the timing light into the spark plug circuit.

Caution: Do not puncture the spark-plug cable in an attempt to obtain contact between the timing light and spark-plug circuit. Details on how to hook up your timing light are given in the instruction booklet accompanying the timing light. Read it.

3. Disconnect the vacuum hose from the vacuum advance unit on the side of the distributor and stick a pencil in the end of the hose to plug it up (Figure 51). Make sure that no vacuum leaks from the hose. A vacuum leak affects timing.

4. With the engine idling at its specified idling speed, aim the timing light at the appropriate timing mark and adjacent pointer. Sight straight down the center of the light as you would sight down the barrel of a rifle. Do not tilt the instrument.

5. The light will emit blips. As I said before, the ignition is timed properly if the flashes of light "freeze" the timing mark in relation to the index pointer. You should not see the timing mark shift.

If the timing mark is "frozen" you've made the right adjustment

If timing needs readjusting, loosen the distributor housing with a distributor wrench and rotate the housing until the timing mark lines up with the pointer and holds steady. Tighten the distributor and recheck.

As long as the timing light is hooked up, double-check the condition of the distributor and the functioning of the vacuum advance unit. Remove the timing-light lead from No. 1 cylinder and connect it to the alternate firing cylinder.

On a V8 engine, the alternate firing cylinder is the fifth cylinder in the firing order. On six-cylinder engines, the alternate firing cylinder is the fourth cylinder in the firing order. The firing order for your engine is given in the service manual and on the tune-up specification decal in the engine compartment. Usually it is also embossed on the engine block.

Now, check timing. A three-degree or less difference in timing between the two cylinders (No. 1 and the alternate firing cylinder) is acceptable. A greater variation indicates that the distributor shaft or bushings are worn, and the distributor should be overhauled.

Remove the pencil from the end of the vacuum advance hose and hold the end of the hose near the vacuum advance chamber. Have someone in the car gradually increase engine speed as you push and pull the hose on and off the unit.

The timing mark should shift rapidly. If it doesn't move or moves sluggishly, the diaphragm in the vacuum advance unit has ruptured. Replace the unit.

Time to take a breather—you're not so far from the finish

This completes tune-up of the ignition system. Next, turn your attention to the fuel system.

Begin fuel-system service by replacing the filter

A FUEL FILTER may never clog, but then again one can clog at any time. The filter intercepts dirt carried with gasoline before it can reach the carburetor and engine. If a fuel filter gets clogged with dirt, the flow of gas to the engine will be shut off and the engine won't go.

That is why it's a good idea to replace the filter every 12,000 miles— just in case. Your car has one of three types:

1. A bronze or paper element that is located inside the carburetor inlet. Most General Motors cars have this kind.

To replace this type of filter, disconnect the fuel line at the carburetor and remove the large retaining nut. The filter is right behind the nut. Take it out. Also remove the small spring behind the filter, but don't lose it. It can be reused (Figure 52).

Caution: Before disconnecting the fuel line, place a rag or small receptacle beneath the line to catch excess gasoline. No smoking!

2. An in-line filter that is inserted in the fuel line between the fuel pump and carburetor. Generally, Chrysler Corporation and American Motors models are equipped with this kind of filter.

To replace the filter, detach the retaining clips and pull the filter from the fuel line (Figure 53).

Caution: Same as above.

3. An external filter that is screwed directly into the carburetor inlet. Some Ford models use this kind.

To replace this filter, loosen the fuel inlet hose and unscrew the filter.

Caution: Same as above.

Don't overlook the automatic choke

THE PURPOSE OF the automatic choke is to prevent air from entering the carburetor when a cold engine is started. This results in a richer fuel mixture, which permits faster and surer starts.

As the engine starts and warms up, the automatic choke releases. If it didn't, the engine would receive fuel that was too rich and would flood. This would cause it to stall.

All in all, if the automatic choke in your car isn't working properly, you experience hard starting problems and excessive fuel consumption. A faulty automatic choke also makes an engine idle roughly, lose power, and backfire.

Although choke mechanisms from carburetor to carburetor differ somewhat, they all work much the same. All use a bimetallic spring—that's a coil spring which is affected by temperature. When it is cold, the spring winds up tightly. When it is warm, the spring releases tension.

The spring is connected to a butterfly valve (or plate) inside the throat of the carburetor by means of linkage.

When it is cold, the spring is wrapped up tight, exerting pressure on the valve through the linkage. The valve is closed. When it gets warm, the spring releases its tension on the linkage and, thus, on the valve. The valve opens.

However, there is a wrinkle. Once the engine starts, it is important that the butterfly valve be allowed to open slightly so some air is introduced into the carburetor. Otherwise the engine would flood.

A piston or vacuum mechanism is used to exert pressure on the plate immediately.

Figure 53 (left). The in-line fuel filter is detached from fuel line.
Figure 54 (right). This choke system of a late-model vehicle is equipped with an electric assist unit, which lessens emissions.

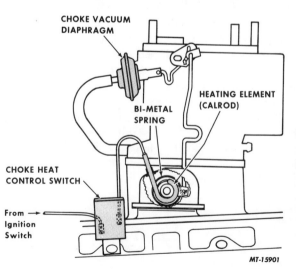

CHOKE VACUUM
DIAPHRAGM

HEATING ELEMENT
(CALROD)

BI-METAL
SPRING

CHOKE HEAT
CONTROL SWITCH

From →
Ignition
Switch

MT-15901

Automatic chokes also work in conjunction with a fast idle cam that allows the engine to idle rapidly when it is cold. Fast idle allows the engine to reach normal operating temperature quickly and also averts stumble and stall.

When the engine gets warm, the fast-idle cam pivots back, permitting a normal idle.

The automatic chokes of many cars since 1972 have been equipped with a device that introduces an electric current to open the choke plate fully as quickly as possible (Figure 54). This is the so-called electric-assist choke and it is employed to help meet exhaust-emission standards.

Another important part of the automatic choke system is an unloader that relieves a flooding condition. The unloader is activated by flooring the accelerator pedal and keeping it to the floor as you crank the engine. Keep this in mind should you ever need help in starting a cold engine that has flooded.

What happens when you floor the accelerator pedal is that a cam trips a linkage, causing the choke plate to open, thereby relieving the over-rich condition in the cylinders.

How to test automatic choke operation

WAIT FOR A COLD DAY and make sure the engine is cold. Remove the carburetor air cleaner.

Have someone in the car press the accelerator pedal to the floor once and release it. The choke plate should close over the carburetor throat.

Figure 55 (left). Keep choke parts clean to reduce chance of trouble.
Figure 56 (right). One type of choke has a stove on the carburetor. This choke is adjusted by loosening and rotating the cover.

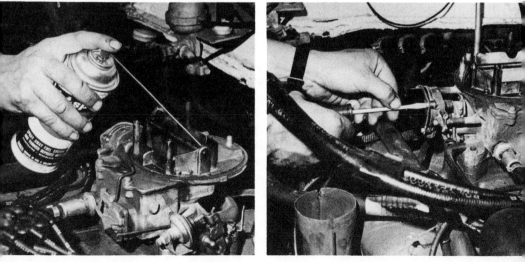

Start the engine. The choke plate should open slightly. As the engine gets warm, the plate should continue opening until it opens fully.

To test the fast-idle mechanism, listen to the engine when it first starts. It should be idling rapidly without stumble.

Now have your assistant tap the gas pedal. The idle should drop off. As the engine gets warmer, idle should drop back even more and reach normal curb idle speed.

If your choke doesn't work this way, it may be dirty or damaged.

Keep choke parts clean

THE CHIEF ENEMY of an automatic choke is dirt. Chokes clogged by dirt work sluggishly or bind completely. When you tune up your engine, clean the choke-plate pivots and all rods and linkages with choke cleaner (Figure 55).

Caution: Never apply oil to any part of a choke system. Oil attracts dirt.

If a choke is clean and doesn't work properly, then you have to hunt for a bent linkage. If everything appears okay, chances are that the bimetallic coil spring is shot. Replace it. How to do this job is outlined below in the discussion on adjusting chokes.

If your carburetor is equipped with an electric-assist choke, and the choke plate doesn't work properly although it is clean and linkages are in good condition, the control switch or heating element has probably burned out. First make sure that the wires connecting components are tight. If they are, have a mechanic test to determine whether the switch or heating element is at fault.

Important: Electric assist chokes cannot be adjusted!

Adjusting a choke to suit the climate

First off, find out whether you have the first or second type of automatic choke

IF AN AUTOMATIC CHOKE is not adjusted right, it won't work right. The right setting isn't always the one recommended by the manufacturer of the car.

Manufacturer recommendations are a compromise. After all, since chokes work on heat and cold, it stands to reason that one on a carburetor in Florida is going to work differently from one on the same kind of carburetor in Minnesota.

In order to set a choke properly, you have to identify the kind you have on your car. There are two general types:

1. A heat-sensitive bimetallic coil spring that is mounted on a housing on the carburetor and is connected to the choke plate by a short rod. This is the so-called stove-type choke (Figure 56).

Heat is concentrated on the spring through a tube that extends from the exhaust manifold. This mechanism uses a small piston to override spring tension when a cold engine is first started, so the choke plate will open slightly and not flood the engine.

2. A well-type choke which has a bimetallic coil spring positioned in the exhaust crossover of the intake manifold or in the exhaust manifold. The spring is connected to the choke plate by a long rod (Figure 57).

This type of choke uses a vacuum-operated diaphragm, which can be adjusted to override spring tension when a cold engine starts; the choke plate opens slightly to prevent engine flooding.

The cover of a stove-type choke is marked in increments denoting "richer" and "leaner." The plate on which the spring of a well-type choke is mounted is also marked in this way. Markings are used in making an adjustment.

The way to get the right adjustment for your choke is to start by setting the adjustment mechanism two marks to the lean side of the mark specified by the manufacturer. For example, if the manufacturer says to set the choke two notches to the lean side, set it four notches to the lean side.

Figure 57 (left). Another kind of choke has a thermostat spring in a well in the manifold. It is adjusted by loosening the locknut.
Figure 58 (right). Remove cover of stove-type choke to replace spring.

Figure 59 (left). If a stove-type choke clogs because of the presence of internal dirt, change the heat tube.
Figure 60 (right). Vacuum break of well-type choke should be tested.

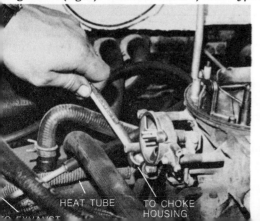 

HEAT TUBE   TO CHOKE HOUSING

STEM

The manufacturer specification for the choke is given in the service manual and on the decal in the engine compartment.

Save this for a cold day

BE SURE THE ENGINE is cold (wait for a cold day, too) and start the engine to see if it starts easily and idles without stumbling and stalling. If it doesn't perform properly, move the choke adjustment mechanism one notch at a time toward the rich side until the engine starts and runs normally.

Adjust a stove-type choke by loosening the cover retaining screws and rotating the cover. In most cases, clockwise rotation reduces choking action (makes it leaner). Counterclockwise rotation increases choking action (makes it richer).

Adjust well-type chokes by loosening the mounting-post locknut and turning the post until the desired mark lines up with the index. Place the mechanism back into its well and attach the choke rod to the choke plate.

Make sure that the coil spring of a well-type choke doesn't come into contact with the sides of the well. Lift the covering disc, and open and close the choke plate by hand to determine if the connector rod clears the sides of the hole in the cover without binding. If the rod binds, it is bent. Replace the entire unit.

Here's how to adjust both types of chokes and make repairs

If you can't get a choke setting with either type of choke, the thermostatic coil spring has probably lost tension and should be replaced. The coil spring of a stove-type choke is inside the cover (Figure 58).

When you take off that cover, check to see if there is dirt or carbon in the choke housing. If there is, it means that the heat tube from the manifold has developed a leak. Replace the tube and clean inside choke parts with kerosene or choke cleaner (Figure 59).

If you are working on a well-type choke, check out the vacuum diaphragm unit, which is also called the vacuum break (Figure 60). Disconnect the vacuum line and inspect it for splits and holes.

Depress the stem of the diaphragm and place your finger over the vacuum opening. Release the stem. If the stem moves more than $\frac{1}{16}$ of an inch in 10 seconds, the diaphragm is leaking. Replace the unit.

To adjust the vacuum break, close the choke plate and hold the vacuum break against its stop. Measure the distance between the edge of the choke valve and the wall of the air horn. This measurement must be to manufacturer specification, so check the service manual.

Other carburetor adjustments that need attention

WHEN YOU ARE tuning up an engine, other carburetor adjustments you should make are curb-idle speed and fast-idle speed. If your car is equipped with an anti-stall dashpot, that part also deserves attention. There is another adjustment that I want to mention before getting into detail on the others. It is idle mixture—that is, adjusting the proportion of gasoline to air. Before 1968, the car owner could make this adjustment by turning a screw. Times have changed.

In 1968, the mixture screws of new cars were capped. This was done to comply with federal law requiring a reduction in exhaust emissions.

The mixture is set at the factory and should not be tampered with unless the carburetor is overhauled (Figure 61). Then, a combustion analyzer is needed to record the carbon-monoxide content of the exhaust gas. The setting is made exactly to specification.

We have already discussed how to adjust curb-idle speed. If idle speed is too fast, the engine races and consumes more fuel than necessary. If idle speed is too slow, the engine lopes and can stall.

On cars built prior to 1968, the idle speed is set by turning an idle-speed adjusting screw (Figure 62). Since 1968, most carburetors have been equipped with an idle-stop solenoid, and are adjusted by using this device.

Idle speed, as you have seen before, is set using a tachometer. It must be made to specification.

The fast-idle mechanism uses a fast-idle screw that comes into contact with graduated steps on a fast-idle cam (Figure 64). As the engine gets warmer and warmer, the screw steps down from one cam to another, letting idle speed taper off.

When the engine is warmed to normal temperature, the screw is off the cam completely, the fast idle is disconnected, and the engine runs at normal idle speed.

Generally, fast idle is set with the engine warm and turned off, but you should check manufacturer instructions. The throttle is usually open and the choke plate is closed. The throttle is then closed manually to place the fast-idle screw on the highest step of the fast-idle cam.

Figure 61 (left). Do not remove caps that cover idle-mixture screws. Figure 62 (right). A tachometer is used when setting idle speed. This car is pre-1968 and has an idle-speed adjusting screw.

Figure 63. Adjust idle stop solenoid to change idle on post-'68 cars.
Figure 64 (below). Adjust typical screw shown to set fast idle speed.

Figure 65. Leave air pump with internal filter to professional.

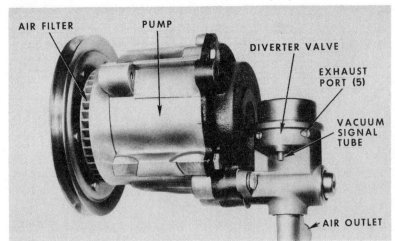

AIR FILTER   PUMP

DIVERTER VALVE

EXHAUST
PORT (5)

VACUUM
SIGNAL
TUBE

AIR OUTLET

Rotate the fast-idle cam until the screw drops to the second highest step. Start the engine and check idling speed with a tachometer to determine if it is to manufacturer specification. If not, turn the fast-idle screw until it is.

Dashpots are installed on carburetors of many cars equipped with manual transmissions to retard the return of the throttle to idle position and prevent stalling. An engine that stalls when hot indicates the need for a dashpot adjustment.

Adjustment is made after idle speed has been set to specification. A tachometer is used to read out specified revolutions per minute (rpm) with the throttle lever in light contact with the stem of the dashpot. If specified rpm is not attained, loosen the dashpot's locknut and move it until the specified speed is attained.

Advice: Our instructions about carburetor adjustments may seem rather vague. They are, because of the significant differences, from one carburetor to another. You should have a service manual available when making adjustments. Another way to try and get information is to get the model number of your carburetor off the nameplate attached to the unit and send it with a request for data to the company.

How to tackle the A.I.R. system

THE FOLLOWING PROCEDURE should be followed when servicing an A.I.R. system (if you don't think you can do it, let a mechanic do it for you):

1. With the engine warmed up, check air output by removing the hose at the air-distribution manifold. If air streams from the hose with the engine idling rapidly, the system up to the check valve is working properly.

2. With the engine turned off, disconnect the air-supply hose at the check valve and inspect the position of the valve plate inside the valve body. It should be lightly pressed against the valve seat.

Depress the valve with a probe. Release it. It should return to its original position.

Start the engine and run it at fast idle. Watch to see if there is an exhaust-gas leak from the check valve.

If the valve doesn't meet these criteria, replace it.

3. Check the anti-backfire (air bypass) valve. Remove the hose connected to the valve. With the engine running at normal idle, see if air flows from the bypass-valve hose connection.

Pinch off the vacuum hose for about five seconds. Release it. Air flowing through the valve should diminish or stop momentarily.

Reconnect the hose and remove the vacuum supply hose at the bypass valve connection. Hook a vacuum gauge to the hose first—and then to the valve with the engine idling. Both readings should be the same.

If the valve reading is lower than the reading you got from the hose, replace the valve. If the hose's reading is lower, check the hose for loose connections and damage.

4. Replace the air filter every 24,000 miles. Several variations are employed.

Some systems have an external filter. No sweat. Just disassemble the filter housing, remove the filter and replace it with a new one.

If the filter is inside the air pump, then there's a bit of a hassle. The pulley usually has to be removed, and the danger of cracking the housing is present (Figure 65). Better leave this to a professional who knows how to tackle it.

How to clean the exhaust-gas recirculating valve

CLEAN THE EGR VALVE every 12,000 miles.

Remove it from the engine and hold it tightly in your hand. Do not put it into a vise.

Tap lightly on the sides and end of the valve with a plastic hammer to remove deposits from the valve seat. Now, with a wire wheel, buff deposits from the mounting surface and from around the valve.

Depress the valve diaphragm and look at the valve outlet, checking for cleanliness. If the valve or seat isn't perfectly clean, repeat the cleaning procedure.

Check for deposits in the valve outlet and with a screwdriver remove any you find. Clean the mounting surfaces of the valve assembly and intake manifold. Install the valve assembly back on the intake manifold, using a new gasket.

No tune-up is complete without a road test

A ROAD TRIAL is the true test. Get the car on the highway and vary its speed—accelerate rapidly and then drop back quickly; accelerate slowly from a dead stop; and accelerate quickly from a dead stop.

The engine should perform flawlessly. If it misses, stalls, surges, or demonstrates flat spots in acceleration, recheck what you have done. If you are certain that everything is adjusted and connected properly, and that all parts are in good condition, then your engine problem is something that can't be repaired by a tune-up.

Engine problems and causes other than "tunable" ones are discussed in subsequent chapters.

Chapter 2

How to stretch your fuel dollar as far as it can go

Practically everyone has moaned and groaned about the high price of gasoline, but what are they doing about it? Be smart. Investigate the methods outlined here for getting every bit of use from your fuel dollar.

LET'S START WITH a basic question: which gasoline should you be using in your engine?

Some drivers may answer simply, "The gasoline specified by the manufacturer for my car in the owner's manual."

Unfortunately, the type of gasoline you should be using isn't always spelled out in the manual in clear terms. Even when it is, some drivers have doubts. They question the manufacturer's judgment.

For instance, a manufacturer may say to use a "regular" grade of gas. There are those drivers who believe that they should use a "premium" grade instead, because they get "more power" or "better mileage."

This is so much nonsense. All they are doing is spending money for nothing.

It all revolves around octane rating

YOU ARE LIKELY to find at least three grades of gasoline sold at any service station. They are referred to generically as regular, premium, and no-lead (or low-lead) regular.

Regardless of designations, all gasolines are basically the same. They are blends of a variety of refined petroleum products to which certain chemicals are added to prevent engine problems. These additives include rust and gum inhibitors, detergents, and anti-icing compounds.

It doesn't matter whether the gasoline is called "super-duper," "premium," or "economy." They all contain pretty much these same ingredients.

So what is the difference? Octane rating!

Octane rating is a numerical designation that represents the ability of gasoline to resist detonation. The degree to which the gasoline must resist detonation depends for the most part on engine design, but also on the region in which the car is driven.

Thus, anti-detonation substances are blended into gasoline in varying amounts. It is the difference in the quantity of these substances from one grade of gasoline to another grade which is really the only basic difference between grades of gasoline.

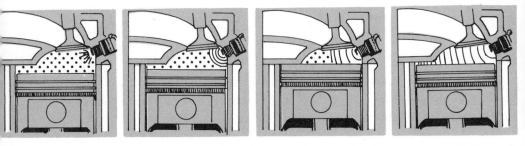

Figure 1. In normal combustion, flame front races at a controlled speed across the combustion chamber to burn the fuel mixture completely.

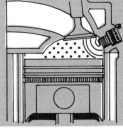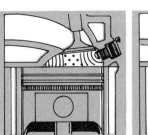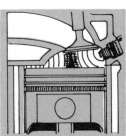

Figure 2. Detonation is abnormal combustion that results in knock (ping). The spark plug fires and the mixture starts burning normally, but then a portion of the unburned mixture starts burning independently. When the two flame fronts meet, they explode, causing knock, loss of power.

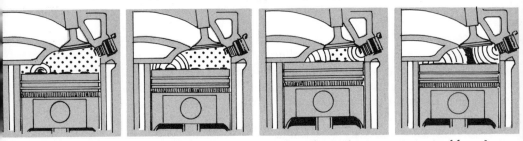

Figure 3. Preignition occurs when the fuel mixture is ignited by a hot spot or glowing deposit before the timed spark ignites the mixture.

How to prevent detonation—for less money

DETONATION REFERS TO a rapid, rattling knock that comes from an engine, particularly on acceleration. Many drivers call it "ping." But it is *not* preignition although some drivers call it this, too.

Detonation occurs when gasoline is unable to withstand the heat and pressure occurring in the engine's cylinders. Instead of burning smoothly and evenly as it should, the gas ignites violently after it has been ignited by the spark plug (Figures 1 and 2). This sudden burst of violent ignition of the gasoline remaining in the cylinder rattles the engine's cylinder head and makes the noise that you hear.

Preignition, on the other hand, is premature combustion of fuel within a cylinder (Figure 3). The gasoline is ignited by a foreign substance, such as a piece of red-hot carbon, before normal ignition actually occurs.

Light-intensity detonation is not usually harmful to an engine. However, heavy detonation can cause internal damage.

There is no such thing as "light" or "heavy" preignition. There is no such thing as "harmless" detonation. When gasoline ignites out of time in a cylinder, it puts intense strain on moving parts and will ruin the engine. Piston heads can have holes blown in them and connecting rods can be bent.

Unfortunately, the untrained cannot always tell the difference between the noise made by detonation and that made by preignition. So the best advice I can offer is this:

If you cannot get a knock that you think is detonation to disappear by trying the methods outlined here, then the noise is probably preignition. Get the car to a mechanic for a carbon-purging job as soon as you can.

The way to prevent (or get rid of) detonation is to make sure the ignition is timed properly, see to it that the engine is not overheating, and then select a gasoline which has an octane rating that meets the engine's requirements.

Let's look a little closer at octane rating

WE SAID ABOVE that octane rating is a numerical designation. The average octane rating of so-called regular grades of gasoline sold in the United States in recent years has been about 93 to 94, while the average octane rating of so-called premium grades of gasoline has been 98 to 100.

Before we go further, we had better clear up exactly how this numerical designation is determined. Two methods are used. They are called the research method and the motor method. Each gives an octane number different than the other for the *same* gasoline.

The research method defines the octane rating of gasoline according to laboratory test procedures. The motor method provides an octane rating by actual in-engine use.

The motor method gives an octane designation that is numerically lower for the same gasoline than the rating provided by the research method.

The fact that there are two ways of arriving at an octane rating for a particular grade of gasoline has heightened motorist confusion ever since gasoline stations have been required to post octane ratings on gasoline pumps. Generally, the octane numbers recommended in owners' manuals by automobile manufacturers are research-method numbers. The octane number posted on pumps are lower, but they are not motor-method numbers.

Let's take an example. Suppose your owner's manual says to use a regular grade of gasoline having a 91-octane rating. The regular grade of gasoline sold at the local service station, however, is rated at 89 or 90. You wonder if you have to use a premium gasoline to meet your car manufacturer's requirements.

However, the posted octane ratings are derived by adding the research method number and the motor method number, and dividing by two. For example, suppose a gasoline has a research octane number rating of 94 and a motor octane rating of 84.

The octane number that will be posted on the gasoline pump delivering that product will be 89 . . . $94 + 84 \div 2 = 89$.

If the engine doesn't knock, no need for higher octane

When you come right down to it, though, the true test of the gasoline you use is whether or not it prevents detonation. The money-conscious motorist is the one who buys the least expensive gasoline he can get which fulfills this need.

How resistance to detonation is "added" to gasoline

FROM 1923 TO THE PRESENT, the chief ingredient put into gasoline to add resistance to detonation has been lead—tetraethyl lead in particular. The more lead that is added to gasoline, the greater will be its resistance to detonation.

The octane rating is a reflection of this resistance. Gasoline having an octane rating of 100 (research method), for instance, has a greater resistance to detonation than gasoline having an octane rating of 94.

The actual octane rating of a gas is obtained by comparing its resistance to detonation with a blend of isooctane and n-heptane (the *n* stands for "normal").

Isooctane has maximum resistance to detonation and possesses an octane number of 100. N-heptane has no resistance to detonation and has been given an octane number of 0.

Take a gasoline that has an octane rating of 94. This means that this gas has the same resistance to detonation as a mixture of 94 percent isooctane and 6 percent n-heptane.

Octane ratings of the same grade of gasoline (regular, premium, or whatever) differ significantly from one section of the country to another. This is because altitude affects resistance to detonation. Cars driven in higher elevations have less tendency to develop detonation. Thus, gasoline of lower octane is generally sold in these areas.

Throughout the country, the octane numbers for regular grades of gasoline vary from 90 to 96. The octane ratings of premium grades of fuel vary from 97 to 103.

The importance of unleaded gasoline

ADDING LEAD TO GASOLINE is not the only way to add resistance to detonation. Unleaded gasoline uses no lead, but yet it has resistance. In fact, unleaded gasoline is the "wave of the future." Within a decade, it is expected to replace leaded gasoline.

The reason for this is the fight against air pollution. By using unleaded fuel, car manufacturers are able to equip vehicles with a highly effective pollution-control device called a catalytic converter (Figure 4).

Lead in gasoline is expelled through the car's muffler. The catalytic converter is actually used as a muffler. Lead particles destroy the catalyst within a few thousand miles.

Leaded gasoline can quickly destroy the top anti-pollution device

However, by using unleaded gasoline, the life of the device can be extended to at least 50,000 miles. Catalytic converters cost about $200, so you can see the importance of this.

In a catalytic converter, harmful exhaust gases (hydrocarbons, carbon monoxide, and nitrogen oxide) are converted to harmless water vapor, carbon dioxide, and nitrogen when they come into contact with the catalyst, which may be platinum.

Another benefit in removing lead from gasoline is that the expulsion of lead particles into the air will be eliminated, putting to rest once and for all the argument that has raged for decades about whether lead particles in the air constitute a health hazard.

Nonleaded fuel achieves resistance to detonation by means of complex and expensive refining techniques. Nonleaded fuel has a research-method octane number of 91. This is low when compared to leaded fuels, and it necessitated a changeover in engine design beginning with the 1971 models.

Figure 4. The job of the catalytic converter is to tranform pollutants into harmless substances.

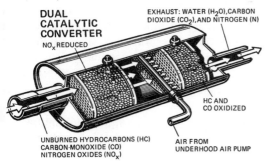

DUAL CATALYTIC CONVERTER
NO_x REDUCED

EXHAUST: WATER (H_2O),CARBON DIOXIDE (CO_2),AND NITROGEN (N)

HC AND CO OXIDIZED

UNBURNED HYDROCARBONS (HC) CARBON-MONOXIDE (CO) NITROGEN OXIDES (NO_x)

AIR FROM UNDERHOOD AIR PUMP

Practically every pre-1971 car requires gasoline having an octane rating of at least 92. With few exceptions, every engine built from 1971 onward can operate without knocking on the nonleaded (or low-lead) 91-octane fuel.

(Low-lead gasoline is an interim step employed by some oil companies in making the transition from leaded to nonleaded fuel. Leaded gasoline contains as much as 4.2 grams of lead per gallon. Low-lead gas contains only 0.5 gram per gallon or less.)

How to find the gasoline your car needs

AS I SAID before, first make sure ignition timing is to manufacturer specification and that the engine is not overheating. Now, use the grade of gasoline (regular, premium, or unleaded or low lead) suggested by the manufacturer of your car in the owner's manual.

Switching gasoline brands—not grades —may be the way to cure engine knock

If the engine performs without knocking, you have found the gasoline to use. If detonation starts, switch to a different brand of the *same* grade.

From one oil company to another in the same area, grades of gasoline can differ by two octane numbers. It can take only one to stop knock.

When you find the right gasoline for your car, the engine will stop knocking within a tankful.

Remember: If you can't get the knock to stop, consider the possibility of preignition.

Above all, keep in mind that excess octane is of no value. It doesn't give the engine more power. It doesn't keep an engine clean. All it does is cost you more money.

Testing: the next step

ONCE YOU HAVE established which gasoline is best for your engine, the next step in your effort to conserve fuel is to determine exactly how much gasoline your car is actually using. Unless you can check results before and after applying conservation methods, there is no way of telling if those methods are successful.

Checking gasoline mileage should be done with a gas-per-mile gauge, or similar device (Figure 5). The test should be made over a planned test course with you driving. A mileage test conducted with someone else behind the wheel is not an accurate test, since each driver causes a car to consume a different quantity of gasoline. This is due to individual driving habits.

In laying out the test course, make sure that the following types of driving conditions are included:

1. A trip at highway speed in one direction, and then back to the original destination over the same route. This will equalize the effects of any head and tail wind.

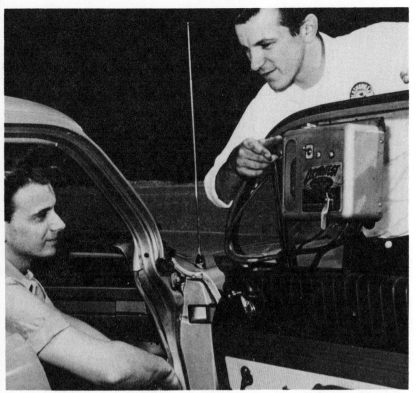

Figure 5. Establish how much gasoline your car actually uses with a professional miles-per-gallon gauge, as here, or with the homemade instrument described in the text.

2. A drive through a light-traffic residential area.

3. A drive through a heavy-traffic business area.

An instrumented gasoline mileage test costs about $10 or $15 if you have a professional serviceman help you. You don't need the serviceman, but you do need his equipment.

How to make your own gasoline mileage detector

However, you can devise a test instrument of your own from a quart can, fittings and tubing. It will be crude, but it will be effective.

The tubing you use should be the same diameter as the fuel-pump-to-carburetor fuel line. Attach one fitting, which should be the same size as the existing carburetor-inlet fitting, to one end of the tube.

Drill a hole in the bottom of the quart can and solder in the other fitting. Make sure that your homemade gasoline-mileage meter doesn't leak.

Fashion a handle or wire hook for the instrument so you can hang it from the window on the driver's side of the car. Place the can outside and roll the window up against the handle to hold it as steady as possible.

In preparing for the test (whether you use a factory- or homemade testing instrument), inflate tires to specification. Underinflated tires increase fuel consumption.

Make sure the car's brakes aren't dragging. By rights, the engine should be tuned up. Nothing wastes gasoline more than an untuned engine.

Also test to see that the exhaust system is not restricted. A restriction in the exhaust wastes power, which leads to use of more gas.

Accelerate the engine at idle to a high speed momentarily, and back off on speed. A hissing sound, which will be most noticeable at the tailpipe, signifies a restriction.

Check the tailpipe for mud, and clean any out with a screwdriver or other pointed instrument.

Check to see if the tailpipe is kinked. Frequently, a pipe can be straightened by inserting a bar and gently pushing out the collapsed area.

If the tailpipe is in satisfactory condition, a restriction may exist because of carbon in the muffler or a loose muffler baffle. For maximum fuel economy, the restriction should be eliminated even if this means replacing the muffler.

See to it, too, that the manifold heat control valve moves freely. If your engine possesses this valve, you will find it beneath the exhaust manifold.

A stuck manifold heat control valve may be robbing your fuel

Be sure the engine is cold before putting your hand down there. If the valve does not move as you turn the counterweight, try to free it by lubricating around the counterweight with manifold heat control valve solvent (Figure 6).

Another step to take in preparation for the mileage test is to inspect the carburetor air-cleaner element. A dirty element can increase fuel consumption by as much as one mile per gallon.

Remove the air cleaner cover and take the element from place. Inspect it by placing a lamp so the light shines from the inside out. If you can't see the light clearly, the element is clogged. Replace it.

If you are employing a homemade testing instrument, hook it up by disconnecting the fuel line at the carburetor. Plug the end of the line with a small cork or some other suitable object to prevent gasoline from spurting out.

Run the engine until fuel remaining in the carburetor is consumed. Now, connect the test instrument to the carburetor. Be sure to mount the can higher than the carburetor so fuel will flow into the carburetor by gravity. Pour exactly one quart of gasoline into the can.

Caution: Remember that you are handling gasoline. No smoking or other act that will cause a spark or flame.

Jot down the reading on the odometer and make your test drive over the planned course. When the car runs out of gasoline, note the odometer reading again to see how far you have traveled.

Multiply that distance by four since there are four quarts to a gallon. This provides the fuel consumption rate for your car.

For example, if you run out of gas after going 4.3 miles, your car is getting 17.2 miles per gallon.

If the test is being done with professional mile-per-gallon equipment, there is no need for the mathematical manipulations just discussed. The meter "tells all."

How to improve gas mileage

IF YOU WANT to take the biggest step you can toward maximum fuel economy, apply the procedures outlined in Chapter 1—tune up your engine periodically. Once this is done, look for leaks. Gasoline that is lost before it reaches the engine is money down the drain.

Tighten fittings at the fuel line where it connects to the carburetor and fuel pump (Figure 7). Be sure that carburetor assembly bolts are tight and give carburetor mounting bolts a turn, too (Figure 8).

Start the engine and trace the fuel line from the carburetor as far back toward the fuel tank as you can see. Perhaps a pinhole has developed and gasoline is being lost. Also inspect to see if the fuel tank and filler neck have developed leaks, especially at seams.

Figure 6. Manifold heat control valve solvent can be applied around the counterweight of the valve to free the valve.

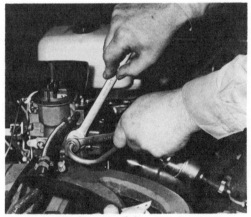

Figure 7. Tighten fuel-line connections, where the line connects to the carburetor and fuel pump, to prevent gasoline leaks.

Figure 8. Carburetor assembly bolts should also be tightened to stop leaks. If a carburetor bowl keeps leaking, replace gasket.

There is another cause of "leakage" that is always avoidable. Make sure that the gas-tank cap is always as tight as possible.

Don't trust service-station attendants. A busy guy can fail to tighten the cap. Get out of the car and give the cap a twist yourself. Gasoline fumes that escape from around a loose gas-tank cap not only pollute the air—they also represent a loss of gas.

In line with this, keep one more thing in mind: avoid overfilling the fuel tank, especially in hot weather. Gasoline expands. If the tank is filled to the brim, gas might overflow and be lost.

Maintain an air space in the tank between the gas and the top of the filler neck. The best way to do this is to stop the attendant from pumping in more gasoline after the automatic shut-off on the gas pump snaps off.

Look out for overcooling

AN INSPECTION OF spark-plug tips can inform you of two conditions that may be causing your engine to use an excessive amount of gasoline (Figure 9). If spark-plug tips are covered with black, sooty deposits—(1) the engine may be failing to operate at a temperature that is needed to assure complete combustion; or (2) the fuel mixture may be too rich.

Consider what happens if water-jacket temperature inside the engine fails to reach operating range. Fuel that concentrates itself next to the cylinder walls in particular, where it is cooler, may not get hot enough to burn. It will be exhausted out the tailpipe in a "raw" state. This is wasteful and also contributes to air pollution.

Unfortunately, the main reason for low engine-temperature operation is short-trip driving, and sometimes that is unavoidable. However, another cause is something that you do have control over: a faulty cooling system thermostat or failure to use a thermostat.

You should always have your engine equipped with the thermostat specified by the manufacturer of your car. And that thermostat should be in peak operational condition. See Chapter 5 on overheating and overcooling for a discussion of thermostats.

An overrich fuel mixture is a mixture that doesn't contain sufficient oxygen to burn completely. This means that a portion of every charge which is drawn into the combustion chambers does not produce power, but instead is blown out the exhaust system in an unburned state.

The following is a summary of those conditions that can cause an overrich fuel mixture:

• **A dirty carburetor.** If the carburetor has not been cleaned for many thousands of miles (30,000 miles is the limit usually given) and gasoline consumption has been getting steadily worse, the carburetor should be disassembled and cleaned.

Depending upon the availability of service data and your own desires, you may or may not want to do this job yourself. If you decide

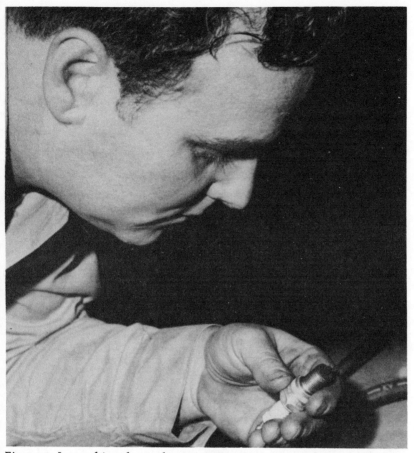

Figure 9. In tracking down the reason for excessive fuel consumption, important clues may be found by examining spark plug tips.

not to do it yourself, get estimates from several professional carburetor mechanics. Then see how much a new carburetor will cost you. The cost of labor may almost equal the cost of a new carburetor.

At the time that the carburetor is overhauled, certain adjustments bearing on fuel economy should also be made. Depending on the type of carburetor you are dealing with, adjustments may include the accelerator pump stroke, idle vent, choke unloader, dashpot, float, idle mixture, and vacuum break (Figure 10).

Note: Unfortunately, it is not possible in this book to go into greater detail on carburetor overhaul and adjustments than we do here and in other chapters. There are simply too many different types of units and scores of variations. However, if you get the name and model number of your carburetor from the nomenclature plate that is normally attached to the carburetor and send it to the manufacturer, the company normally will be willing to send you overhaul and adjustment instructions. These instructions are also contained in the service manual published by the manufacturer of the car who may or may not

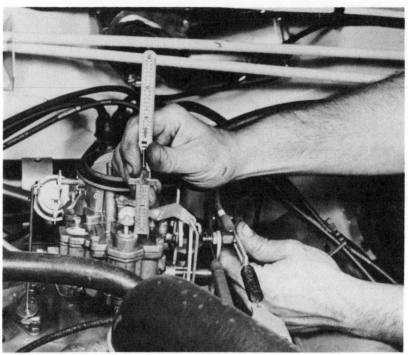

Figure 10. Every carburetor requires certain adjustments. Here, for example, we are adjusting the accelerator pump stroke.

be the manufacturer of the carburetor.

• **Sticking accelerator linkage.** Have someone press down on the gas pedal as you watch the action of the accelerator linkage. Does it bind? Is it sluggish?

If so, clean off all dirt with carburetor cleaner and see to it that parts are straight and not hanging up. Replace a damaged linkage.

If the stroke is not smooth, you might be able to adjust the linkage by loosening an adjustment nut and taking up on the linkage. Not all linkages are set up this way, though.

• **Improperly adjusted automatic choke.** This is discussed in great detail elsewhere in this book, but we mention it here again to remind you of its importance. The choke should be set to the leanest possible setting that still allows easy starting. Any richer setting only wastes fuel.

• **Remember the carburetor air-cleaner element.** This, too, is mentioned in several other parts of this book, but it is extremely important to fuel economy. An engine needs at least 9000 gallons (volume equivalent) of air for every gallon of gasoline that it consumes.

If air is blocked from reaching the engine because of a dirty carburetor air-cleaner element, the fuel mixture will become overly rich.

• **A restricted carburetor venturi.** Deposits that accumulate on the

Figure 11. Clean the inside of the carburetor throat (venturi) if there are signs of deposit buildup.

venturi wall from oxidizing gasoline vapors can build up and restrict the intake of air.

Examine the carburetor throat. If you see a dark covering on the walls, brush out the inside of the venturi with a small brush and some carburetor cleaner or combustion-chamber conditioner (Figure 11). Brush until the walls are shiny and smooth.

Needed: sensible driving

WHEN ALL IS SAID and done, the main reason for excessive use of gasoline, other than an untuned engine, is stupid driving. If you want to save gasoline, keep two facts in mind:

1. The more times you hit that gas pedal, the more gasoline your car is going to consume.

2. The more times that a car's engine is allowed to idle, the more gasoline it is going to consume.

With these points in mind, here are several driving tips that will save gasoline that might otherwise be wasted:

• **Avoid needless idling.** An engine that is allowed to idle for three minutes uses as much gasoline as a car that is driven one-half mile at 30 miles per hour. If you must sit at idle this long, shut off the engine.

The gasoline you use to restart the engine will come nowhere near equaling the amount you will use if you allow the engine to keep idling.

• **Use a steady, light foot on the accelerator pedal.** When starting off from a stop, press down on the accelerator pedal steadily and slowly. Avoid jackrabbit starts and stops.

Flooring the accelerator and then backing off burns up gasoline that is not needed to accelerate in the first place. Let the other guy act like a big deal. It's his money.

• **Use proper passing procedure.** Avoid running up on the car ahead of you, slamming on the brakes, and then hitting the accelerator pedal to pass him.

The fuel-saving way to pass a car is to start your maneuver well in back of him to permit yourself a smooth swing out and a smooth swing in.

In line with this, don't tailgate. Not only is it dangerous, it also wastes gasoline since a tailgater is a guy who is constantly on and off the accelerator and brake pedals.

• **Drive at moderate speeds.** Once the car shifts into driving gear, gas consumption increases as you increase speed!

• **Avoid unnecessary braking.** Time traffic lights so you can keep rolling without stopping. You will use more fuel by stopping and starting off again than by coasting to the light and reapplying steady pressure on the gas pedal as the car is still moving and the light turns green.

• **With a manual-shift car, use your brakes instead of the clutch when waiting for a traffic light on an uphill grade.** "Riding" the clutch and revving the engine to keep from stalling wastes gasoline and wears out the clutch.

Shift into Neutral or keep the clutch disengaged by keeping the pedal on the floor, and use your brakes.

Chapter 3

Here's the easy way to revive a faltering battery

Battery failure probably is the leading reason autos refuse to run. Yet, there's nothing simpler than preventing this familiar mishap. What to do when it happens; how to keep it from happening.

EVERY WINTER, DEAD BATTERIES leave almost 40 million motorists in this country stranded. You can avoid becoming part of this group by taking the following steps before cold weather strikes:

• **Test the battery** in your car to determine if it is on the verge of failure, and charge or replace it according to what the tests tell you.

• **Service the battery** so it will provide you with quick starts for the entire winter. This means that you should clean it and make sure, above all else, that its water level is maintained.

Although a battery can fail at any time of the year, it is particularly susceptible to cold. According to the American Automobile Association, road service calls to revive dead batteries account for 25 to 46 percent of that association's emergency service. However, during cold weather, this figure soars to nearly 70 percent, which is sufficient proof that winter makes dire demands on a battery.

Even a brand-new battery that has not been prepared can fail to start an engine if the weather gets cold enough. At 0° F, a fully charged battery loses about 50 percent of its strength. At this reduced strength, a battery possesses enough energy to start an engine. However, if the battery wasn't fully charged to begin with, it doesn't stand a chance in really cold weather. This is why drivers should perform preventive battery maintenance in October or November. Waiting until January or February may create trouble.

Is your battery ready for cold weather?

BATTERIES FAIL for two reasons: (1) a dead cell; (2) loss of charge.

Although a battery with a dead cell may have enough energy to start an engine in warm weather, it will not survive for long; certainly it will fail with the first cold snap. A battery with a dead cell cannot be "repaired." You can try and charge it to bring it back to life, but the outcome is very much in doubt, and chances are that you will have to replace the battery with a new one.

A battery that has lost, or is losing, its charge and doesn't have, or won't have, sufficient energy to turn the starter is one that can usually be revived and returned to service. The time for you to do the "reviving" is before you find yourself in a bind with a lifeless battery.

Incidentally, a battery that fails because of a dead cell or low charge generally allows an engine to "turn over," but with such little life that ignition can't take place. The engine will emit low, lifeless growls.

If there is no response at all from an engine when the ignition key is turned on, do not discount the likelihood of battery failure. If cells are dead, the battery may not have sufficient energy to evoke a whimper from the engine. Replace the old battery with a good one to see if the battery is really to blame.

You can find out if your battery has a shorted cell or is low in charge by making a specific-gravity test with a battery hydrometer. Specific gravity is a measure of the weight of battery electrolyte as compared with water. Sulphuric acid is heavier than water. Since the mixture of sulphuric acid and water (electrolyte) is heavier than just water, therefore, it is possible to test the difference between the two. Plain water has a specific gravity of 1.000.

Here's how the hydrometer tells that a battery is losing its charge The specific gravity of a fully charged automobile battery is 1.260 or more. This is interpreted to mean that a given amount of electrolyte from a fully charged battery weighs 1.26 times (or more) as much as an equal quantity of water.

When a battery loses its charge, the specific gravity lessens because the heavier sulphuric acid breaks up and the resulting lead sulphate unites with the battery plates. When very heavy sulphation takes place, an internal short circuit results. In any event, the remaining electrolyte in the cell becomes lighter and lighter as sulphation progresses. Thus, it is possible to determine battery condition by measuring specific gravity with a battery hydrometer.

A battery hydrometer (make sure it is a *battery* hydrometer; hydrometers are also made for testing engine coolant) consists of a gauged float inside a glass barrel. To use the instrument properly, draw electrolyte from one cell into it (Figure 1). Make sure the float rides freely, hold the tube at eye level, read the scale, note the temperature of the electrolyte if the hydometer is equipped with a built-in thermometer, and return the electrolyte to the cell from which it was taken. Repeat the procedure for each cell.

Compare each reading you obtained with the others. Look for a difference of .050 specific gravity points or more. For example, if readings are 1.250, 1.250, 1.180, 1.240, 1.250, and 1.240, this tells you that the cell reading 1.180 has developed a short.

You can try charging the battery. Perhaps the bad cell will have its specific gravity increased to approach that of the other cells, but

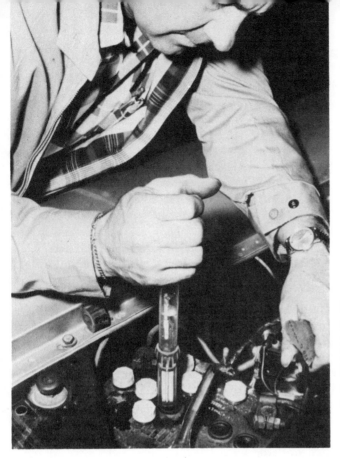

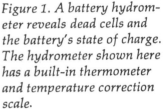

Figure 1. A battery hydrometer reveals dead cells and the battery's state of charge. The hydrometer shown here has a built-in thermometer and temperature correction scale.

this is unlikely. Chances are the battery will have to be replaced.

After checking for shorts, add up the readings you obtained and average them. When doing this, you must compensate for electrolyte temperature. Specific gravity readings may be taken directly only if the electrolyte temperature is at 80° F.

Battery hydrometers with built-in thermometers usually also have temperature-correction scales that tell you how many specific gravity points to add or subtract from the readings you obtained. For instance, if the thermometer levels out at 100° F, the accompanying scale tells you to add .008 specific gravity points to each reading. If one reading is 1.245, the actual specific gravity (corrected for temperature) would be 1.253.

Battery hydrometers equipped with temperature-correction scales are more expensive than ones without, but worth the money. However, if a hydrometer does not have scales, you can make temperature corrections by first inserting a separate thermometer into the center cell of the battery to get a temperature reading. For every 10° that electrolyte temperature is above 80° F, add four (.004) specific-gravity points to the readings. For every 10° that electrolyte temperature is below 80° F, subtract four (.004) specific-gravity points.

Here is what specific-gravity readings mean:

Overall Specific Gravity	Condition of Battery
1.260+	100% charged
1.250–1.260	75% charged. Return to service.
1.225–1.250	50% charged. Charge the battery.
1.190–1.225	25% charged. Extensive sulphation has occurred. Charge the battery and retest. If specific gravity doesn't approach 50% charge, it is unlikely that the battery will last the winter.

Never make a specific-gravity test right after water has been added to the battery. Water makes electrolyte lighter, resulting in an inaccurate reading. The battery should be charged, so first run the engine for a while.

An inaccurate hydrometer reading will also result if you test soon after the battery has been discharged at a high rate. Discharging occurs when the engine is cranked for a prolonged period. Rapid discharge weakens acid temporarily.

The odor and color of electrolyte can give you a clue to a problem inside the battery or in other parts of the electrical system. However, before you can be sure that electrolyte in a hydrometer is actually discolored, you should be sure that it hasn't been tinged by a dirty hydrometer. A hydrometer should be taken apart and washed in soapy water after (or before) use.

Check the electrolyte in the hydrometer tube for the following:

• **Does the fluid** have an odor of rotten eggs, is it milky white, or are there black specks floating in it? The battery is being overcharged. Check the integrity of the voltage regulator.

• **Does the electrolyte** look brown or red? The positive plates have worn out, probably because of lack of water, freezing, or a short circuit.

How to forecast a battery's reliability

THERE IS ANOTHER TEST to make if you want to be 100 percent certain that a battery won't fail you in the dead of winter. It is the battery-capacity test, which is also called the variable-load or high-rate discharge test. Its purpose is to find out if the battery can meet the demands put on it by the starter motor.

A variable-load tester is needed. This instrument measures battery output at the same time that it imposes a load equal to that imposed during starting.

If you decide to buy and use a variable-load tester, follow instructions accompanying the unit. Generally, testing is done in this way:

• **Connect the unit** to the battery and adjust the load-control knob

Figure 2. The battery capacity test is made with a voltmeter/ammeter that imposes a load to tell if the the battery can meet stiff demands.

so the ammeter points to the ampere-hour rating stamped on the battery case (Figure 2). If that rating is not provided, assume a 60 ampere-hour rating if the battery is a 12-volt unit and a 100 ampere-hour rating if the battery is a six-volt unit.

• **Read the voltmeter.** If it shows 9.6 or more volts for a 12-volt battery, or 4.8 or more volts for a six-volt battery, the battery is in good condition. However, if voltage is below these specifications, charge the battery and test again.

A few helpful hints about charging

THERE ARE TWO WAYS of charging a battery: fast and slow. A fast charge is normally done with a portable high-rate charger that is rolled up to a car and connected. It charges a battery in about one-half hour, but restores only approximately 80 percent of capacity. If the car's alternator is functioning properly and the car is driven extensively, a fast charge will suffice.

However, if alternator output is not sufficient, either because of a malfunction or because the car is confined to low-speed or short-distance driving, the battery will not approach full charge. It will begin to lose charge.

The advantage of a slow battery charge is that it charges the battery completely and reverses discharging action by drawing sulphate off the plates. Slow charging can be done with a relatively inexpensive unit called a trickle charger that you can buy from an auto-supply dealer. Most trickle chargers take from 12 to 24 hours to fully charge a battery, depending upon the condition of the battery to begin with.

During the charging period, you should check specific gravity frequently to make sure that the battery does not overcharge. This should be done even though the charger is equipped with an automatic charge control that tapers down output as the battery approaches full charge. Automatic devices do go bad.

When charging a battery, remove the battery caps and place a rag loosely over electrolyte holes in case electrolyte bubbles up. The battery should be placed on a wooden platform to keep the electrolyte from spilling on the floor.

Warning: As a battery charges, it emits highly explosive gases which can be ignited by a spark, causing the battery to explode. Do not smoke near a battery. Do not bring any flame near a battery. Keep a battery away from appliances, especially from water heaters. Don't even switch on a light in an area where a battery is charging.

Extend your battery's life by giving it a bath

CORROSION AND DIRT that form on a battery act like a conductor, "pulling" charge from the battery. A battery's life can be extended many hundreds of miles by periodically removing it from the car and washing it.

Removing a battery should be done carefully to keep from seriously damaging an otherwise sound unit. Never use a screwdriver or similar prying tool to take cables off battery posts. Never bang on terminals with a hammer.

Instead, loosen the bolts holding the terminals, if bolts are used, and try to lift off the terminals by hand using a rotating motion. If terminals are stubborn, purchase a battery terminal puller from an automotive parts store. This tool is designed to remove terminals from battery posts without damaging the battery. The puller fits over the terminal so that straight, firm, even pressure can be applied (Figure 3).

Always disconnect the ground cable first. In most cars, the ground cable is the one attached to the negative (−) post of the battery. If you aren't certain whether the negative (−) cable or positive (+) cable is ground, trace the cables. The one that is attached to the engine or frame is ground (Figure 4). The one going to the starter motor is the "hot" cable.

By disconnecting the ground cable first and reconnecting it last, you lessen the chance of sparks being created. Sparks can ignite the hydrogen gas emanating from the battery. Be certain, too, that the ignition switch and all accessories have been turned off, and take care not to let a tool or other metal object fall across the battery terminals. This will cause sparks.

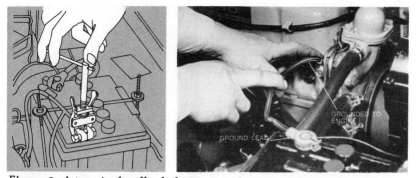

Figure 3. A terminal puller helps to guard against battery damage.
Figure 4. The way to identify the ground cable (above, right) is to
trace it. The ground cable attaches to the engine or frame.

Figure 5. Washing a battery with a mixture of baking soda (or ammonia)
and water neutralizes acid and makes the battery clean.
Figure 6. Rinse battery thoroughly after applying cleaning solution.

With cables detached, remove the battery from the car. Make sure
the battery caps are tightly in place, and cover them with small strips
of masking tape. The caps possess tiny holes that permit gas to escape
from inside the battery. The purpose of the tape is to keep cleaning
solution from getting inside the battery and neutralizing battery acid.

Mix a solution of baking soda or ammonia and water. Use one part
of baking soda or ammonia to one part of water. Wash the top, sides
and bottom of the battery with the solution (Figure 5). Follow with a
thorough flushing of the battery with water from a hose (Figure 6).
Repeat the cleaning procedure until a fresh application of cleaning
solution doesn't "fizzle" when it is applied. Clean the battery carrier
in the car in the same way.

Before placing the battery back into the car, inspect the battery
cables and clean the terminals. Replace a cable if it is frayed and internal wires are exposed, or if insulation is brittle and cracked.

Clean the terminals with a battery-cleaning tool, which can be purchased at an auto-supply counter (Figure 7). You may use sandpaper
instead, but the wire-brush cleaning tool is more effective.

Place the battery back on its carrier, and reconnect the "hot" cable

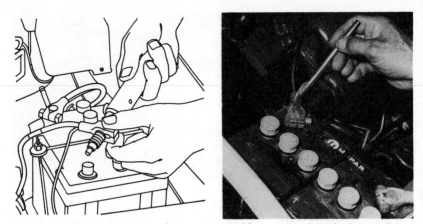

Figure 7. A battery terminal cleaning tool has a wire brush that makes short work of corrosion and dirt that have formed on terminals.
Figure 8. Apply thin coating of petroleum jelly (right) to terminals.

to the "hot" post first. In most cars, this will be the positive (+) cable and post. Now, reconnect the ground cable to the ground post. Make sure of connections before making them. Reversing connections may damage the car's electrical system.

Make sure that terminals are tightly connected to battery posts. A loose connection can result in an electrical failure. Apply a thin film of petroleum jelly to terminals and posts to help retard corrosion (Figure 8).

Thirst can kill a battery

MOST BATTERY FAILURES are caused by neglect. If a battery is forced to function without an adequate supply of water, its chemical action is impaired and its plates begin deteriorating.

You should check the water in your battery at least once a week. If water has to be added, it is desirable to use distilled or pure water, such as rain water that you catch in a clean container. Pure water doesn't contain chemicals that may react adversely with battery plates.

However, remember this important point: in the absence of pure water, add tap water if a battery needs replenishment. Tap water is far less detrimental to a battery than allowing it to operate without sufficient water.

Do not overfill the battery. Excess water will create excess electrolyte, which will vent and cause corrosion. Fill to the level mark, which is usually at the bottom of the fill hole. If you aren't sure where the level mark is, make certain at least that the battery plates are covered with water.

Chapter 4

How to get your dead car started in cold weather

At no other time of the year is your car's engine more likely to fail you than during the winter. Fortunately, there are methods, including some of the Rube Goldberg-type, that will get you going again practically every time.

SUPPOSE YOU GET behind the wheel of your car some cold morning or evening and twist the key to discover that the engine simply will not start. Some people would accept the fact and start trudging to the train station or in search of professional help.

But not the knowledgeable car owner. Instead, he will size up the situation, go into his tool chest if he needs a piece of equipment (which he, of course, has armed himself with since he knows that hard starting is a likely problem in cold weather) and proceed to apply a surefire method that will get him going.

Sizing up the situation? That's easy. Just determine in what way the engine is not starting. Your conclusion will be one of three—

- The engine cranks normally, but does not start!
- The engine starts but fails to keep running!
- The engine cranks sluggishly or not at all!

Engine cranks normally but doesn't start or stalls

WHEN THIS HAPPENS, immediately suspect that the engine has been flooded because of a careless starting procedure. Too many of us have a tendency in cold weather to pump away on the accelerator pedal, thinking that the more gas you give an engine, the faster it will start. This is bad thinking.

If an engine is given too much gasoline, it will load up and won't start at all. Or, if it does start, it will fail to keep running.

To start an engine correctly in cold weather, place the transmission gear selector lever of an automatic transmission in Park or Neutral.

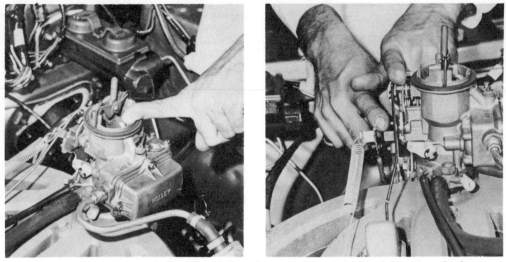

Figure 1 (left). The choke plate (at fingertip) should be closed when a cold engine is started in cold weather. If it's not, starting is hard. Figure 2 (right). To move plate, release choke arm from fast idle cam.

If the car is equipped with a manual transmission, press the clutch pedal to the floor.

Note: Earlier-model cars with manual transmissions will start if you place the shift lever in Neutral and keep your foot off the clutch pedal. However, late-model cars with manual transmissions are equipped with a starter interlock that prevents cranking if the clutch pedal is not fully depressed.

Now, follow one of these starting procedures, depending on the circumstances:

(1) If the engine is warm, do *not* pump the gas pedal at all. Instead, press it half-way to the floor and crank the engine. Do not crank for more than 15 seconds at a time.

(2) If the engine is cold, press the gas pedal right to the floor once only and release it slowly. Keep your foot off the pedal as you turn the ignition key. If the engine starts but fails to keep running, repeat the procedure. Do not crank for more than 15 seconds at a time.

(3) In extremely cold weather (0° or below) when the engine is cold, fully depress and release the gas pedal slowly two or three times. Remove your foot from the pedal and crank the engine. Do not crank for more than 15 seconds at a time.

(4) If you should happen to flood the engine (most times, you will smell gas), press the gas pedal right to the floor and keep it there as you turn the ignition key. This action activates the choke unloader, which trips the choke plate, causing it to open wide. A rush of air pours into the cylinders, which leans out the flooding condition.

When the engine starts, hold the gas pedal to the floor until the engine speed increases and smooths out. This gives the cylinders a chance to clear themselves of excess gasoline. As the engine starts to run bet-

Figure 3 (left). A folded matchbook can keep a choke plate open.
Figure 4 (right). To determine if gasoline is getting to the cylinders, operate the throttle by hand as you look down the carburetor throat.

ter, ease off on the gas pedal. Again, do not crank for more than 15 seconds at a time.

Important: In each of these four cases, if the engine fails to start after two or three attempts (allow a rest period of one minute between attempts), do not keep at it. Chances are that the cause of hard starting is something besides a faulty starting procedure. Further cranking may add a weak battery to your problem.

Now is the time to look to the choke plate

ANOTHER PRIMARY REASON why engines crank normally but don't start in cold weather (or start and stall) is an inoperative automatic-choke plate. Get beneath the hood and remove the carburetor air-cleaner cover.

When a cold engine is started in cold weather, the choke plate should be closed

If the engine is cold, the choke plate should be closed to provide an enriched fuel mixture to the cylinders (Figure 1). But suppose the plate is open.

Trace the choke arm to the fast idle cam and pull back on the cam. You should now be able to move the choke plate and close it (Figure 2).

If the choke plate won't stay closed unless you hold it, push it closed and prop it in that position by wedging a screwdriver between the carburetor air-cleaner holding bracket and the carburetor. Start the engine. As soon as it is running, remove the wedge so the plate can open.

If the engine starts but fails to keep running, the choke plate may be sticking in the closed position, which is causing the engine to load up with gas. Again, release the choke arm from the fast-idle cam in the

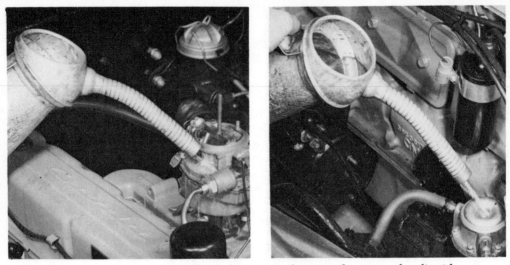

Figure 5 (left). To melt ice impeding gas flow, pour hot liquid over carburetor inlet at fuel bowl and over fuel line going to fuel pump. Figure 6 (right). Also pour hot liquid over the fuel pump.

event that it is stuck. Keep the plate open by wedging it with a scrap of wood, screwdriver or anything that will fit snugly between the carburetor plate and carburetor (Figure 3). You can drive this way until you reach a shop where the cause of the malfunction can be traced and repaired.

An inoperative choke in cold weather results frequently when dirt on pivots and linkage gets wet and freezes. The way to prevent choke problems is to keep the choke mechanism clean.

Is gas getting to the carburetor?

AT THIS POINT, you should find out whether a lack of gasoline to the cylinders is preventing your engine from starting although it cranks briskly. Keep the carburetor air cleaner off and operate the throttle lever once or twice by hand. Peer into the carburetor throat.

See if you can squirt gasoline into the carburetor

You should see, and also hear, a strong spray of fluid squirting into the carburetor venturi (Figure 4). If there is no gasoline entering the carburetor, then there is a blockage aft of the carburetor. That blockage may be a piece of ice that has formed in the fuel bowl, fuel line or fuel pump.

Caution: You only have to work the throttle linkage once or twice to determine if gas is flowing into the carburetor. Continuous manipulation will flood the engine.

The first thing to do if you suspect that ice is preventing a free flow of fuel is to get some hot liquid. If you are stuck in your driveway or in a populated area, that should present no problem.

However, let's suppose you have gotten stranded in a remote area.

Figure 7 (left). In an emergency, warm coolant from the radiator, poured from a hubcap, may serve to de-ice the fuel system.
Figure 8 (right). Snip bit of PCV hose to replace clogged fuel filter.

Hopefully, you will have a thermos of hot coffee with you. Pour it slowly over the fuel pump, fuel line, fuel filter (if external), and carburetor fuel bowl (Figures 5 & 6).

Lacking a thermos? Perhaps the engine is warm. Remove a hubcap if no other receptacle is available and open the drain plug in the bottom of the radiator. Drain out some warm coolant, but not too much (Figure 7).

If there is just no hot liquid around, but there is snow or cold water, gather some in a receptacle or hubcap and start a fire. Make hot water. This is an emergency.

Once this has been done, and you still have not gotten started, look at that fuel filter. Ice in it may not have melted or dirt may be clogging the works, keeping fuel from the carburetor. The fuel filter can be removed and the engine, if it then starts, run without it.

How to get rid of a gas-blocking fuel filter

A CAR EITHER has an external or internal fuel filter. Examine the fuel line going to the carburetor. If you see a small cylinder (plastic or metal) cut into the line, it is an external filter. If there is no filter, then the filter is located out of sight in the carburetor inlet.

Removing an external filter is no problem. But you have to have a length of hose to tie the two ends of the fuel line together. It might be a good idea to keep a length of hose of the correct size to fit the fuel line (and a knife to cut it) in your tool kit.

However, if spare hose is not available, look under the hood of the car for a piece that you can cannibalize. It has to be a length that once

Figure 9. Slide clamps off fuel line to remove external fuel filter.
Figure 10 (right). Then place the length of hose on the fuel line in
place of the filter. Fasten it in place with the filter's clamps.

removed will not keep the engine from starting and running.

One possibility is the windshield washer hose. Another is a piece of positive crankcase ventilation (PCV) system hose (Figure 8). Using the PCV system hose will cause the engine to lose vacuum, but it will start and keep running until you can reach help although it will balk.

To remove an external fuel filter, slide the clamps off the fuel line and pull the filter from place (Figure 9). Tie the piece of hose between the two ends of the fuel line. Use the clamps off the filter to keep the hose in place if they haven't been damaged (Figure 10). If they can't be used, tie the hose to the fuel line with wire or cord.

To remove an internal fuel filter, you have to detach the fuel line at the carburetor. Be sure that you equip your tool kit with the right-size wrenches in the event of an emergency (Figure 11).

Remove the filter and just reconnect the fuel line to the carburetor inlet (Figure 12).

You can run your engine without a fuel filter for a long time, but it is advisable to get a new filter as soon as you can. Filters keep dirt from getting inside engines.

If it isn't lack of gas, it may be lack of spark

AS LONG AS the engine cranks normally, which means that the battery is in good shape, there is no reason to suspect that cold weather has caused a malfunction in the ignition system. The sparks generated by a sound system are not affected by cold.

However, it is possible that snow, sleet or rain has been driven beneath the hood and has settled on ignition parts. Moisture can dampen spark. The possibility is even more likely if you have allowed dirt to build up on ignition parts. Dirt retains moisture.

Therefore, the very first thing you should do when it comes to igni-

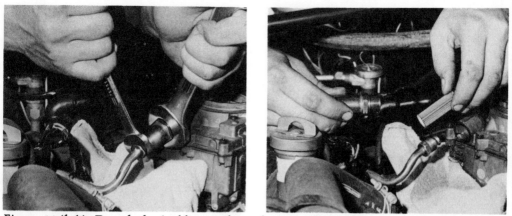

Figure 11 (left). Detach the fuel line at the carburetor to remove
an internal fuel filter. It's hard without the right-size wrenches.
Figure 12. Remove and pocket filter, reset the line and start engine.

tion is to remove the distributor cap and wipe it out with a clean rag.
Remove cables from the distributor-cap towers one at a time so each
can be replaced in its proper tower before removing another. This will
prevent confusion.

Wipe out each tower. Then wipe dry every cable terminal (Figure 13).

Remove the cable from the coil tower, too, and wipe out the tower.
Also wipe dry the cable terminal and the coil primary connections.

Turn your attention to the spark plugs. Plugs of new cars are
equipped with tightly sealed boots. However, boots can dry out and
crack. When they do, moisture can get on spark plugs and cause an
interruption of spark.

Pull each boot from its spark plug by grasping the boot.

Caution: Do not pull on cables. You may damage them!

Wipe each spark plug dry (Figure 14). Work the spark plug boot
back if you can, but do not destroy the molded bond between cable and
boot if one exists. If you can work the boot back onto the cable, wipe
the terminal dry.

Important: Make certain that the cables are tightly reconnected.
Poor connections, especially in cold weather, will hamper starting.

If the engine does not start now, there may be an ignition-system
failure, which would have occurred whether the weather was cold or
warm. But let's suppose it happens in cold weather and you are in a
remote area.

The engine doesn't start. It is cold enough to freeze the tail off a
brass monkey. What can you do to get going again so you can reach
help?

First make sure that the problem is related to the ignition system.
Disconnect one of the cables from a spark plug.

Pull back the boot, exposing the terminal, if possible. If you can't do
this without destroying the molded bond between the boot and cable,

**Wiping off the
spark plugs may
do the trick**

91

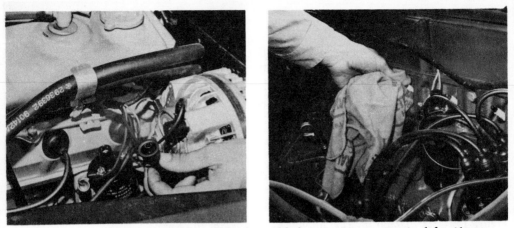

Figure 13 (left). Pull back a cable boot to wipe a terminal dry if you can do so without destroying a bond between the boot and cable.
Figure 14. Wiping moisture from ignition parts may improve starting.

insert a screwdriver inside the boot so it makes contact with the terminal (Figure 15).

Hopefully, you will have someone with you who can crank the engine while you make the test beneath the hood. If not, you will have to forget about the test.

Hold the exposed terminal about one-quarter inch from a clean ground on the engine. Or hold the screwdriver about one-quarter inch from a clean ground on the engine.

Have your helper crank the engine. If a fat, blue spark jumps the gap to the engine, the ignition system is in great shape. The cause of your starting problem is elsewhere.

If there is no spark, forget it. You won't be able to get the engine started. There is a bad component in the ignition system that must be found and replaced.

But if the spark is kind of weak and yellow, you have a chance. Remove two or three spark plugs. Carefully tap the ground electrode of each on the engine (or use an electrode bending tool) to close the electrode gap to the width of a matchbook cover (Figure 16).

Reinstall the spark plugs and try to start the engine. Hopefully, the narrower gaps will permit the weak spark to jump between the ground and center electrodes, which will ignite the fuel and get the car moving toward help.

How engine oil is used to affect cold-weather starting.

THANKS TO THE DEVELOPMENT and perfection of multiviscosity oil, cold-weather starting caused by thickened oil is no longer the problem it once was. Viscosity refers to the flowability of oil. Multivicosity oil possesses polymers that allow oil to flow well in cold weather and to resist thinning out when the engine gets warm.

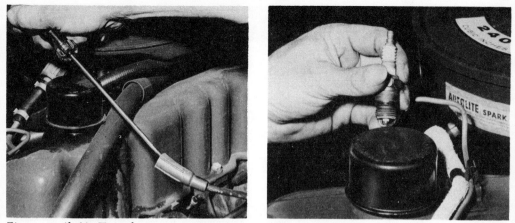

Figure 15 (left). Test the ignition system: ground a screwdriver, insert it in spark-plug cable, watch for spark when engine is cranked. Figure 16 (right). Narrowing spark-plug gaps may help a weak spark.

In the old days, when only single-viscosity oils were available, you would have had starting problems had you been caught with the wrong-viscosity oil in the crankcase when cold weather struck. If the oil was too thick (and made thicker by the cold), excessive friction would have been created, making it difficult, if not impossible, for the starter to turn the engine over.

Multiviscosity oils are those bearing such designations as SAE 10W-30 and SAE 10W-40. SAE stands for Society of Automotive Engineers, which devised the classification system. The letter W (for winter) means that the oil is suitable for use in cold weather.

You should use only the viscosity of oil recommended by the manufacturer of your car in the owner's manual (Figure 17). In most climates, oil having a designation of SAE 10W-30 or SAE 10W-40 would be suitable.

In very cold regions, however, the manufacturer of your car probably recommends either an SAE 5W-20 or SAE 5W-30 oil.

If you are using the oil suggested by the manufacturer, but find it is becoming too thick, impeding engine starting, you can buy an engine heater to keep the engine warm overnight. It keeps the oil from thickening.

A dipstick heater will keep your car engine cozy on the coldest night

One popular type is a dipstick heater. It is nothing more than a heating element with an electric cord that plugs into an ordinary wall socket (Figure 18).

To use it, remove the oil dipstick from the dipstick tube and lay it aside. Insert the dipstick heater element into the dipstick tube. Plug the device into an electric wall socket.

When the engine cranks sluggishly or not at all

WITHOUT DOUBT, DEAD OR WEAK BATTERIES top the list of reasons why engines fail to start in cold weather. Cold saps battery

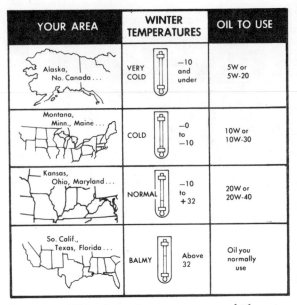

YOUR AREA	WINTER TEMPERATURES		OIL TO USE
Alaska, No. Canada...	VERY COLD	−10 and under	5W or 5W-20
Montana, Minn., Maine...	COLD	−0 to −10	10W or 10W-30
Kansas, Ohio, Maryland...	NORMAL	−10 to +32	20W or 20W-40
So. Calif., Texas, Florida...	BALMY	Above 32	Oil you normally use

Figure 17. This chart gives you a general idea of the type of oil to use in your car in the winter. For exact details, refer to your owner's manual.

strength—even that of a fully charged battery.

According to the American Automobile Association (AAA), battery failure accounts for 25 to 46 percent of all emergency road calls.

However, when cold weather strikes, the AAA claims that the number of emergency calls which are caused by dead batteries that are received by its members who provide emergency road service soars to 70 percent.

Although the battery is at fault in most cases, let's not jump to conclusions. If the engine cranks sluggishly or not at all, make sure that the shift lever is shoved firmly into the Park position if your car is equipped with an automatic transmission. If the engine still refuses to start, set the shift lever into Neutral and try again.

Failing this, work the shift lever back and forth on both sides of Neutral a few times, and try once more to start the engine. The shift is equipped with a starter safety switch to keep the engine from starting when the transmission is in gear. If this switch has become misaligned, it may be shorting out the starting circuit.

Safety switches don't go bad very often, but if your engine now starts, replace the one in your car as soon as you can.

Once this is out of the way, you can turn your attention to the battery. One way to confirm the existence of a dead battery (or of a problem in the battery circuit which is restricting the flow of current) is to turn on the headlights and try starting the engine. If lights dim sharply or emit a yellow or orange glow, that's it. You have battery problems.

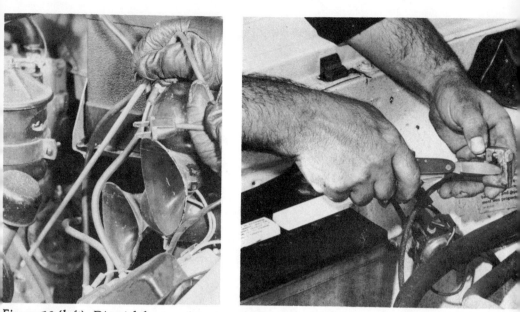

Figure 18 (left). Dipstick heater plugs into any electric outlet.
Figure 19 (right). Corrosion on battery terminals and posts may be creating resistance that is impeding starting circuit. Scrape it off.

What to do when battery troubles strike

OKAY, THE WEATHER IS COLD, but you are going to have to get beneath the hood and do some work. Check first to make sure that battery-cable connections are tight. Also see to it that terminals haven't become so badly corroded that good contact with the battery posts have been impeded.

Remove the cables from the battery posts and scrape out their insides with a knife (Figure 19). Reattach the cables tightly.

If cable bolts or clamps that hold the cable terminals to battery posts have been eaten away by corrosion, you may not be able to tighten cables sufficiently to get good contact. This may prevent starting.

To overcome this problem, force the tip of a screwdriver between the cable terminal and the battery post. This will help complete the circuit and may permit the engine to start.

Cables may also be loose or affected by corrosion at their other ends. Trace the cable attached to the battery's positive post to the starter switch, or to the solenoid on the firewall, and then to the starter. Make sure that connections are clean and tight (Figure 20).

Trace the ground cable from the battery's negative post to the engine. Make sure that this connection, too, is adequate.

If cables are damaged, the engine will refuse to start. You can frequently spot a bad cable. Its insulation is cracked and frayed, especially around terminals.

A trick you can try to get started in cold weather if cables are

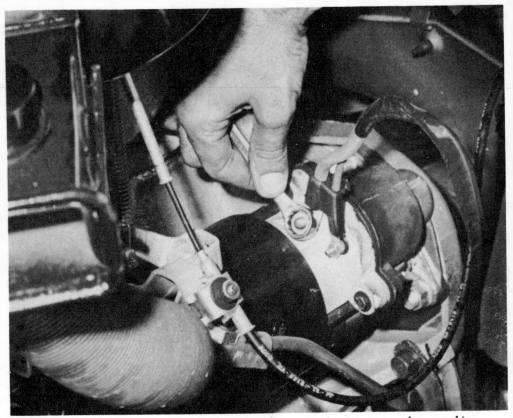

Figure 20. *If you can get to the starter (some are tough to reach), check for corrosion and loose terminal connections.*

damaged makes use of the set of battery jumper cables you should carry with you. Simply substitute the jumpers for battery cables (Figure 21). Naturally, this should only be employed if you get stuck in a remote region and must get to help.

Connect one of the jumper cables between the battery's positive post and starter switch. Connect the other cable between the battery's negative post and ground.

If the engine starts, drive very slowly to keep cables from slipping off because of vibration. Stop frequently and touch the cables to see if they are hot. If they are, stop the engine and let them cool.

If the cables are in good shape and tight, then the battery is probably too weak to start the engine. You can get started if you have a set of jumper cables and another car comes along (or if you are equipped with a booster battery). If your car is equipped with a manual transmission, you may also get started by getting a push.

Caution: Automobiles equipped with automatic transmissions cannot be started by pushing. Do not try it! You can damage the transmission.

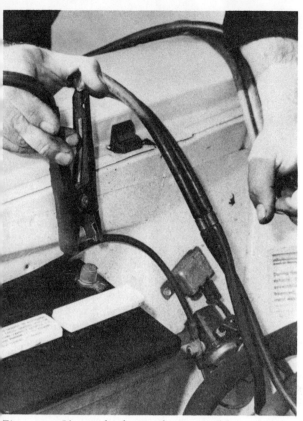

Figure 21. If you think your battery cables might be the cause of hard starting, use your booster cables as substitutes.

The right way to boost a dead battery

FOLLOW THIS SIMPLE PROCEDURE:

1. Drive the car with the good battery close to the car with the dead battery, but see to it that the two cars don't touch. Make sure, too, that the ignition switches of both are turned off.

2. Remove the vent caps from both batteries, and cover the vents with lengths of clean rag. Vent caps are removed so that highly explosive hydrogen gas that forms in the battery may escape freely. Vents have to be covered, however, to catch battery acid that may splash.

3. If the weather is very cold, check to see if the battery acid is frozen. If it is, do not attach the jumper cables! Pockets of hydrogen gas may have formed beneath the ice and may explode when current is introduced.

A frozen battery must be thawed before jumpers are connected. Get the battery into the warmest of the two cars. Or, if there is an electrical outlet nearby, place a light bulb near the battery.

Figure 22. A good
set of jumper cables
is one of the most
important pieces
of emergency
equipment you
can carry.

Naturally, out in the boondocks, you will have no electricity available, but in this presentation we try to present all conceivable possibilities so that your options are as many as possible.

4. Attach one jumper cable to the positive posts of both batteries.

5. Attach only one end of the second jumper cable to the negative post of the good battery. Bring the other end of this cable to your car and attach it to a clean, unpainted part of the engine. If necessary, scrape paint and dirt from an engine spot before securing the cable.

Make sure that all connections are tight and won't slip.

Caution: Do not attach the ground jumper cable to the negative post of the dead battery. Sparks may occur when the connection is broken. If hydrogen gas has gathered near the battery, it may explode and cause injury and damage.

6. Make sure that all accessories in both cars are turned off, and start the engine of the helper vehicle. Now, start the engine of the disabled car.

7. When both engines are running, remove the ground booster cable from the ground on the engine of the car that was disabled. Then, remove the ground booster cable from the negative post of the helper battery.

8. Finally, disconnect the other jumper cable from the positive posts, take the rags off the vents, and replace the vent caps.

How to start a car by pushing it

REMEMBER: THIS APPLIES ONLY to cars equipped with manual transmissions.

Line up the bumpers of the two vehicles. Put the shift lever into second gear, turn on the ignition key, and depress the clutch pedal.

As you begin to accelerate, keep your eye on the speedometer. When the needle reaches about 10 miles per hour, let out the clutch pedal gradually. If the car does not start, the problem is probably something more severe than a dead battery.

Chapter 5

Your engine runs a temperature too: overcooling and overheating remedies

As in the human body, a fever or subnormal temperature has a great variety of possible causes and is a clue that something needs to be corrected. Either condition can damage an engine severely.

WHEN THE TEMPERATURE gauge or indicator light in your car shows that the engine is overcooled or overheated, you can assume that a problem exists in the cooling system. The cooling system consists primarily of the radiator, radiator pressure cap, radiator hoses, thermostat, water pump, fan, and drive belt.

When an engine overcools, the temperature gauge barely budges or the indicator light indicating a cold engine (in some cars, this is a green light) doesn't go out. Of course, the temperature-indicating system may have malfunctioned. This is why a more positive indication of overcooling is needed.

When the car has been driven far enough for the engine to be warm, set the heater to deliver maximum heat. If it blows cool air instead, overcooling exists.

An overcooled engine can cause serious damage and a major repair bill. An engine that runs in a cool state all the time doesn't evaporate internal condensation. Condensation mixes with oil, forming sludge, which can gum up moving parts.

Likely culprit: a temperamental thermostat

A FAULTY THERMOSTAT is the main cause of overcooling. A properly working thermostat allows an engine to attain normal operating temperature rapidly and to maintain that temperature at proper level. A faulty thermostat causes overcooling *or* overheating, depending upon how it fails.

The heart of most thermostats is a temperature-sensitive pellet resembling wax. When an engine is cold, the pellet is in a constricted state, and is not applying pressure to the thermostat valve. The valve remains closed, blocking off the flow of coolant to the radiator. Instead, coolant flows through the engine.

As the engine gets hotter and hotter, the coolant gets hotter and hotter, and this heat causes the temperature-sensitive pellet to expand. The swelling pellet pushes a piston that forces the thermostat valve open. Coolant now flows through the radiator, where it is kept at a more or less constant temperature (Figure 1).

Suppose the thermostat valve sticks in the open position. When you start a cold engine, coolant will flow through the radiator instead of remaining in the engine. This results in coolant never getting hot enough (overcooling). Conversely, if the thermostat valve sticks in the closed position, coolant won't reach the radiator, and overheating will result.

To check thermostat functioning, first determine the temperature at which the thermostat in your car is supposed to open. This varies from 185° to 212°, so check the data in your car owner's manual or in the car's service manual. If neither manual is available, call the service manager of a dealership in your area that sells your make of car. He will be able to tell you your thermostat's temperature rating.

It's normal for the radiator to hiss as you begin to loosen the cap

Now, drive the car for about 10 minutes. Stop, shut off the engine, and place a heavy cloth over the radiator pressure cap (for your protection against scalding). Turn the cap slowly counterclockwise to the first stop. *Do not go past this point, and do not apply downward force on the cap.*

Allow the cooling system pressure to relieve itself. When the hissing ceases, press down on the cap and take it off.

Insert a cooling-system thermometer into the coolant. (You can buy such a thermometer in an automotive-parts supply store.) Make sure the bulb is submerged. The thermometer should immediately register at least 212°F.

Start the engine and let it idle. The temperature of the coolant as revealed by the thermometer should stabilize itself at 8° to 10° below the rating of your thermostat. For example, if the rating is 205°, the thermometer should stabilize at 195°–197°. (If it does, your thermostat is okay.)

Another way of determining whether the thermostat is functioning properly is to buy a temperature stick with about the same rating as your thermostat—188°, for example. The temperature stick is a pencil-like device that has a chemically treated wax compound that melts at the designated temperature.

Rub the stick on the thermostat housing. Allow the engine to warm up. The mark will melt if the coolant heats to the rating of the thermostat. If the coolant is not heating up enough, the mark will not melt.

Replacing the thermostat

IF THE THERMOSTAT is faulty, it should be replaced. Here is how:

1. Allow the engine to cool. Open the drain valve in the base of the radiator and let about four quarts of coolant drain into a clean pan (Figure 2). This is done so the coolant is drained from the thermostat housing.

2. Unscrew the bolts holding the thermostat housing to the engine, and bend hose and housing out of the way (Figure 3).

3. Note the position of the thermostat for future reference. Remove the gasket and thermostat. Discard the gasket.

4. Take the old thermostat with you when buying a new one so you can get a replacement of the exact type and rating. Also buy a new gasket.

5. Install the new thermostat in the exact position in which the old one had been.

Throw away the gasket, but take the old thermostat with you when you buy a new one

Figure 1 (below). A properly working thermostat allows coolant to flow through radiator at proper time, to maintain engine temperature at norm. Figure 2 (right). Drain coolant by opening valve. Figure 3. Unbolt thermostat housing. Figure 4. Assemble parts and tighten the housing.

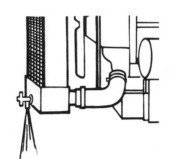

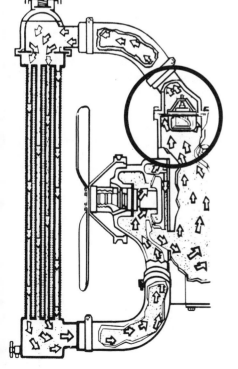

6. Clean housing and engine surfaces with a wire brush, and install the gasket. Rebolt the thermostat housing to the engine (Figure 4).

7. Carefully pour coolant back into the radiator, but first make sure that the radiator drain valve is closed.

8. Start the engine and check for leaks around the thermostat housing.

Overheating: a case for detective work

NOTHING HAS TO be mechanically wrong for an engine to overheat. I can think of four "non-mechanical" reasons that will cause a temperature gauge to soar or a "hot" warning light to flash. They are:

1. *Prolonged idling* with the air conditioner operating.
2. *Prolonged driving* in city traffic jams.
3. *Pulling a trailer* with a car not equipped for the strain.
4. *Improper installation* of an aftermarket air conditioner.

In the case of numbers 1 and 2, revising driving techniques should solve the problem. When caught in traffic and when sitting with the engine idling for long periods, place the transmission in Neutral as often as possible and press the accelerator pedal slightly to increase engine speed. This action causes greater air and coolant flow to cool the engine. If the car is equipped with air conditioning, turn it off.

Pulling a medium- or heavyweight trailer is no problem for a car equipped for it. However, if the car has a normal-duty cooling system rather than a heavy-duty cooling package (required by most automobile manufacturers if the trailer weighs over 2,000 pounds), the engine will overheat.

An aftermarket air conditioner is one not installed by the vehicle manufacturer. A heavy-duty radiator and special fan are generally needed in cars equipped with air conditioning. If an aftermarket air conditioner was installed without this equipment, it is probably the reason for overheating.

From a mechanical standpoint, overheating is usually caused by one or more of the following:

- Loss of coolant
- Loose drive belt
- Collapsed radiator hose
- Bad radiator pressure cap
- Faulty thermostat
- Blocked radiator
- Defective fan

Let's examine each of these in detail:

• **Loss of coolant.** A cooling system is pressurized so any leak results in a loss of coolant. When coolant is lost, engine heat can't dissipate and overheating ensues.

Therefore, examine the following areas visually for leaks (this examination should be done with the engine turned *off*):

Figure 5. Hoses are examined by "feel." One that feels mushy or shows cracks under pressure should be replaced.

Figure 6. Never position a clamp right at the end of a hose. Pressure can cause a bulge and failure, so leave space.

1. Top and bottom radiator hoses. Squeeze each hose (Figure 5). Replace one that feels mushy or shows cracks under pressure. Also look around hose clamps. See any wetness, or whitish or rust-colored deposits? These signify a leaky hose. Replace the hose and clamps.

When an old hose and clamps have been removed, clean off connections to which the hose attaches with a wire brush. Coat the connections with a water-resistant sealing compound. Shove the new hose firmly into place and position the new clamps no closer than ⅛-inch from the end of the hose (Figure 6). In other words, don't place the clamps right at the very end of the hose. Tighten the clamps firmly.

2. Radiator. Examine the radiator for corrosive-looking or rust-colored deposits. These indicate a leak.

If the leak is small, you may be able to plug it chemically. Add a can of leak sealer. Ethylene glycol antifreeze that contains a leak sealer is also effective. If the leak doesn't stop, the radiator has to be removed for repair or replacement.

3. Water pump. Run your hand around the water-pump housing. If it comes away wet, the water pump is leaking. Replace it.

4. Thermostat housing. Examine the housing-engine joint. Whitish or rust-colored deposits indicate a leak—probably a defective gasket. Replace the gasket. If the leak continues, the housing probably is warped and should be replaced.

5. Heater hoses and heater. The heater is part of the cooling system, since it uses the same coolant. Test heater hoses as you did radiator hoses. The heater is merely a miniature radiator, so examine it in the same way as you did the radiator.

A cooling-system pressure tester, which costs about $20, makes leak detection easier (Figure 7). Remove the radiator pressure cap, and place the tester on the radiator filler neck. Pump up pressure to the rating designated on the radiator pressure cap.

Wait 10 minutes and check the dial. If the pressure has dropped off, there is a leak. Check all the spots we've just mentioned. Pressure in the system exerted by pumping up the tester again may cause coolant to spurt from the leak, making detection no trouble at all.

A leak isn't always external. There may be an internal leak caused by an internally cracked engine that is permitting coolant to leak into oil galleries and mix with the oil. The way to determine if this is happening is to draw the oil dipstick from its tube and examine the oil or let some of it drop onto a hot exhaust manifold. If the oil looks white or sizzles when it meets heat, an internal leak exists. This calls for a major repair—maybe even for replacement of the engine.

Let's hope you don't find water in the oil—and perhaps have to replace your engine

Loss of coolant may result from a cause other than a leak. Air or combustion gas entrained in the cooling system can raise the coolant level in the radiator and force it out the overflow tube (in those cars that don't have a coolant reserve system). A coolant reserve system allows overflow coolant to flow into a plastic reserve tank (Figure 8).

The overflow tube acts as a vent to relieve pressure. The tube is connected to the radiator filler neck and extends down the side of the radiator so that the other end is aimed at the ground (Figure 5). If the radiator is overfilled, coolant expands when it gets hot and flows out the overflow. Coolant is thus wasted, which is one good reason for never overfilling a radiator. Consult your car owner's manual to determine the correct coolant level for your car, or check the radiator. Some have a mark to indicate this level.

Anyway, air or combustion gas entrained in the cooling system can cause a normal amount of coolant to overflow. Air may be drawn into a cooling system through a bad water-pump seal. Combustion gas may

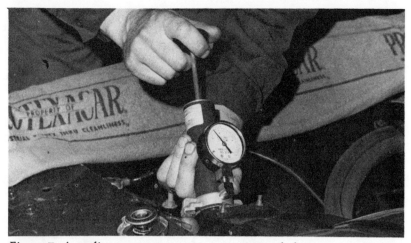

Figure 7. A cooling-system pressure tester is needed to test a radiator pressure cap, and can be used to discover leaks.

be forced into the cooling system through a leaky cylinder-head gasket.

To determine if this is happening, first make sure that the coolant is up to the proper level and that the engine is cold. Buy a *non*pressurized radiator cap and tighten it to the radiator filler neck. Disconnect the overflow tube from the side of the radiator and place the output end in a jar of water. Keep the other end connected to the filler neck. Make sure the tube runs straight—no bends or kinks.

Let the engine run at a fast idling speed until it warms up. If during this time water begins to bubble, an air or combustion leak exists (Figure 9). Consult a professional service technician.

• **Loose drive belt.** Look for glaze on the inside of the belt. Also check pulleys for glaze. Glaze causes a belt to slip. A slipping belt can't adequately drive the fan and water pump. When these cooling mechanisms are impeded, overheating may result. Replace a glazed belt. If a pulley is glazed, see if it can be repaired.

Figure 8. Cars equipped with a coolant-reserve system don't lose coolant through overflow. Instead, it flows into a tank.

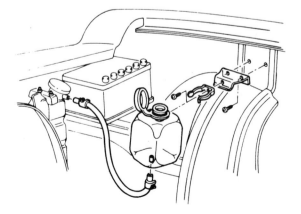

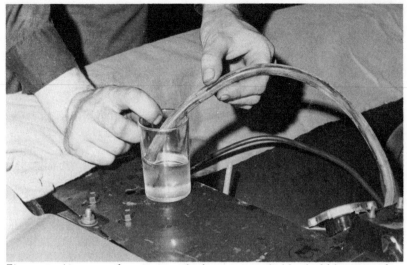

Figure 9. Air or combustion-gas leaks are revealed by bubbles caused when overflow tube is inserted in glass of water.

A loose belt also impedes water pump and fan output. The best way to check belt tension is with a drive-belt tension gauge. The gauge's tang is hooked onto the belt and the knob is pushed down with maximum pressure. When the knob can't be pushed further, read the dial. The reading is the belt's tension (Figure 10).

This instrument costs about $20, which is why many car owners use the "old-fashioned" way of checking tension. Press in on the belt with your thumb midway between the pulleys. If the belt "gives" no more than ½-inch under heavy pressure, tension is satisfactory.

You can tighten a drive belt by bringing pressure against the center of the alternator (or air conditioner compressor) and tightening-bracket nuts.

• **Collapsed radiator hose.** The hose we are speaking of is the *lower* radiator hose (Figure 11). It contains a coiled spring that keeps the hose from collapsing when high pressure that occurs at high speed produces a partial vacuum. Thus, if your car's engine suddenly begins overheating only at high speeds, for no apparent reason, suspect that this spring has lost its tension and that the hose is collapsing, closing off the flow of coolant. Replace the hose.

• **Bad radiator pressure cap.** The job of the radiator pressure cap, other than to keep coolant in the radiator, is to build up pressure in the cooling system. When a liquid (coolant) is pressurized, its boiling point increases.

The boiling point of a mixture of ethylene glycol that protects an engine from freezing at 20°F below zero, for example, is 224°F. Most engines today, especially those with air conditioners, but also those that travel at turnpike speeds, produce more heat than this. Were it not for the radiator pressure cap, the coolant would boil.

Figure 10. The best way to check belt tension is with a gauge. The reading should match tension "spec" in car's service manual.

A radiator pressure cap raises the boiling point of coolant 3°F for each pound of pressure at which the cap is rated. A 15-pound cap, therefore, increases the boiling point of coolant by about 45°, which means that instead of the coolant mentioned above boiling at 224°F, it won't boil until its temperature reaches 269°F. This is enough of a safety margin to keep engines from overheating.

When a radiator pressure cap loses its ability to hold pressure, the boiling point of the coolant decreases and overheating becomes a possibility. No radiator pressure cap retains its capability forever. This is why the cap should be tested periodically and, of course, when overheating occurs.

Figure 11. A bad spring inside the lower radiator hose will cause overheating at operational speeds.

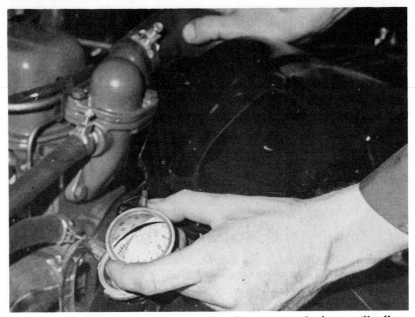

Figure 12. A thermometer and your hand squeezing the hose will tell you if the thermostat is causing overheating.

A cooling-system pressure tester may be needed, but before proceeding hold the cap to the light upside down. If light shows between the vent valve and rubber gasket, or if the gasket is split, distorted or damaged in some other way, replace the cap.

If the cap passes this inspection, wash it in water and attach it firmly to the cooling-system pressure tester. Pump up the pressure until the tester's dial records the pressure rating of the cap. The rating is stamped on the cap. Now, if the dial's needle drops more than two pounds, the cap is defective. Get a new one, but be sure to buy one that bears the same model number as the old cap.

A cap may be in perfect condition, but may not be seating firmly because of a damaged radiator filler neck. Examine the neck. A strip of emery cloth or a wire brush can be used to get rid of nicks or raised spots that may be keeping the cap from seating. If the filler neck shows serious damage, such as a broken or badly worn cap-retainer tang, have a radiator specialist remove the neck and replace it with a new one. There is no need to replace the entire radiator.

A loose radiator cap can set the coolant to boiling —and you won't know it

Coolant can boil if the radiator cap isn't tightened to the neck all the way. What is dangerous about this is that boiling can take place without activating the temperature warning light.

In an Oldsmobile, for instance, the temperature-sensing switch closes and lets the warning light come on at 248°F, plus or minus 2°. If the radiator pressure cap is left loose and the strength of the coolant is 20°F below zero, the coolant will start boiling at 224°F. This is 24° below the temperature at which the warning light will glow. Make

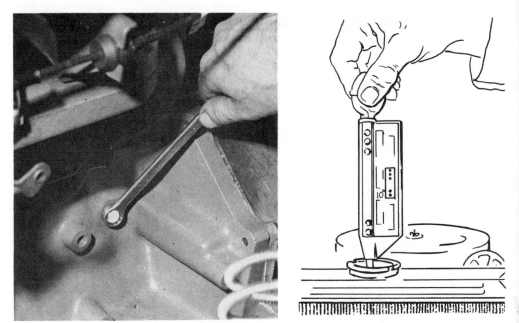

Figure 13 (left). For full drain, remove engine plugs. One shown here is hidden. Figure 14. Check antifreeze with hydrometer.

sure the radiator pressure cap is tight!

• **Faulty thermostat.** As pointed out in the discussion of overheating, a thermostat valve stuck in the closed position will cause overheating. To test the thermostat for this, start with a cold engine and insert a cooling-system thermometer into the coolant, making sure the bulb is completely submerged. Start the engine.

When the thermometer records the temperature at which the thermostat is rated, squeeze the upper radiator hose (Figure 12). You should feel coolant begin surging through the hose. If you don't and the temperature soars past the rating specification, the thermostat is shot. Get a new one.

• **Blocked radiator.** A blocked radiator takes two forms. First, dead bugs and other debris can become embedded in and on the radiator core, blocking the flow of cooling air. If the clogging is bad enough, the coolant will boil and overheating will result.

Bugs and debris can be cleaned out by directing a burst of air pressure through the core from the rear. If air pressure isn't available, carefully use a soft-bristle brush to brush foreign matter from the radiator.

Maybe the bugs in your system are bugs—and they're smothering your radiator

The second form of radiator blockage is more serious. It is caused by lack of maintenance. Corrosion and rust build up until they clog radiator tubes. If fluid can't flow through tubes, the coolant can't cool, and overheating results.

If a radiator reaches this sad condition, it will have to be removed

109

from the car and boiled out in acid, physically cleansed (the procedure is called "rodding"), or replaced. It's much less expensive to practice preventive maintenance (see below).

• **Defective fan.** The fan referred to here is the one employing a clutch. Cars with air conditioners or those equipped for trailering usually have one. It is a thermostatically controlled device that delivers more air when more cooling is needed and less air when less cooling is required.

When the air conditioner is not operating, for example, less cooling is required. The clutch controlling the fan is decoupled, and the fan is allowed to revolve at a normal rate of speed (about 1200 revolutions per minute).

Now, when the air conditioner is turned on, and the temperature starts rising, a thermostat allows the clutch to engage. This causes the fan to start rotating at a much faster speed—2,400 revolutions per minute, for instance. This creates a greater cooling effect.

Ever hear of a two-speed radiator fan? You probably have one if your car is air-conditioned

Check the fan with the engine cold and turned off. Spin it by hand. It should turn freely. If not, the clutch has locked up and repairs are needed. Also look for a fluid leak, which probably indicates that the clutch bearings have failed.

Stopping trouble before it starts

EVERY TWO YEARS, at least, do the following:

1. Check the cooling system for leaks, and inspect the radiator cap, thermostat, hoses, drive belt and water pump as explained above.

2. Drain the cooling system. With the engine heated, open the radiator drain valve and remove the engine drain plug(s) (Figure 13). Six-cylinder engines normally have one plug and V8's, two. The heater should be turned on as draining takes place, so coolant can drain from it, too.

3. Flush the system. Close the radiator drain valve and reinsert the drain plugs securely. Fill the system with water and add a commercial fast-flush cooling-system solution. This compound is sold at service stations and auto-parts supply stores. Follow directions on the can.

4. When the system is clean, fill the radiator with a mixture of a well-known ethylene glycol antifreeze to meet the lowest anticipated temperature in your area. Directions on the container will allow you to prepare the correct mixture.

Ethylene glycol should be replaced every second winter and checked for potency every winter with a cooling-system hydrometer (Figure 14).

One final tip: if your car is equipped with a temperature warning light instead of a gauge, keep your eye on it. It should glow when you turn on the ignition key and go out as soon as the engine starts. If your light doesn't work this way, the bulb has burned out, the fuse has blown, or a defect has developed in the circuit. Get it fixed or you won't be able to tell until too late that overheating has occurred.

Chapter 6

Rough engine idle:
a step-by-step guide to finding
its cause

Rough engine idle, which is also called missing, loping, and rolling,
may stem from any one of a dozen different malfunctions. **Here is a veritable "road map" that will lead you through this maze to the source of your engine's trouble.**

START WITH WHAT has become one of the most common causes of rough engine idle: a dirty carburetor air-cleaner element.

As you know, air that enters the carburetor must first pass through an element (filter) that cleans the air. This keeps dust and dirt carried by air out of the engine interior. These foreign particles can scar cylinder walls and piston skirts, reducing the life of the engine.

When a carburetor air-cleaner element becomes clogged by this dirt and dust, however, the amount of air which is permitted to enter the carburetor is reduced. This alters the engine's normal air:gasoline ratio.

Instead of consuming a properly proportioned amount of air and gasoline, the engine is forced to run on a mixture that is weighted in favor of gasoline. The engine, in other words, must run on a fuel mixture that is too rich. This causes the engine to gallop while it is idling. It may also cause hard starting.

Does your car gallop at the starting gate? Its feed is too rich

In any event, if you suddenly notice that the engine in your car lopes, and you realize that you haven't replaced the carburetor air-cleaner element in many thousands of miles, look for a clogged filter. Manufacturers generally recommend that an air filter be replaced every 15,000 to 24,000 miles, but more often if the vehicle is operated in regions that are dusty.

The easiest way to find out if a clogged carburetor air-cleaner element is causing your rough-idling problem is to start the engine and let it idle—rough. Now, just remove the filter (Figure 1).

111

Figure 1. Remove the air filter to see if it is causing rough idle.

Carburetor adjustments may need re-setting

THREE BASIC ADJUSTMENTS made to carburetors affect the way an engine idles. These are slow idle (also called "curb idle") speed, idle-mixture adjustment, and fast-idle speed.

As its name implies, the slow-idle speed adjustment controls the engine's idling speed after the engine warms up. And as *its* name implies, the fast-idle speed adjustment controls the engine's idling speed when the engine is cold. The two are not the same.

The idle-mixture screw adjustment controls the amount of gasoline that is permitted to enter the carburetor and mix with air before entering the cylinders.

The slow-idle speed adjustment can change as an engine assumes mileage. Every engine has a specified speed which it runs at when idling. This specification is given in the car's service manual and on the tune-up specification decal in the engine compartments of late-model cars. The specification may also be printed in your owner's manual.

Along with the specification, instructions are provided by the manufacturer that explain the conditions under which the slow-idle speed adjustment should be made. This varies from car to car.

You may have to turn on the headlights or keep them off. Some

Figure 2. A typical tach-dwell meter has high and low RPM scales.

manufacturers want the adjustment made with the air-conditioner compressor operating. The manufacturer will also specify in what gear the transmission should be placed.

A tachometer is needed to adjust an engine's slow (and fast) idle speed. Connect the instrument as you are instructed to do in the manual that accompanies it. The typical tachometer, which is normally combined with a dwellmeter in one instrument, is connected as follows (Figure 2):

- Black lead to a clean ground on the engine.
- Red lead to the distributor primary terminal at the coil.

Allow the engine to warm up so the automatic choke plate is wide open. Observe the rpm (revolutions per minute) scale on the tachometer. If the engine is not idling to specification, make the adjustment for the correct slow-idle speed by turning the slow-idle-speed adjusting screw or the lug on the idle-stop solenoid.

Some carburetors have a slow-idle-speed adjusting screw only (Figure 3). Some carburetors have an idle-stop solenoid only (Figure 4). This solenoid has been placed on some carburetors to provide positive closing of the throttle plate when the ignition is turned off. This prevents the engine from dieseling—that is, from continuing to run after the ignition is shut down.

Other carburetors have both a slow-idle-speed adjusting screw and an idle-stop solenoid. Where this setup prevails, the adjustment procedure usually is to first make the slow-idle-speed adjustment to specification by turning the lug on the idle-stop solenoid.

Disconnect the solenoid by pulling the solenoid wire from the quick-disconnect plug. Now, if necessary, readjust the slow-idle speed to specification by turning the slow-idle-speed adjusting screw. Don't forget to reconnect the solenoid wire.

The story behind idle mixture

MOST CARBURETORS BUILT since 1968 have had locking tabs placed over their idle-mixture adjusting screws. If your car is pre-1968 (or if it doesn't have these tabs, which limit idle-mixture-screw travel), you can easily adjust the mixture.

Try to find the happy medium between "too rich" and "too lean"

With the engine warmed up and idling (rough, of course), turn the mixture-adjusting screw ⅛ turn at a time clockwise. This is toward the lean side.

Wait 30 seconds after each turn to see if the engine stabilizes. When the engine speed drops off, slowly turn the adjusting screw in the opposite direction (counterclockwise), while counting the number of turns. Stop turning when the engine speed again drops off.

The proper idle-mixture adjustment is midway between the extremes. For example, if you had to turn the idle-mixture-adjustment screw two full turns between lean "drop-off" and rich "drop-off," then set the screw back one turn. If the engine is still idling rough, then the idle mixture is not to blame.

A one-barrel carburetor has one idle-mixture-adjusting screw. Two- and four-barrel carburetors have two idle-mixture-adjusting screws. One must be adjusted before the other one is adjusted.

After making the idle-mixture adjustment, double-check your slow-idle speed to see that it has held.

Figures 3, 4. The screw of a slow-idle-speed adjusting screw or the lug of an idle-stop solenoid is turned while the engine is idling until the tachometer records the specified slow speed for the engine.

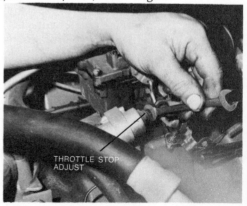

THROTTLE STOP
ADJUST

Incidentally, idle-mixture screws have a tendency to be damaged by overzealous turning. A damaged screw can be the cause of rough idle (Figure 5).

If you can turn the idle-mixture-adjusting screw all the way in without getting the engine to stumble and stall, remove the screw and examine it. If the screw is bent or grooved, replace it.

Caution: When turning an idle-mixture adjusting screw, use a "light" touch.

As we said, since 1968 idle-mixture screws have been capped to limit their range of travel and prevent car owners from setting carburetors for excessively rich fuel mixtures that contribute to air pollution.

If your carburetor has locking tabs over the mixture screws, they can be turned a limited distance to set the carburetor for the best mixture. Just turn the screw or screws until the engine is idling as smoothly as possible (Figure 6).

There is usually no reason for removing the locking tabs from idle-mixture screws unless the carburetor is overhauled and the adjustment has to be made, or unless the setting that was made at the factory during manufacture was not done properly. If your engine cannot be made to idle smoothly by applying the procedures outlined in this chapter, this may be the case.

Locking tabs on the idle-mixture adjusting screw probably won't cause trouble

Some manufacturers suggest that if locking tabs have to be removed for making an idle-mixture adjustment, that the adjustment be made with the aid of an exhaust-gas analyzer only. Since this is an instrument you are not likely to own, the car should be taken to a professional mechanic.

Other manufacturers suggest that the preferred method of setting idle mixture is with an exhaust-gas analyzer, but that an alternate method is acceptable. This involves removing the locking tabs and adjusting the idle-mixture screws as we discussed above. New locking tabs must then be placed over the screws.

Figure 5. Replacing a damaged idle-mixture screw may cure rough idle.
Figure 6. Even when the idle-mixture screw has locking tabs over it,
it can be turned a limited distance to obtain a smoother idle.

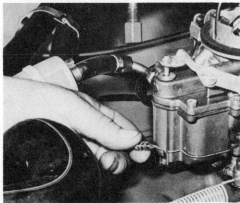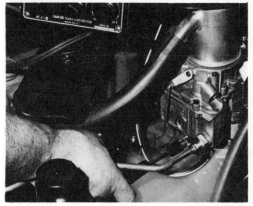

To determine which method the manufacturer of your car recommends, consult the service manual. The procedure may also be printed on the tuneup decal in the engine compartment.

Consider the fast-idle-speed adjustment for a minute

A COLD ENGINE, as you know, requires a faster idling speed than the specified slow-idle speed to keep from stalling. However, if the fast-idle speed is too slow, the engine will lope and can stall. Conversely, if the fast-idle speed is too fast, the engine will consume gasoline needlessly and unnecessary stress will be placed on engine parts.

There is an ideal fast-idle speed. It is the one given in the owner's or service manual, or on the decal in the engine compartment. Set it while using a tachometer.

Adjusting the fast-idle cam may cure a car of stalling —or save gas

Carburetor manufacturers suggest different ways of adjusting fast-idle speed, depending on the carburetor, so you will have to consult service instructions. Generally, though, the engine is warmed up and the fast-idle cam is rotated until the fast-idle screw rests on the highest or second highest step.

Now, the fast-idle-speed adjusting screw is turned until the tachometer records the specified fast-idle speed (Figure 7).

After making the adjustment, open the throttle slightly and release it quickly to slow the engine down to the slow-idling speed. Double-check the slow-idle-speed adjustment to make certain it hasn't varied.

Maybe the engine is all choked up

AS YOU KNOW, your car's automatic choke permits a butterfly plate in the carburetor to close over the throat of the carburetor when a cold

Figure 7 (left). The fast-idle speed is adjusted with a tachometer.
Figure 8 (right). Adjust well-type automatic choke by rotating post.

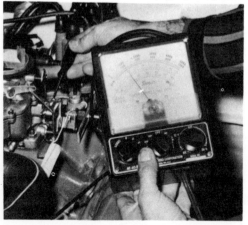

engine is started. This cuts the air intake to the carburetor and provides a richer fuel mixture for easier starting.

As the engine gets warm, the tension on the butterfly plate is supposed to relax, permitting the plate to open and allowing air to enter the carburetor.

However, if the automatic choke is set to provide a mixture that is too rich, the butterfly plate won't open fast enough after the engine starts. This may cause a temporary rough idle—temporary, that is, until the choke plate does finally open.

There are two different types of automatic chokes and therefore two different ways to approach adjustment. One type works by means of a thermostatic coil spring which is inside a well in the intake manifold.

This spring is connected to the automatic choke butterfly plate in the carburetor by a comparatively long choke rod. Unhook the choke rod from the choke-shaft lever. Unbolt the thermostatic spring housing from the manifold (Figure 8).

The culprit may be a too-tense butterfly

Now, loosen the mounting-post locknut so the mounting post can be rotated. Notice the index marks.

Adjust the choke to manufacturer specification (see the service manual or engine compartment decal) to determine if rough idle straightens out. Be sure the engine is cold when you are performing this test.

If the choke is already adjusted to manufacturer specification, reset it a notch or two to the lean side. During the test, if the engine is hard to start, it means that the choke is set too lean.

The other type of automatic choke has the thermostatic spring mounted on the carburetor. It is inside a cap that is usually held to the choke housing by three screws (Figure 9).

To adjust this type of choke, loosen the screws and turn the cap to its correct position by consulting the index marks on the housing. The

Figure 9 (left). Stove-type choke has thermostatic spring inside cap.
Figure 10 (right). If heat tube appears to be damaged, replace it.

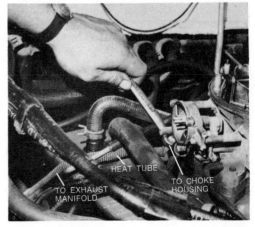

adjustment is made in the same manner as above with the well-type choke.

A damaged choke may also be causing rough engine idle. For this reason, check choke operation after assuring proper adjustment.

Remove the carburetor air cleaner so you can see the choke butterfly plate. With the engine cold and turned off, tap the accelerator pedal to the floor once only. The butterfly plate should close.

Start the engine. The plate should open slowly until it is completely open when the engine has become warm.

Note: If the choke is equipped with an electric assist element, as many chokes in post-1972 cars are, the automatic-choke butterfly plate should open almost right after the engine starts.

If the butterfly plate does not react in this way, examine the complete choke assembly for dirty or damaged parts. You may find that dirt is hampering operation, so clean off the choke rods and apply automatic choke or carburetor cleaner to butterfly-plate pivot points.

Figure 11 (above). The basic instrument you'll need for checking vacuum is a vacuum gauge.

Figure 12 (right). The vacuum gauge is connected to a vacuum port. Every engine has at least one port.

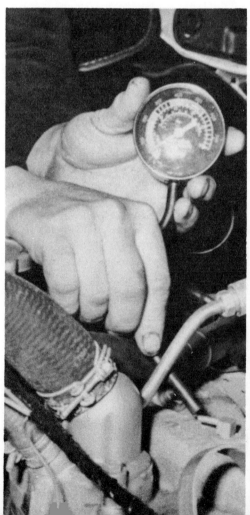

The thermostatic spring may have lost its resiliency and may have to be replaced. In the case of chokes mounted on the carburetor, the heat tube between the choke housing and manifold may have sprung a leak (Figure 10). An indication of this is carbon-like particles inside the choke housing which are restricting thermostatic-spring operation. Replace the tube.

Vacuum leaks: a number one bugaboo

ENGINE (or intake manifold) VACUUM refers to the rush of air into an engine's induction system to fill the void left in the cylinders by the downward strokes of the pistons. As the pistons rush downward, they leave empty spaces into which air rushes.

As air rushes in to fill these voids, it does so with sufficient force to create energy to activate several components. For example, the brake power-assist unit (power brake) works because of engine vacuum.

When you press the brake pedal down, you create an area of high pressure on the pedal side of the diaphragm in the power-brake booster chamber. The area on the other side of the booster diaphragm is a low-pressure area.

The difference in pressure causes the diaphragm to "collapse" toward the area of low pressure, which is the brake master-cylinder side. This permits activation of the braking system with minimum force by the driver on the brake pedal.

This area of low pressure on the master-cylinder side of the booster diaphragm exists because of engine vacuum. A vacuum hose between the power-brake booster unit and the intake manifold literally pulls air from inside the brake unit.

In other words, the pulling power of the low-pressure area existing inside the engine causes a rush of air from the brake-power assist unit into the engine. If engine vacuum failed, there would be no brake assist.

Other accessories on cars that are usually dependent on engine vacuum include the air-conditioner controls, heater-system controls, automatic door locks, automatic speed controls, automatic trunk lids, headlight covers and tilt-away steering wheel.

The engine itself depends on engine vacuum. If the engine could not develop adequate vacuum or if it leaked vacuum, it would idle rough and stumble on acceleration.

Vacuum controls the intake of air and gasoline for the air : fuel mixture. It takes a proper amount of vacuum to deliver a properly proportioned ratio of gasoline and air. Vacuum also controls vacuum (spark) advance, which is necessary to assure smooth acceleration.

Obviously, then, if your engine is idling rough and/or is stumbling on acceleration, or if one of your vacuum-operated accessories is not functioning, you must check vacuum.

Vacuum checks: tighten, squirt and watch

YOU CHECK VACUUM in much the same way that you would check an electrical component that failed. Just as electricity must be complete from its source to the component, so must vacuum be complete from its source to its components.

The tools you need to make vacuum checks are a simple vacuum gauge, some motor oil, a tachometer, a pair of pliers and a length of vacuum hose (Figure 11). Start at the source of vacuum, which is the engine, because if vacuum is lacking at the source, everything will suffer, including engine performance.

Tighten the intake-manifold bolts to specification and in the sequence outlined by the manufacturer in the service manual. Even a slight leak at the manifold will cause enough vacuum to be lost to hamper engine performance.

With the engine warmed up and idling at the specified curb-idle speed, and with the vacuum gauge connected to the main vacuum-source port on the manifold, you should get a steady reading on the vacuum gauge (Figure 12). The needle should not flutter.

A reading of 15 to 21 in. Hg. is considered normal for most engines, but you had best check specifications for your engine to determine what "normal" vacuum is. This varies from engine to engine, because there is a difference in valve overlap between engines.

For example, a vacuum reading of 13 in. Hg. would be a normal reading for some engines, while it would show that other engines are losing vacuum (Figure 13).

If the vacuum gauge flutters or shows some other irregularity, it indicates an abnormal condition. For example, if the needle registers a reading lower than normal, but does not flutter, you know that vacuum is being lost. Chances are that it is leaking past a bad intake manifold or carburetor gasket.

When a vacuum-gauge needle drops back to a low reading, perks up to normal, drops back again, and so forth it usually means that there is a burned valve or insufficient valve-tappet clearance in the engine that is causing a valve to leak.

If the vacuum gauge needle flutters intermittently, you know there is a leaking valve, weak valve spring, intake-system leak, or defect in the ignition system.

A slowly fluttering needle means that the gas : air mixture is too rich, there is a leak in the intake system, or there is a restriction in the positive crankcase ventilation system.

If the vacuum gauge shows that an air leak exists, a can of heavy oil and a tachometer can serve as detection implements. With the tachometer connected and the engine idling, apply oil along the intake manifold joint and around the carburetor (Figure 14).

If there is an increase in engine idling speed, and/or engine idle smooths out after running, and/or oil is sucked into the joint, you

Vacuum gauge reading	Problem	Remedy and comments
Needle floats over range of four to five inches	Faulty carburetor adjustment	Perform appropriate adjustment or repair
Needle steady but below normal	Faulty ignition timing	Perform appropriate adjustment or repair
Needle drops intermittently about four inches	Valves are sticking	Check by injecting penetrating oil into the intake manifold. If intermittent vacuum drop stops temporarily, you can be sure valves are sticking. Remove them for reconditioning
Needle drops back to constant low reading, returns to normal, drops back, and so on	Burned valve or insufficient valve tappet clearance causing leaky valve	Gauge needle drops back whenever the burned valve or the valve that isn't closing is in operation. Replace or adjust valve
Normal and steady reading at engine idle, but vibrating reading at high engine speed	Weak valve springs	Perform appropriate adjustment or repair
Needle vibrates excessively at idle, but steadies as engine speed is increased	Worn valve guide stems	Perform appropriate adjustment or repair
Excessive needle vibration at all speeds	Leaky head gasket	Perform appropriate adjustment or repair
Steady, but low reading	Improper valve timing	Failure to obtain normal reading could also mean that ignition timing is off, but this possibility should be eliminated beforehand as indicated above. If necessary, adjust valve timing
Slow drop of needle to zero as engine speed is increased	Restricted exhaust system	Perform appropriate adjustment or repair
Needle holds steady but below normal	Stuck throttle valve or leaky intake manifold or carburetor gasket	Verify by turning ignition off, closing throttle valve by backing out throttle stop screw and connecting a jumper lead from distributor primary terminal to ground. Crank the engine. The needle should quickly rise to normal. If it does not, one of the problems noted is the cause. To pinpoint vacuum leak, squirt oil around joints and test again. A temporary normal reading indicates a faulty gasket

know at once that you have found the reason for rough idle. Tighten the bolts to see if you can stop the leakage. If you can't, replace the gasket.

Once you have established that vacuum at the source is normal, finding a leak or failure in a vacuum component and its branch-off hose is pretty much cut-and-dried. Keep in mind that a vacuum leak through any one of these "branch circuits" can be the cause of rough idle.

Also keep in mind that in trying to find a vacuum leak you must be methodical. The reason for the failure of a vacuum component lies either in the hose or in the component. There is no other place for it to hide.

Hoses often become damaged. This is the place to start when you have a vacuum-operated system that fails, whether failure is accompanied by rough idle or not or whether the only symptom is rough idle and you have already established that vacuum at the source is okay.

Trace each vacuum hose branching from the engine to make sure it is connected securely at each end and that it is perfectly straight. If a hose is kinked, bent, or squashed, vacuum will be cut off from a component that needs vacuum to operate.

A hose that is torn and leaking may emit a hiss that you can hear. A leaking hose is one that disrupts engine balance; it will cause the engine to idle rough and stumble on acceleration.

You can uncover which hose is leaking by pinching each hose in turn with a pair of pliers at the vacuum source as the engine is running. When the offending hose is pinched off, the hissing will stop and engine idle should smooth out.

Another way of checking hose integrity is by disconnecting each hose in turn at a component and hooking up your vacuum gauge. If

Figure 14 (left). To verify the existence of a vacuum leak, apply oil around the manifold and carburetor as you observe a tachometer.
Figure 15 (right). To make sure a float is not causing rough idle, adjust it to specification. It should ride freely in the fuel bowl.

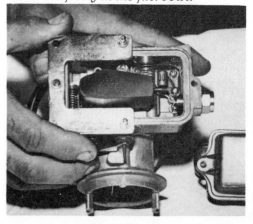

the gauge does not show the same reading that it did when you had it connected to the main vacuum port on the engine, there is a leak or restriction in the hose.

Naturally, if a system that uses vacuum fails, the problem may be a bad component. If the system also employs electricity, the trouble may be caused by a bad electrical connection.

You can easily verify if vacuum is the cause of the problem by by-passing the component with a jumper as you would when checking out an electrical circuit. Hook a length of vacuum hose to the main vacuum port at the engine. You know there is vacuum there.

Disconnect the hose from the output nipple of whatever component is causing the problem. Hook up the "jumper" hose to the output hose, turn on the system and see what happens.

If the system now functions properly, you know that the component has failed internally. Many times, diaphragms inside vacuum-operated components spring a leak. This necessitates replacement of the component.

Some other reasons for rough engine idle

HERE IS A RUNDOWN of the other major reasons for rough engine idle:

• **Stuck or improperly adjusted carburetor float** (Figure 15). Look for this especially if the engine starts idling rough soon after the carburetor has been disassembled and overhauled. If the float has been set either too high or too low, the air : gas ratio will be disrupted. This will result in rough engine idle.

• **Dirty gasoline filter.** If a gasoline filter is partially clogged with

Figure 16 (left). If your carburetor is dirty, it will cause rough engine idle. Get it cleaned and adjusted properly.
Figure 17 (right). Be sure that the point dwell and ignition timing are adjusted to specification.

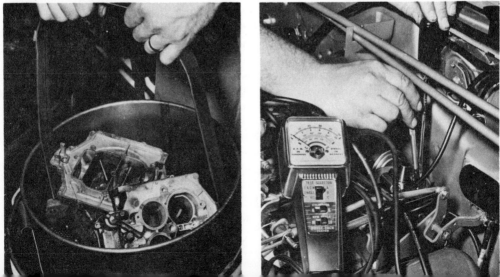

dirt, some gasoline will get through, but not in a sufficient amount to feed the engine properly. The engine will starve for gasoline, and when that happens it starts bucking. Replace or clean a filter (if it is the cleanable kind) that has not been serviced in 12,000 miles.

• **Dirty carburetor.** A carburetor that has seen 30,000-plus miles without having been cleaned may be loaded up with dirt, which is restricting the flow of fuel. This can be the cause of rough engine idle (Figure 16).

• **Faulty distributor breaker-point dwell angle.** If the ignition spark is reaching the spark plugs too early or too late, a bad rough-idling condition can be created. Timing the ignition spark is directly related to distributor-point dwell angle—that is, to the number of degrees of distributor—cam rotation during which the points remain closed.

If the points open too soon, the spark arrives too early. If the points open too late, the spark will be retarded.

Check the distributor breaker-point dwell and ignition timing as we discussed in Chapter 1 (Figure 17).

Other services related to tune-up that have a direct bearing on whether an engine idles rough or not include faulty spark-plug gap and worn spark-plug cables and boots. These conditions must not be permitted to exist if you expect to obtain overall adequate engine performance, including smooth engine idle.

• **Leaking valve.** A valve that is not closing properly is one which is not sealing off the combustion chamber. This causes a leak that can cause the engine to idle rough.

To check the condition of hydraulic valves, which most cars use, allow the engine to warm up. Attach a vacuum to the main vacuum port and let the engine idle. If the needle demonstrates a steady pulsation, the valve covers should come off and the valves should be checked.

• **Erratic fuel-pump pressure.** This isn't common, but it may happen. Too much or too little fuel-pump pressure will upset the air : gas ratio. Check the fuel pump with a fuel-pump pressure tester. Make sure it is putting out the pressure specified for it in the service manual —no more, and no less. If it isn't correct, replace the fuel pump.

• **Stuck manifold-heat control valve.** Yes, the manifold-heat control valve may be causing rough idle, too. If the valve is stuck, it can be making the fuel mixture too lean when the car is first started. Check the valve as we have discussed in several other chapters of this book.

• **Restricted positive crankcase ventilation system.** A plugged PCV system affects engine ventilation. The system must be unrestricted for you to maintain a smooth engine idle.

Test the PCV valve by removing it from the engine and shaking it near your ear. You should hear a clicking. If not, replace the valve.

Start the engine and let it idle. Hold your finger over the open end of the PCV valve. You should feel a strong suction, and the engine idle should vary as you cover and uncover the end of the valve.

Weak suction or the lack of engine idle variance indicates a bad PCV valve or some other problem, such as a damaged hose.

Chapter 7

Where to look for the cause of engine stumble

Some people call the condition "hesitation." Others refer to it as "flat-spot acceleration" or "lag." Whatever, here are the major reasons why engines lose power momentarily on acceleration.

THERE ARE NINE major causes of hesitation and a few others that aren't so major. Unfortunately, there is no quick way to determine exactly which malfunction is causing your trouble. Each reason has to be investigated until the real cause is uncovered.

That being the case, we present here the reasons for engine stumble in the order of prevalence; that is, we start with the reason that most often causes the problem and proceed down through the list in logical order to the least-common reason.

It is suggested that you proceed to troubleshoot this problem in the order given here.

Is the accelerating pump quick on the trigger?

This is the part most likely to break down and cause engine stumble

WHEN YOU PRESS DOWN on the gas pedal in order to accelerate rapidly, the amount of air that the carburetor suddenly ingests is increased. Since gasoline is heavier than air, the gas supply lags behind the flow of air.

If it were not for a part in the carburetor called the accelerating pump, the critical air-to-fuel ratio would be thrown out of balance, and the engine would starve for gasoline. This would cause the engine to stumble.

The job of the accelerating pump is to shoot a supply of gasoline into the carburetor when you accelerate rapidly; this balances out the increase in air. The extra shot of fuel mixes with the air to prevent a momentary thinning of the mixture that would cause hesitation (Figure 1).

The accelerating pump performs this important job, that is, if it is in good condition. But a faulty accelerating pump is as useless as no

125

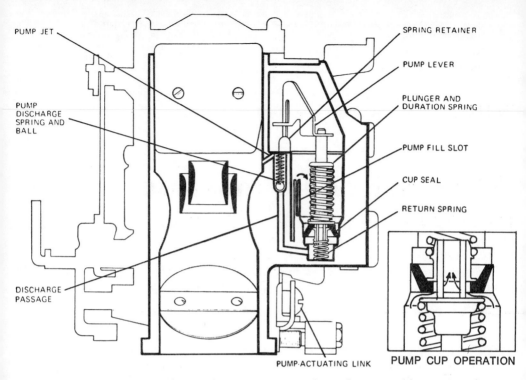

PUMP JET

SPRING RETAINER

PUMP LEVER

PLUNGER AND
DURATION SPRING

PUMP
DISCHARGE
SPRING AND
BALL

PUMP FILL SLOT

CUP SEAL

RETURN SPRING

DISCHARGE
PASSAGE

PUMP ACTUATING LINK

PUMP CUP OPERATION

Figure 1. The accelerating pump in the carburetor adds gasoline during rapid acceleration. If the pump goes bad, hesitation will result.

accelerating pump at all. Since this part has a tendency to go bad—frequently, the cup on its tip that does the pumping dries out—it should be the first thing you check when engine stumble crops up.

To test the accelerating pump and, for that matter, the accelerating-pump circuit through the carburetor, warm up the engine to operating temperature. Make sure the choke butterfly plate is wide open.

Turn the engine off and remove the carburetor air cleaner so you can see down the throat of the carburetor. Now, have someone in the car quickly step down and up on the gas pedal two or three times. Or you can manipulate the accelerator yourself from beneath the hood by actuating the throttle lever to simulate rapid acceleration.

You should see and/or hear streams of gasoline squirting into the carburetor each time the gas pedal is pressed.

Before condemning the accelerating pump if the squirts of gasoline are weak or nonexistent, examine the way in which the throttle linkage moves. This is the linkage from the gas pedal to the throttle lever.

The linkage movement should be smooth. There should be no binding. A dirty or bent throttle linkage can impede accelerating-pump movement and result in engine lag. Clean or fix the linkage.

If linkage action is smooth and proper, then the lack of gasoline moving into the carburetor upon rapid acceleration is probably being caused by an inoperative accelerating pump and/or a defective accelerating-pump circuit. In either event, the carburetor should be disassembled for servicing, but not before you investigate the possibility of a defective fuel filter.

Fuel filters, chokes and other hesitation causes

A PARTIALLY CLOGGED fuel filter can cause engine lag on acceleration by not permitting enough fuel to reach the carburetor. There is no way of determining whether a fuel filter is clogged.

Generally, manufacturers call for replacing a fuel filter every 12,000 miles, so if you haven't done this in a long time, replace the filter now and see if the hesitation problem clears up. If it does, you have averted the expense of having to have the carburetor disassembled to repair the accelerating pump and accelerating-pump circuit.

The fuel filter is either in the fuel line between the fuel pump and carburetor, or inside the fuel inlet at the carburetor. Instructions in previous chapters tell how to remove and replace both types.

Now, let's assume that your hesitation difficulties occur only when the engine is cold. The major reasons for this phenomenon are—
- (1) A misadjusted automatic choke;
- (2) a malfunctioning vacuum break; or
- (3) an improperly working exhaust-emission control system.

The automatic choke is always a likely source of trouble whenever an engine develops a problem involving too little or too much gasoline flow. To prevent hesitation with a cold engine, the automatic choke is supposed to provide a richer fuel mixture. If the choke is not working properly or is not adjusted correctly, engine acceleration can lag until the engine warms up.

The way to find out if the choke is at the root of the problem is to wait for a cold day and begin with a cold engine. Remove the carburetor air cleaner so you can watch the choke plate and depress the accelerator pedal one time before starting the engine. The choke plate should close over the throat of the carburetor if it isn't already in this position.

Start the engine. As it starts and idles, the choke plate should open partially, and then open wider and wider until it is fully open as the engine gets warm.

If the choke plate is sticking, you have probably found the cause of the lagging condition. To repair the malfunction, clean dirt off the choke linkage and from around the plate's pivot points with one of the several different brands of choke cleaner that are available in automotive parts supply stores.

Make sure that hesitation isn't being caused by an improperly adjusted choke by readjusting the mechanism to provide a richer fuel mixture. This is a trial-and-error method, but it is worth the effort.

Make the adjustment for the type of choke in your car as explained in a previous chapter. You either have a stove-type choke—this is the

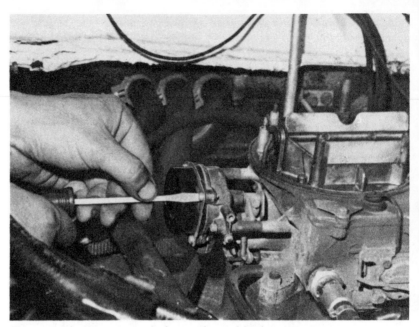

*Figure 2. The automatic choke is adjusted by loosening screws
and rotating the cover one notch at a time between tests.*

kind with the control mechanism on the carburetor—or a well-type
choke which has the control mechanism located in a well in the intake
manifold.

Reset the choke one notch more to the rich side from where it is
set now (Figure 2).

After making the adjustment, let the engine get cold and test engine
pickup while taking a short drive. If hesitation persists, readjust the
choke one more notch to the rich side and road-test again.

Now if the problem continues, you can rule out the choke as the
cause. Move the control back to its original setting and continue your
search.

Overchoking or
underchoking re-
sults from a mal-
adjusted vacuum
break

Now check the vacuum break

THE PURPOSE of a vacuum break is to prevent overchoking. When
you start a cold engine, manifold vacuum is transmitted through a
channel to a vacuum-break diaphragm that opens the choke plate
partially, so the engine can operate without loading up.

If the vacuum break is not adjusted correctly, hesitation becomes a
possibility since the choke plate may not open enough or it may open
too much.

Do not confuse the vacuum break with the choke unloader. The job
of the choke unloader is to allow the fuel mixture to lean out if the
engine is accidentally flooded as it is being started.

The choke unloader, which has no bearing on hesitation, comes into play when you depress the accelerator pedal to the floor and keep it there as the engine is being cranked. The unloader mechanism forces the choke plate open to allow extra air into the carburetor to lean out the excessively rich fuel mixture which is causing flooding.

To adjust the vacuum break and rule it out as a cause of flat-spot acceleration, you have to consult service data to determine, first of all, if your carburetor is equipped with a vacuum break (not all are). If it does have a vacuum break, then service literature provides exact details of how to adjust it.

Get out your service manual to make this adjustment

(Carburetors not equipped with a vacuum break usually have small pistons that cause the choke plate to open partially upon engine starting. These pistons seldom go bad.)

Generally, the vacuum-break adjustment is made by seating the vacuum diaphragm and placing a specific-size gauge between the lower edge of the carburetor plate and the wall of the carburetor.

If the opening is too small or too wide, the vacuum-break rod, choke rod, or vacuum-break link should be bent until the gauge fits properly (Figure 3). The vacuum break is now adjusted correctly.

Figure 3. The vacuum break of this carburetor is adjusted by inserting gauge of correct size between the choke plate and air horn wall, and bending the choke rod. Vacuum break is seen just below left hand.

The effect of emission controls on hesitation

CARS OF 1968 and newer vintage generally are equipped with thermostatically controlled air cleaners. These are characterized by a valve in the air-cleaner snorkel which is controlled by a temperature sensor.

The valve controls the amount of air that is allowed to enter the carburetor as the engine is started and warms up. This permits a tighter control of the fuel mixture. In other words, a leaner fuel mixture is maintained than in cars without thermostatically controlled air cleaners. Leaner fuel mixtures produce less emissions.

You can see what would happen if the thermostatically controlled air cleaner in your car weren't working properly. The valve in the snorkel would either stay closed too long or would not close at all. In either event, engine stumble could occur.

Checking the functioning of the thermostatically controlled air cleaner is easy enough. Look inside the snorkel before starting a cold engine. The valve should be closed (Figure 4).

Start the engine. The valve should begin to open and be fully open when air around the snorkel reaches 100°–110°F.

Have you checked the snorkel of your thermostatically controlled air cleaner?

Figure 4. The butterfly plate in the thermostatically controlled air cleaner is often overlooked as a cause of hesitation. The valve should open when underhood temperature reaches about 105 degrees F.

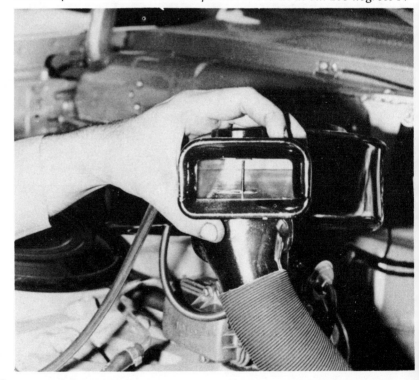

If the valve does not work in this manner, make sure that all hoses are tightly connected. Failing this, the temperature sensor has probably gone bad (Figure 5). Have the unit checked by a mechanic.

Here are the rest of the reasons for stumble

LET'S SUM UP some of the less-common causes of hesitation that you should investigate if you haven't found the trouble by now. Details of how to approach testing and repair of these are provided in other parts of this section:

Refer to other chapters in this section to perform these last-ditch measures

- Weak fuel pump—test fuel pump pressure.
- Improperly adjusted carburetor float—readjust to specification.
- Dirty carburetor—clean and overhaul.
- Air leaks around manifold, carburetor, and vacuum-actuated components—check engine vacuum for signs of a leak, and tighten bolts (Figure 6).
- Faulty distributor spark-advance unit—test unit.

Figure 5. Hand points to the temperature sensor inside a thermostatically controlled air cleaner. It is the part that goes bad most often, affecting butterfly valve operation.

• Incorrect ignition timing—set timing to specification with a timing light.

• Improper distributor-point gap and dwell—readjust properly as spelled out in the chapter dealing with engine tuneup.

• Spark plugs worn or fouled—check and replace plugs, if necessary.

Figure 6. Loose screws can cause air leaks that lead to engine hesitation.

Chapter 8

Don't let engine dieseling drive you daffy

Although it may disturb you when your car's engine continues to run after the ignition is shut off, dieseling will not harm your engine. Still and all, it is best to get rid of the problem. Here's how.

DIESELING IS IGNITION in the absence of spark. It occurs when fuel in the combustion chambers is ignited by heat. The condition is also called "run-on" and "after-run."

Dieseling is not a modern phenomenon although it is more prevalent in 1968 and later-model cars. With earlier models, it could happen when the carburetor's idling speed went out of whack.

The cause of dieseling since 1968 is not much different. It happens primarily because of the higher idling speeds at which engines have been set to run (to help overcome the rough idling brought about by the leaner fuel mixtures adopted to reduce exhaust emissions).

Whether pre-1968 or post-1968, then, an increase in engine idling speed may give unburned fuel a greater chance to enter and remain in the cylinders when the engine is turned off. All that is needed to cause dieseling is heat to ignite this unburned fuel.

Where the heat comes from

IN PRE-1968 CARS, a misadjustment of ignition timing and/or a clogged cooling system could provide the heat. In post-1968 cars, the heat source in many cases is also timing and greater heat produced by the engine, but they cannot be referred to as "misadjusted" or "clogged." These conditions are normal.

Since 1968, ignition timing has been set to occur later. This retarded setting has been made to compensate for the leaner fuel mixtures, which burn more rapidly than the rich fuel mixtures of the past.

A retarded timing setting contributes to a buildup of heat in the engine. Because spark occurs later in the combustion cycle, the period of time that heat has to escape is reduced. Some heat is retained in the cylinders.

Keep in mind, too, that the modern engine runs at a higher temperature than its predecessors. Higher temperatures provide more efficient performance.

But there is another factor—the greater number of accessories that work off the engine, such as power steering and air conditioning. These place a greater load on the engine and cause it to run hotter.

Another factor concerning this business of dieseling is the kind of gasoline engines use. More and more of them are operating on fuel that is lower in octane rating than in years gone by. Lower octane fuel burns hotter than higher octane fuel, so this too is a contributing factor to the high temperature which builds up inside engine combustion chambers.

In fact, in some cases drivers have found that they can eliminate dieseling just by switching from a regular grade of fuel to a premium grade. Considering the high cost of gasoline, though, this is an expensive solution, especially when there are other methods to employ.

How to trick your engine out of dieseling

YOU CAN PREVENT dieseling by "stalling" your engine. Here's what I mean.

Suppose your car is equipped with an automatic transmission. Vehicles with automatic transmission are more susceptible to dieseling than those with manual transmission.

The usual way of bringing a car with automatic transmission to a halt is to shift the transmission selector lever from Drive to Park, and then turn off the ignition key. But what this does is take the load off the engine and cause an increase in idling speed. I'm sure you have noticed how the engine speeds up when you shift from Drive to Park.

What happens is that the increase in idle speed gives unburned fuel more of an opportunity to get inside the combustion chambers before you turn off the ignition. If the degree of heat is sufficient to ignite this fuel, dieseling occurs when you switch off the key.

The way to trick your engine and prevent dieseling is to shut off the ignition with the transmission selector lever still in Drive. This reduces the chance of gasoline getting inside the combustion chambers. However, be sure that the parking brake is set and that your foot is solidly on the brake pedal.

If you have a car with manual transmission and it insists on dieseling, it too can be tricked. Stall the engine instead of shutting it off in the normal manner.

Figure 1 (left). Idle-stop solenoid closes carburetor throttle
valve as soon as the ignition is turned off, thus preventing dieseling.
Figure 2 (right). The solenoid plunger controls the throttle lever.

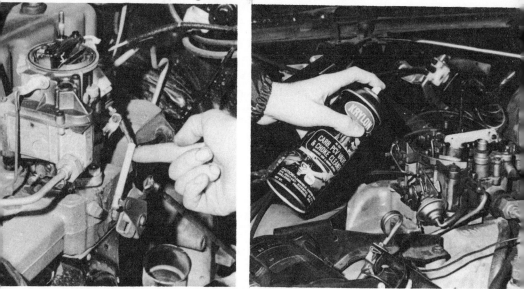

Figure 3 (left). Excess fuel can get into combustion chambers if throttle
linkage hangs up and keeps valve open after engine is turned off.
Figure 4. Clean off dirt that can cause the throttle linkage to bind.

Keep the transmission in gear, engage the brake and release the
clutch. Then shut off the ignition.

These "gimmicks" will work, but they really can't take the place
of finding out why dieseling is occurring and taking steps to stop it
properly.

Figure 5. The curb idle of engines equipped with idle-stop solenoids is adjusted by altering the length of the plunger drive. The idle speed would be set exactly to manufacturer's specs.

Taking steps that may cure a dieseling condition

BECAUSE DIESELING HAS BEEN a widespread problem on post-1968 cars, automobile manufacturers have developed methods to stop the condition without retarding air-pollution control systems. Chief among these methods has been the addition of an idle-stop solenoid or, as some call it, an anti-dieseling device (Figure 1).

The idle-stop solenoid has been placed on the carburetors of many cars equipped with automatic transmission. Its job is to allow the throttle to close at once when the ignition is shut off, thus preventing excess fuel from entering the combustion chambers. The solenoid works like this:

When you turn on the ignition, an electric coil is activated. This drives a plunger at the base of the solenoid against the throttle lever, and sets the throttle to provide the specified idling speed.

Now, as soon as you turn the ignition off, the electric coil is de-energized. The plunger retracts immediately, and the throttle valve closes—snap, at once (Figure 2). This blocks the flow of gasoline from the carburetor into the combustion chambers. Without fuel, dieseling cannot occur—no matter how much heat builds up inside the cylinders.

You can easily check the solenoid to see if it is operative. You simply watch it to see if it is working. Naturally, if the idle-stop solenoid is not working, or is not adjusted properly, dieseling is more likely to occur.

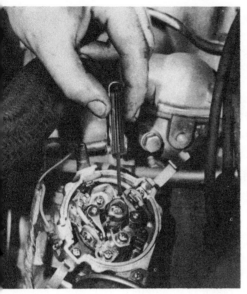

Figure 6 (left). To regulate heat in combustion chambers, make sure breaker-point gap and dwell are set to manufacturer's specification.
Figure 7 (right). Use stroboscopic timing light to set timing.

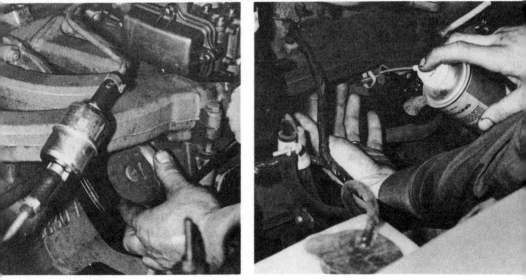

Figure 8 (left). Heat will increase if the manifold heat control valve is stuck. Check its operation with the engine cold.
Figure 9. Periodically apply manifold heat control valve solvent.

Have someone start the engine and let it idle as you watch the solenoid. The plunger should come against the throttle lever and remain there as the engine idles.

Now have your assistant turn off the ignition. The plunger in the base of the solenoid should retract at once. If it doesn't, then probably the device is damaged and should be replaced.

Other steps you can take to try and stop dieseling

MOST OF THE OTHER methods you can try to help solve a dieseling problem have been discussed in previous chapters, so reference will be made to them in the following list:

1. Make sure that the carburetor linkage is not hanging up and keeping the throttle plate open (Figure 3). Also make sure that the linkage and choke plate are clean (Figure 4). Dirt can cause binding that will keep the throttle open when the ignition is turned off.

2. Be sure that the curb idle speed is set exactly to manufacturer specification. The curb idle of engines equipped with idle-stop solenoids are adjusted by adjusting the length of the plunger drive (Figure 5). See Chapter 1 on engine tune-up. It explains in detail how to set curb idle speed.

3. Make certain that the distributor breaker-point gap and dwell are set exactly to manufacturer specification, and then check to see that ignition timing is smack on the button (Figures 6 & 7). Proper ignition adjustments are necessary to regulate heat inside the combustion chambers. A section in the chapter on engine tune-up explains all of this in detail.

4. The manifold-heat control valve, if stuck in the closed position, will trap hot exhaust gases in the engine. Make sure that the valve, which is found beneath the exhaust manifold, is operating freely by seeing that the counterweight moves easily by hand when the engine is cold (Figure 8). If the valve is stuck, try freeing it with manifold-heat control valve lubricant (Figure 9).

5. The engine must not be running hot. Consult the chapter on engine overheating and overcooling for sound advice on how to prevent this trouble.

If none of the solutions discussed in this chapter helps to stop a dieseling problem, then it is possible that the cause of the problem is internal. So-called surface ignition can occur when fuel in the cylinders is ignited by a glowing deposit, such as carbon.

However, keep in mind that surface ignition is accompanied by engine knock. If knock is not present along with dieseling, don't run to have the engine torn down for a carbon-purging job. You will be spending money for nothing.

Chapter 9

Tracking down the cause of engine stalling

The subject of stalling is often difficult to pin down, because "stalls" can be defined in several ways. The information in this chapter, complete with handy chart, will help you put things into perspective.

THERE ARE "EVERYDAY" STALLS and there are "emergency" stalls. There are stalls that occur only in hot weather (these are discussed in Chapter 10), there are stalls that occur only in cold weather, and there are stalls that occur in any weather.

There are also stalls that occur when the engine is cold only; when the engine is hot only; when the engine is neither cold nor hot, but is in that mid-temperature range described as warming up; and when the engine is accelerating from a standing stop.

To help you put all of these into perspective, the chart below outlines the condition prevailing when your engine stalls and what the usual causes are. As you can see, some of the causes dominate for more than one condition.

Scan this "quick guide to stalling," and then proceed to refer to the applicable discussion in the pages that follow to determine what should be done to remedy the situation.

Other facts about the causes of stalling

ONCE YOU HAVE PLACED your car in its particular "condition" category, you then proceed to investigate each cause. Troubleshooting and repairing most of these have been discussed at some length in previous chapters. These causes are the following (see the index to find the pages where they are discussed):

- Clogged fuel filter
- Weak fuel pump
- Loose and badly corroded battery cables
- Sticking choke butterfly plate

Few things are more maddening than a stalled engine; few troubles have more possible causes

Quick guide to stalling problems

Condition that prevails	Causes to investigate
Engine suddenly begins to sputter and jerk, and then stalls, after it has been driving along perfectly (fuel-system failure generally indicated)	• Car is out of gas • Vapor lock or percolation (hot-weather problem—see chapter 10) • Clogged fuel filter • Bad fuel pump • Dirt (or ice in winter) has wedged between needle valve and seat, and engine has flooded
Engine dies suddenly, without warning, after it has been driving along perfectly (ignition-system failure generally indicated)	• In rainy (or snowy) weather, after splashing through a puddle, ignition parts may have drowned out • Ignition-switch failure • Loose ignition wire at bulkhead connector • Loose electrical connections at spark plugs, distributor tower, or coil-to-distributor primary wire • Weak condenser or coil
Engine stalls when cold, but not when hot	• Choke butterfly plate is sticking (Figure 1) • Carburetor fast-idle adjustment is set too low • Manifold-heat control valve is stuck in the open position
Engine stalls when hot, but not when cold	• Carburetor idle speed is not set properly (if engine stalls when it idles) • Vapor lock or percolation (see Chapter 10) • Carburetor is flooding • Fuel pump is defective
Engine stalls while warming up	• Carburetor icing • Manifold-heat control valve is stuck in the open position
Engine stalls as you accelerate from a standing stop	• Fouled spark plugs • Defective distributor vacuum advance unit • Distributor primary is grounded • Fuel filter is clogged • Defective carburetor accelerator pump, or the float level is too low • Internal engine problem

Figure 1. A dirty choke is one that can stick, causing the engine to stall. Keep the plate and linkage clean.

- Incorrect fast-idle adjustment
- Stuck manifold-heat control valve
- Incorrect carburetor idling speed
- Fouled spark plugs
- Defective distributor vacuum advance unit
- Defective carburetor accelerator pump and an improperly set float

How to check out those sneaky problems

WHAT WE WILL discuss in the rest of this chapter are those causes of stalling that we haven't dealt with before. In some cases, they are the devious ones that aren't often considered.

- **Dirt or ice** wedged between the needle valve and seat. If this happens, the needle valve will be kept off its seat, which means that gasoline will keep flowing into the carburetor and from there into the engine. This will cause the engine to flood and stall, since the job of the needle valve is to regulate gas flow.

If you get stuck on the road, a quick way to try and clear the trouble

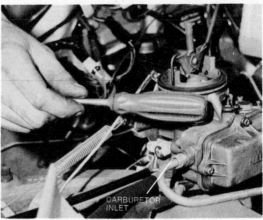

Figure 2. Try to free dirt or ice from the needle valve by tapping the carburetor inlet. If ice may exist, pour hot water over carburetor bowl.

is to tap the carburetor bowl with the handle of a screwdriver (Figure 2). This may loosen the dirt or ice enough to let the needle valve close.

If it doesn't, the bowl cover will have to be removed, and the dirt or ice physically ejected from beneath the needle valve.

• **Drowned-out ignition parts.** If your car stalls right after you splashed through a deep puddle, or snow has driven beneath the hood, the ignition may have drowned out. With a dry rag, wipe off the ignition parts, including all spark plugs, the distributor cap, and the coil. Also wipe dry all cable terminals.

• **Ignition-switch failure.** If your car stalls suddenly, perhaps the

Figure 3. By jiggling a loose or defective ignition switch, you may be able to restore a contact enough to get a stalled engine started.

Figure 4 (left). If car stalls, push in wires in bulkhead connector.
Figure 5 (right). A loose wire can cause a stall. Tighten primary
wire, as here, and also coil-to-distributor secondary cable.

ignition switch has failed. If you can, reach beneath the dashboard and jiggle the switch (Figure 3). This may shake it sufficiently and put enough life back into it to let the engine start.

If this doesn't work and you are stuck in an area where help is not available, it may be necessary to bypass the ignition switch. Attach one end of a jumper cable to the positive post of the battery and the other end to the ignition terminal on the starter solenoid.

If the starter solenoid is mounted on the firewall, and not on the starter, attach one jumper cable between the positive post of the battery and the ignition terminal of the solenoid on the firewall. Attach another jumper cable from the positive post of the battery to the ignition terminal on the starter motor.

• **Loose ignition wires** at the bulkhead connector. Examine the firewall. Most cars have wires meeting at a large connector block. If ignition wires vibrate loose, the car will stop dead in its tracks. Push all wire terminals firmly into the connector (Figure 4).

• **Loose electrical connections.** Other ignition wires may have vibrated loose. Push all spark-plug cable terminals firmly onto plugs and into the distributor-cap towers.

Pay particular attention to the cable from the coil tower to the distributor tower. If this one vibrates loose, the car will stop.

Tighten the primary wire between the coil and the distributor (Figure 5). This is the thin wire. One end is connected to the coil and the other is usually attached to the distributor contact points. To tighten the wire at the points, you will have to remove the distributor cap (Figure 6).

• **Weak condenser or coil.** To determine which of these two parts has failed, if either, disconnect the condenser and place it so it isn't grounded on the distributor plate.

Turn on the ignition key, and open and close the distributor contact

Figure 6 (left). Tighten that part of the ignition primary wire that is hidden inside the distributor. Make sure it isn't grounding out.
Figure 7 (right). Moving throttle may break carburetor ice jam.

points with a screwdriver. If a spark jumps the gap between the points, the condenser is bad. If there is no spark, the coil may be at the root of your stalling problem.

• **Carburetor icing.** This condition can occur when air temperature is between 30°F and 50°F, and the relative humidity is about 65 percent. Moisture from the air rushing into the carburetor can collect around the throttle plate. It can turn to ice, thus closing off the narrow bore, and cut off the supply of gasoline to the engine. This will cause stalling.

You can try breaking the ice jam by operating the throttle plate manually (Figure 7). However, if your carburetor is prone to carburetor icing, then it would be useful to buy an anti-icing additive that can be added to the gas. This will prevent icing. You can buy the additive at a service station or automotive parts supply store.

• **Grounded distributor primary.** This is one of the most devious of all conditions that cause stalling. It happens when the insulation on the ignition primary wire wears off, leaving the wire exposed. The wire comes against the metal body of the distributor, which means that it grounds out. When the ignition primary grounds, the engine comes to an abrupt halt.

To check the condition, you have to remove the distributor cap. Examine the primary lead closely, looking for exposed wire. If wire is exposed, wrap electrician's tape around the spot until you can get the car to a garage. Then, replace the wire.

• **Internal breakdown.** Low compression can cause an engine to stall. Thus, as a last check, take a compression test of the engine (see the chapter on engine tune-up for procedure). If compression is low, the engine should be overhauled.

Chapter 10

What to do when your car keeps stalling in hot weather

Vapor lock and percolation still create problems, even though their causes and remedies have been known for many years. Here's how to cope with them.

CAR REPAIR OFTEN IS two-thirds diagnosis and one-third fixing, but you don't have to wrack your brain too much to troubleshoot a hot-weather stalling problem. Odds are that the cause of the trouble is either vapor lock or percolation.

Let me be more emphatic: if your engine doesn't stall in cold weather, but stalls or is hard to start in warm weather, save yourself a lot of work and immediately troubleshoot for vapor lock and percolation.

This is not to say that some other condition isn't causing the stall, such as a weak fuel pump or clogged fuel filter. But these conditions do not fluctuate with the weather.

Vapor lock and percolation are not the same

THAT IS RIGHT, but you would never know it to hear some people talk. They say "vapor lock" when they mean percolation. The reverse isn't usually the case, because "percolation" is not a popular term.

Anyway, the cause of vapor lock and percolation *is* the same: gasoline boiling. When it happens (and it happens when the temperature of the gasoline climbs to between 80° and 100°), percolation or vapor lock results.

Which one? That depends in what area of the fuel system the boiling takes place.

Vapor lock is the boiling (vaporization) of gasoline at any point in the fuel system before gasoline reaches the carburetor. **Percolation** is confined only to the carburetor.

Vapor lock usually occurs in the fuel pump or in the fuel line from the fuel pump to the carburetor. These two components often lie close to the engine, and engine heat aggravates the problem.

Figure 1 (left). This is an anti-percolation device on a carburetor. Pressure of cam on spring lever keeps the lever over ventilation hole. Figure 2. Gap between lever and hole must be to specification.

This is one reason why you may hear of someone having a vapor-lock problem in cool weather. When fuel-system components lie against the engine (poor design) fuel passing through those components tends to vaporize.

Vapor lock may also occur in the fuel line from the fuel tank to the fuel pump, but this is rare. This fuel line usually is not subjected to engine heat. If vapor lock does occur here, it is because of intense atmospheric heat.

Boiling of gasoline produces bubbles and vapors that partially or completely block the flow of gasoline to the carburetor. The engine won't run with its fuel supply shut off, so it stalls.

A hot carburetor causes gasoline inside to boil. Result: percolation

In an automobile that is prone to percolation, the carburetor lying on top of the hot engine is subjected as well to intense heat from the sun-beaten hood of the car. As the carburetor bowl gets hotter and hotter, gasoline starts boiling.

What occurs is the same as what happens when you boil water in a coffee percolator. Bubbles of fuel and fuel vapors boil up through the circuits of the carburetor into the carburetor's air horn.

Since vapors and bubbles are heavier than air, they fill the air horn and bleed past the throttle valve into the intake manifold. This inundates the engine with too much gas. Flooding takes place, and the engine stalls.

However, unlike vapor lock which can stall an engine while the car is traveling at a fast rate of speed, percolation usually stalls an engine that is running at a slow speed or is idling. During this time, the "cool" airflow around the carburetor is reduced.

Percolation also occurs when a hot engine is turned off. This is why it is frequently difficult to restart a hot engine on a hot day several minutes after it has been turned off.

Did you notice the difference between vapor lock and percolation? With vapor lock, the engine doesn't get enough gasoline. With percolation, the engine gets too much gasoline. Yet, the two problems are caused by the same thing: intense heat.

146

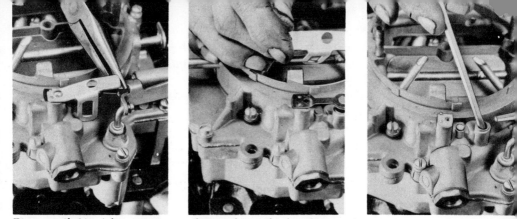

Figure 3 (left). Adjust anti-percolation device by bending spring tang.
Figure 4 (center). This is a closer view of the controlling spring.
Figure 5 (right). Be sure, too, that this ventilation hole is clear.

How to know whether it's percolation or vapor lock

AN INDICATION OF whether a stalling problem (or refusal of a warm engine to start) is caused by vapor lock or percolation is the way in which the problem occurs.

Percolation occurs usually **after a slow drive** in hot weather. As I said before, when you drive fast, there is usually ample circulation around the carburetor to prevent boiling. However, this doesn't mean that percolation can't occur after a fast drive in hot weather. It can, but it usually happens after slowing down or stopping.

Vapor lock can occur when the car is being driven **fast or slow.**

Percolation usually is accompanied by a **strong odor** of gasoline from beneath the hood. **Vapor lock** results in **no odor.** Lift the hood and determine if there is a gas smell.

Many carburetors on models prior to 1971 have a built-in anti-percolation system in the form of a venting arrangement that allows vapor pressure to escape. This is usually referred to as the anti-percolation device.

(Carburetors from 1971 onward are sealed and vented internally. This was made necessary by federal law establishing control of emissions.)

1971 and later-model cars have an anti-percolation unit much different from those on most older autos

The typical anti-percolation device is a spring lever that is controlled by your foot on the accelerator pedal (Figure 1). At highway speeds, your foot on the gas pedal exerts sufficient pressure to keep a cam pressing on this flat lever. Pressure keeps the lever over the vent hole in the carburetor. There is no venting.

In traffic, with a lesser amount of pressure (or none at all) on the accelerator pedal, the spring lever pops open so the hole is vented to the atmosphere. Vapor pressure that builds up in the carburetor escapes.

If percolation problems hit your car, the first thing you should do is to check the clearance of the anti-percolation lever, if one is used on the carburetor. This clearance is the gap between the lever and vent hole. With no pressure on the accelerator pedal and the engine warmed up and idling, a gap of approximately 1/32 of an inch should exist (Figure 2).

To reduce clearance, bend the spring lever down. To increase clearance, bend the spring lever up (Figure 3).

Now, increase engine speed. The lever should close down over the ventilation hole. If it doesn't, replace the assembly with a new one, which can be purchased from a dealer who sells your make of car or from an auto-parts supply store (Figure 4). Failure of the lever to act in this manner means that it has lost its spring.

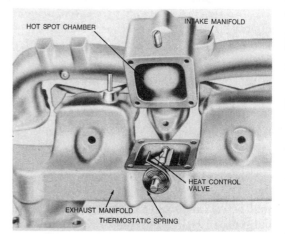

Figure 6. The manifold heat control valve in the exhaust manifold is controlled by a thermostat spring.

Figure 7. During cold starts, the valve plate is closed (left), preventing most of the hot exhaust gases from being expelled. Gases are circulated through a chamber that surrounds part of the intake manifold where fuel vaporization takes place. As the engine gets warm, the thermostat spring loses tension, the valve opens (right) and exhaust gases are permitted to flow out the exhaust.

Another thing you should do is check the ventilation hole itself. If it is clogged, pressure can't escape. Make sure it is clear (Figure 5).

The role of the manifold heat control valve

ANOTHER PART OF the engine that affects heat is the manifold heat control valve, which is also called the heat riser.

The manifold heat control valve is a thermostatically controlled device in the exhaust manifold that helps a cold engine to warm up

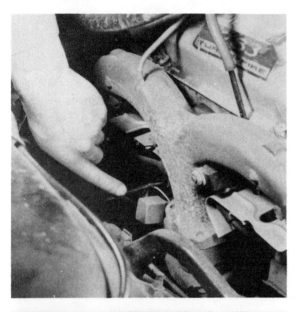

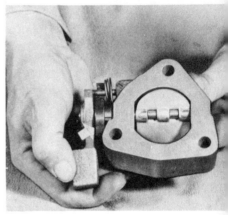

Figure 8 (above, left). Presence of a counterweight below the exhaust manifold means that your car possesses a manifold heat control valve.
Figure 9 (above). This shows how the valve thermostat spring (arrow) and counterweight work together as a unit.
Figure 10 (left). Out-of-sight won't be out-of-mind if you attach a reminder regarding the manifold heat control valve to a spot somewhere in the engine compartment. The valve should be lubricated each time the oil is changed.

149

Figure 11. Apply lubricant to the manifold heat control valve to prevent sticking.

Figure 12. If percolation is a problem, it may be necessary to remove the insulator pad beneath the hood.

rapidly. It closes off the manifold to trap hot exhaust gases (Figure 6). These gases circulate and help an engine reach operating temperature.

As the engine gets warmer and warmer, heat causes the valve's thermostatic spring to lose tension, and the valve opens (Figure 7). If the valve remained closed or partially closed, excessive heat would result that could cause percolation or vapor lock. Other problems caused by a stuck-closed manifold heat control valve are engine overheating and blistered spark plugs.

Not every engine is equipped with a manifold heat control valve. Check your engine by reaching below the exhaust manifold to see if there is a counterweight (Figure 8). The counterweight is part of the valve assembly. The valve itself is inside the manifold.

Absence of a counterweight means that the car does not possess a manifold heat control valve. Fast warm-ups in cars without a heat riser are made possible by an electric heating device.

Caution: Make sure the engine is cold before putting your hands near the exhaust manifold. If the engine is hot, a severe burn may result.

Test the manifold heat exhaust valve by trying to move the counterweight by hand (Figure 9). If the counterweight is stuck, the manifold heat control valve is inoperative.

Apply a liberal amount of manifold heat control valve lubricant or graphite to the counterweight pivot points. If necessary, tap the counterweight lighting on all sides with a hammer.

If the valve doesn't work free so that counterweight movement is easy, replace the unit.

The best way to keep the manifold heat control valve in working order is to lubricate it whenever you change engine oil. Use manifold heat control valve lubricant or graphite (Figures 10 & 11).

Here's the test to see if the manifold heat control valve is stuck

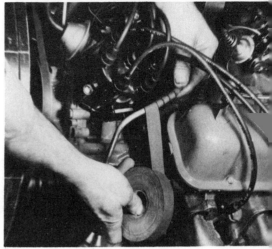

Figure 13. Extra carburetor gaskets or a fiber block will lessen heat by raising the carburetor off the engine.

Figure 14. Insulating tape may protect fuel line from heat enough to prevent vapor lock.

Other steps that may help prevent percolation

IF THERE IS an insulator pad attached to the bottom side of the hood, remove it to allow more air circulation around the carburetor (Figure 12).

If percolation persists, remove the carburetor and insert a couple of carburetor-to-manifold gaskets under the carburetor (Figure 13). The extra height you raise the carburetor off the engine may be just enough to reduce heat on the carburetor, bringing temperature below percolation level.

You might also want to check with a dealer to see if a fan with more blades is available for your car. The extra air a multi-blade fan circulates may be enough to stop percolation and also vapor lock.

An engine fan with more blades may solve both problems

Vapor lock is tougher to handle

VAPOR LOCK COULD cause an accident. It can hit when you least expect it, on a high-speed highway with traffic whizzing all around you. Vapor lock makes your engine die, suddenly.

As I mentioned before, one of the main reasons for recurring vapor lock is poor design. A fuel line lying against a hot exhaust manifold or against an engine hot spot will have a tendency to lock.

In many cases, poor design of fuel lines can be rectified by taping asbestos insulation or insulating tape around the fuel line (Figure 14). This keeps heat off the line and away from fuel.

Heat radiating onto the fuel pump from a nearby manifold pipe can cause fuel to vaporize in the fuel pump. This is rare in late-model cars, but was a problem in earlier years.

If this seems to be your trouble, fabricate a shield from aluminum or sheet metal, and attach it to a convenient location (perhaps to the manifold bolts) so the shield is between the fuel pump and heat source.

The only things you can do if vapor lock strikes your engine is to let it cool down—or help to hasten the cooling action. You can usually relieve a vapor-lock stall by pouring cold water over the fuel pump and fuel line (Figure 15).

Percolation and vapor lock aren't as prevalent as they once were, because they have been recognized and steps have been taken to prevent them. However, drivers shouldn't be complacent. The combination of high atmospheric temperature and high under-the-hood heat will make any car percolate or become locked with vapor—precautionary design notwithstanding.

Figure 15. If you know your car is prone to vapor lock, keep a thermos of cold water with you to use in an emergency. It is poured over the fuel pump and fuel line.

A safe braking system

Chapter 11

What you need to know to maintain a safe braking system

**This chapter provides tests that every driver can make to assure
that his car's braking system is in A-1 condition. For the more technically able,
we also outline the procedure for doing a brake job.**

EVERY CAR ON THE ROAD should have its brakes tested and inspected every 10,000 miles. This periodic examination allows drivers to uncover problems that are still in a minor stage. Once a brake problem becomes major, it poses a serious safety hazard and becomes more costly to repair.

A brake inspection is done in two phases. The first phase consists of tests performed while the car is parked. The second phase is done while the car is being driven.

Every brake malfunction revealed by tests has more than one possible cause. This is one reason we provide a diagnostic chart of brake problems below—you have to know what is causing the problem.

Suppose you find that the brake pedal is spongy. A spongy pedal is caused by air in the hydraulic system that has to be purged (bled), *or* by damaged brake lines that have to be replaced, *or* by a damaged master cylinder that has to be overhauled or replaced, *or* by damaged brake drums or discs that have to be repaired or replaced.

The point is this: when it comes to repair, you should proceed by doing the easiest and/or least expensive job first to see if that doesn't solve the problem. The information here will allow you to make a determination.

However, before we get to the subject of making an inspection, you should become familiar with the differences in braking systems. These differences are summed up by the terms *drum* and *disc*.

Your car has drums, discs, or both

A CAR MAY HAVE drum brakes controlling all four wheels, disc brakes controlling all four wheels, or disc brakes on the front and drum brakes on the rear.

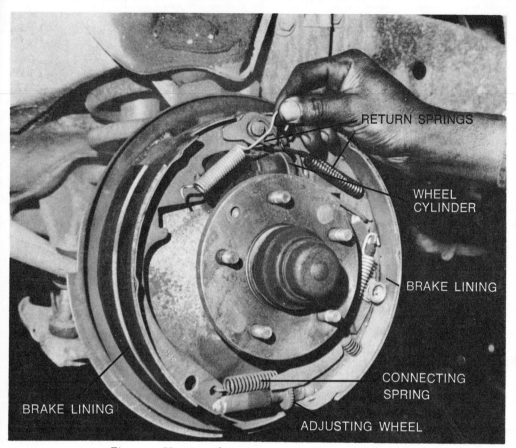

RETURN SPRINGS

WHEEL CYLINDER

BRAKE LINING

CONNECTING SPRING

BRAKE LINING

ADJUSTING WHEEL

Figure 1. Here are the components of a typical drum brake. Only the drum itself is not seen. The parts shown attach to the backing plate.

Four-wheel drum brakes dominated before 1970. Later-model cars are generally equipped with disc brakes controlling the front wheels and drum brakes on the rear wheels. A few makes of cars have disc brakes on all four wheels.

Whether a car has drums, discs, or a combination, the force that activates the brake *per se* is hydraulic. Except for the parts that do the actual braking, everything is pretty much the same, hydraulically speaking.

The reservoir for hydraulic fluid is the master cylinder. When you press down on the brake pedal, as much as 1,000 pounds of hydraulic pressure is forced from the master cylinder through brake lines to each of the four brakes.

The modern braking system is highly efficient. Most are dual types —that is, the master cylinder is split so it activates the front and rear brakes *separately*. If one half fails, the other half will provide adequate braking power temporarily.

Figure 2 (left). A boned lining is seen above; a riveted lining is below. Both work equally well if they are of the best quality.

Figure 3 (below). The major parts of a disc brake are the disc and the caliper that contains the pads. However, other parts should be noted.

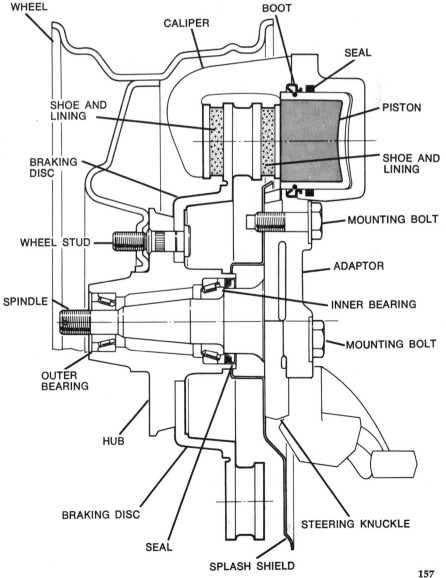

WHEEL

CALIPER

BOOT

SEAL

SHOE AND LINING

PISTON

BRAKING DISC

SHOE AND LINING

WHEEL STUD

MOUNTING BOLT

ADAPTOR

SPINDLE

INNER BEARING

MOUNTING BOLT

OUTER BEARING

HUB

BRAKING DISC

SEAL

STEERING KNUCKLE

SPLASH SHIELD

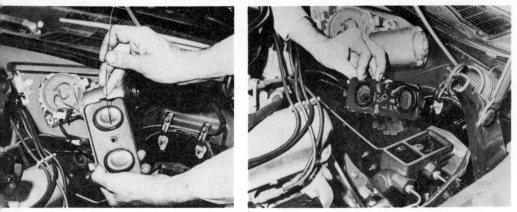

Figure 4. Make sure master cylinder cover vent holes are open.
Figure 5 (right). Check the fluid level in the master cylinder.

Let's look at drum brakes

ALL OF THE WORKING PARTS of a drum brake are enclosed by a hardened metal case (drum). Each wheel has a brake drum attached to the hub so that wheel and drum revolve as a unit.

The other parts of the brake are not attached to the drum, but to a backing plate (Figure 1). Chief among them are the components that provide the frictional force to stop the revolving drum. They are called brake shoes.

There are two brake shoes. Attached to each is a lining made of heat-resistant asbestos. Linings are either riveted or bonded to shoes (Figure 2).

The curved brake shoes are kept away from the brake drum by springs when braking action is not being utilized. But when the brake pedal is pressed, fluid is forced from the master cylinder through brake lines to a wheel cylinder. The brake shoes are attached to the wheel cylinder.

Hydraulic pressure causes the pushrods on each side of the wheel cylinder to push out against the brake shoes with enough force to overcome spring pressure. The wheel cylinder pushrods push the brake shoes and linings against the revolving brake drum. This creates intense friction that brings the revolving brake drums and wheels to a halt.

When you remove your foot from the brake pedal, thus relieving hydraulic pressure, spring tension is permitted to pull brake shoes away from the brake drum.

Here is how disc brakes work

A DISC BRAKE uses fewer parts than a drum brake. Disc brakes are "open"—that is, no parts are enclosed.

The two major parts of a disc brake are the disc itself and the caliper assembly (Figure 3). The disc is a heavy, round metal mechanism that

Figure 6. Use a piece of hose about 18 inches long for the bleeder hose. Attach it firmly to the bleed screw.

is attached to the wheel hub. It revolves with the wheel just as a brake drum does. The disc provides two flat surfaces for braking.

The caliper assembly consists of two brake shoes: an outer shoe and an inner shoe. Linings (also called pads) are attached to these shoes. Like the brake linings of drum brakes, they are made of heat-resistant asbestos.

The outer shoe faces the outer surface of the disc. The inner shoe faces the inner surface of the disc. When the shoes are activated and are forced against the disc, they catch the disc in a vise-like grip.

When you press down on the brake pedal and send hydraulic pressure to braking parts, you actuate a large piston on the inboard side of the disc. The piston actually forces the inboard brake shoe and pad against the disc.

Hydraulic pressure also exerts a back pressure that causes the entire arm of the caliper to move sideways. This brings the outboard shoe and pad tight against the outside of the disc. The revolving disc and wheel are brought to a halt because of this clamping action.

How to test brakes in the privacy of your driveway

IF YOUR CAR is equipped with power brakes, let the engine idle. If it doesn't have power brakes, you can keep the engine off.

Apply heavy pressure to the brake pedal. The pedal should feel firm underfoot. It should not be spongy.

If the brake pedal is spongy, the first thing to do is to make sure that the vent holes in the master cylinder cover, if present, are unclogged (Figure 4). Test the pedal again.

Now if the pedal is spongy, turn your attention to the most common cause of the condition: air that is trapped in the hydraulic system. Air can get into the system if the fluid level gets too low, or if a brake-system part has been disconnected and reinstalled.

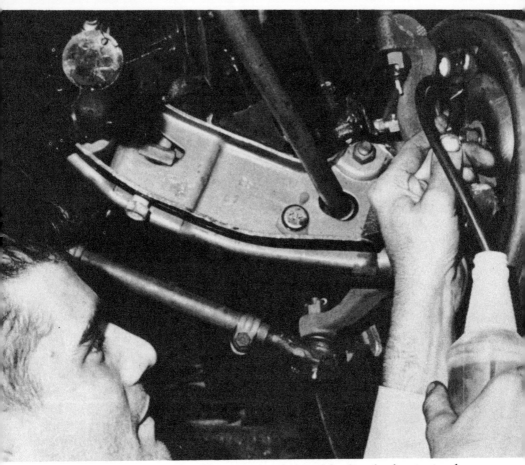

Figure 7. The equipment needed for bleeding brakes is simple—a hose and a container partially filled with fresh brake fluid.

Important: Whenever you work on the braking system, you should bleed the brakes. Bleeding purges air from a brake system. Each wheel is usually equipped with a bleed screw. The following procedure should be observed when bleeding brakes:

1. If the car is equipped with power brakes, depress and release the brake pedal five or six times with the engine off. This gets rid of vacuum.

2. Remove the master-cylinder cover and, if necessary, fill the reservoir with fresh fluid of the type and quality specified by the manufacturer of your car in the owner's manual (Figure 5). Never permit the fluid level to go lower than ½-inch below the top of the reservoir. Reinstall the cover.

3. Attach a bleeder hose to one of the bleed screws (Figure 6). It doesn't matter which one, but be sure that each of the four wheels is serviced. (A piece of vacuum hose about 18 inches long can serve as a bleeder hose.)

4. Place the other end of the bleeder hose into a container that is partially filled with fresh hydraulic-brake fluid (Figure 7). A glass or clear plastic container should be used since you should be able to observe the brake fluid during the bleeding operation.

5. Have someone in the car apply steady pressure to the brake pedal. Open the bleed screw about ¾ of a turn. When the fluid coming out the end of the bleeder hose no longer causes the fluid in the container to bubble, close the bleed screw.

Important: Advise your assistant to maintain pressure on the brake pedal throughout the entire procedure. Releasing the pedal while the bleed screw is open will introduce air into the system. Pressure can be released only when the bleed screw has been tightened.

6. Repeat the procedure for each of the other wheels. Then recheck the brake-fluid level in the master cylinder. Add fluid if necessary.

7. Be sure to discard the brake fluid used for bleeding after you have completed your work. Never pour it back into the master cylinder. It may be contaminated.

Air in the hydraulic system is not the only reason why a brake pedal may feel spongy. Therefore, after bleeding the system, be sure that you test the pedal again. If it still feels spongy, a soft or weak brake hose may be expanding under pressure.

Trace each line branching off the master cylinder over its entire length right to the wheels. Feel every rubber hose. Each should be firm. If a hose is soft, replace it (Figure 8).

Is the brake pedal high enough?

AFTER CHECKING FOR SPONGINESS, notice brake-pedal reserve. If the pedal is too low, the brakes probably have to be adjusted.

Figure 8 (left). Rubber brake hoses can be a source of trouble. They must be firm, tight, and not marred by cuts or cracks.
Figure 9 (right). Tighten connections at master cylinder. Look for leaks.

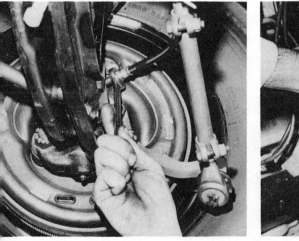

Adequate brake-pedal height is usually a matter of preference. Some drivers prefer a high pedal, and some prefer a lower pedal. However, a brake pedal should not be allowed to sink much below the level of the accelerator pedal. That is too low.

Since the early 1960's, cars have been equipped with self-adjusting brakes. The cause of a low brake pedal in many cases is that drivers do not activate self-adjusting mechanisms as often as they should.

To adjust brakes by means of the self-adjusting mechanism, simply make several forward and reverse stops. But be sure that you come to a complete halt after each forward and reverse movement.

The pedal should come up. If it doesn't, the brake linings are probably worn, or there is another problem, such as a self-adjusting mechanism that has frozen because of little use.

The next phase of your in-driveway brake inspection is to test for hydraulic-fluid leaks. Hold your foot lightly on the brake pedal for about 15 seconds. There should be no pedal movement.

Figure 10 (left). Wheel cylinders of drum brakes are a source of leaks. If fluid oozes from the cylinder when you pull back the boots, the cylinder should be repaired or replaced. Figure 11 (lower left). Brake linings should be measured every 10,000 miles to make sure they are not worn beyond the danger point. Figure 12 (below). Measure the lining at its thinnest point. Use a gauge for accuracy.

BRAKE SHOES

BRAKE DRUM

Now, hold your foot on the brake pedal with heavy pressure. The pedal should not fall away. If the car is equipped with power brakes, repeat this test with the engine running.

If the brake pedal nose dives toward the floor, there is a leak. Your task is to find it.

Inspect the master cylinder first. Look for traces of fluid around connections. Be sure they are tight (Figure 9).

As someone presses down on the brake pedal, check all brake lines and hoses coming off the master cylinder and going to each wheel. If fluid is leaking from a connection, tighten it. Perhaps the connection has worked loose. If not, replace the line or hose.

Wheel cylinders can also leak. To check the wheel cylinders of drum brakes, remove each wheel. If the cylinders are equipped with rubber boots, as most are, pull back both boots (Figure 10). If fluid leaks out, the cylinder should be rebuilt or replaced.

The cylinder of a disc-brake system can also leak. It can be checked when pad thickness is checked, as described below.

If hoses, lines and wheel cylinders aren't leaking, then probably the reason for the fading brake pedal is damage inside the master cylinder. Fluid may be leaking from around the secondary cup into the boot where it is hidden from view. An odor of brake fluid inside the car or beneath the hood tends to confirm this.

Do not waste time rebuilding a master cylinder. It is not practical. Nor is it safe. Buy a new one.

How to inspect the brake linings

IF YOUR CAR is equipped with drum brakes (or disc and drum combination), remove one of the drums (Figure 11). Remove a front drum if the car has drum brakes on all four wheels. Remove a rear drum if the braking system is a combination drum and disc.

Measure brake-lining thickness. Replace the linings (shoes) if thickness is 1/32 inch or less (Figure 12).

Important: If you replace the linings of one wheel, replace the linings of the other wheel on the same axle. Failure to do this will result in unequal braking action.

Disc-brake pad thickness should also be measured during your 10,000-mile inspection. To do this, the pads have to be removed from a caliper. Only one wheel has to be checked.

In most installations, the pads are kept in place by two guide pins. The hairpin-shaped locking clip is removed from each guide pin, and the pins are pulled from place (Figures 13 & 14). Damper springs, if used, should also be removed.

This leaves the pads free for removal. Slide them both straight out (Figure 15). If you can't get a good grip on them, grasp them with a pair of locking pliers and pull.

With both pads out of the caliper, the piston and its surrounding

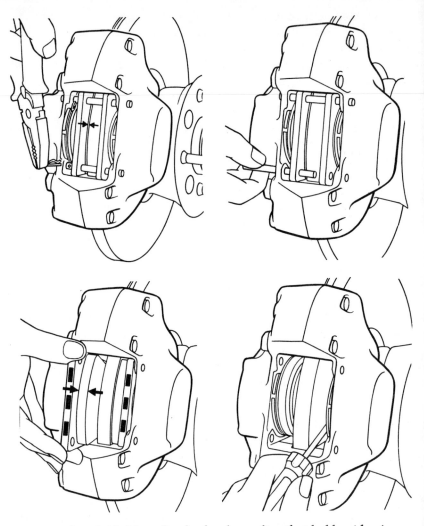

Figure 13 (top left). Most disc brakes have clips that hold guide pins.
Figure 14 (top right). Slide guide pins out to free the pads.
Figure 15 (left). Remove the pads. Check pad thickness.
Figure 16 (right). To position new pads, push piston back into cylinder.

rubber boot are exposed. Make sure that the boot is in good condition. It should not show signs of leaking fluid.

If it is leaking fluid, this is the reason that your brake pedal may be fading. The caliper should be taken apart for overhaul, as described later on in this chapter.

Pad thickness should be more than 1/32 inch. If it isn't, replace both pads and also the pads of the other wheel on the same axle.

To install new pads, which are thicker than the old ones, pistons have to be pushed back into the calipers. Use the shank of a screwdriver to do this, but wrap the tip in a rag so you don't scar any parts, such as the piston head (Figure 16).

When the piston is back in its cylinder, you will have sufficient room in which to slide the new pads into place.

The real test comes on the road

IT IS TIME to put the braking system through its paces on the road to test its functioning under actual operating conditions. Select a dry, clean, reasonably smooth and level highway at a time of day when traffic is light.

Before starting tests, make sure that tires are inflated to manufacturer specification. Uneven or erroneous inflation can cause problems that simulate a brake malfunction.

Caution: You have to be careful not to induce brake-pedal fade during the road test by overapplying brakes. Heat causes fading. If the pedal should fade away, stop the test at once and allow the brakes to cool off for at least 10 minutes before proceeding.

Accelerate the car to between 10 and 15 miles per hour. Make several stops, alternating between light- and medium-pressure pedal applications. Bring the car to a complete halt each time.

Keep aware of the effort you have to exert to make stops. Do the brakes grab? Does the car pull to one side? Is too much effort required to stop the vehicle?

If any of these conditions is present, it is possible that there is a malfunction with the linings (pads), master cylinder, wheel cylinder(s), or drums or discs. A brake-system overhaul may be in order.

However, even if the car pulls to one side when you apply the pedal, there is a chance that overhaul might not be needed. Uneven tire-tread wear, improper tire inflation, loose or worn wheel bearings, loose steering, or improper front-end alignment can cause a car to pull. These should be checked.

Figure 17. Brake overhaul is not a job for everyone. Some special, rather costly tools are needed, such as the ones shown here.

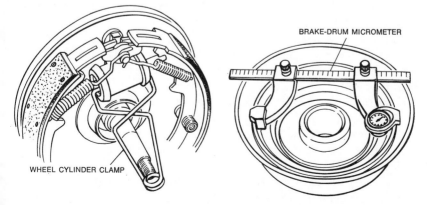

BRAKE-DRUM MICROMETER

WHEEL CYLINDER CLAMP

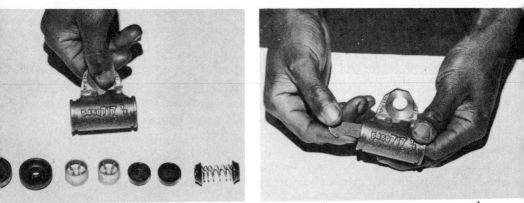

Figure 18 (left). In wheel cylinder are boots, pistons, cups, expanders.
Figure 19 (right). Use crocus cloth to polish the wheel cylinder bore.

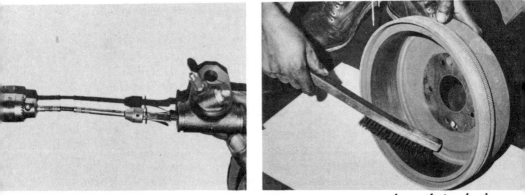

Figure 20 (left). Some manufacturers say you can hone their wheel cylinders to remove scratches. If there is doubt, replace cylinder.
Figure 21 (right). Clean the inside of brake drums with a wire brush.

Continue your road test. Open the windows and turn off all accessories, such as the radio or tape player. Listen for a squealing, clicking, or scraping noise as you drive along at various rates of speed and brake the car.

Try to determine from which wheel the noise is coming. Driving alongside a wall, such as a concrete highway center barrier, will make noises more audible.

When the possibility of noise has been eliminated, accelerate the car to 60 miles per hour and make a few easy-on-the-pedal stops. Is there brake chatter or shudder? It is possible that wheel bearings are worn or loose, but if an inspection determines that bearings are okay, then suspect that brake drums or discs are out-of-round.

From 60 miles an hour, now make several hard-pedal stops.

Caution: Apply the brakes as hard as you can *without* throwing the car into a skid. Bring the car to a complete halt after each brake application. However, do not repeat applications within two miles of each other. High-pressure stopping can induce high temperature, which can result in pedal fade.

Listen for noise and be aware of any extraordinary effort needed to stop the car as you make hard-pedal stops.

Here's your brake diagnosis chart

THE FOLLOWING CHART sums up the causes of various brake problems you are liable to encounter during driveway and road tests. As we pointed out before, check on the easy-to-do conditions first. You may be able to avert a brake overhaul, which is the next subject for discussion in this chapter. It follows the diagnosis chart.

Condition	Cause
1. Low pedal (excessive pedal travel needed to apply brakes)	D E G K
2. Spongy pedal (springy sensation of the pedal upon application)	G I J K
3. Hard pedal (excessive pressure needed to stop the car)	D E H J K L
4. Fading pedal (pedal falls away under pressure)	G I J K L
5. Grabbing or pulling	B C E F G H J L M
6. Noise (squeal, click, scrape)	D E F G H
7. Chatter or shudder	B E G H
8. Dragging brakes	A D E F H J K L

Key:

A—Parking brake improperly adjusted or sticking
B—Loose wheel bearings
C—Front end misalignment or uneven tire-tread wear
D—Brake shoes improperly adjusted; self-adjusting mechanism not working
E—Worn, contaminated or distorted brake linings (pads)
F—Weak or broken brake-shoe return spring
G—Cracked, thin, scored or out-of-round drums or discs
H—Brake-support plate (backing plate) rusted, loose or worn
I—Air in the hydraulic fluid system
J—Brake hoses and lines soft or weak, kinked, collapsed, dented, clogged, loosely connected, or leaking
K—Damaged master cylinder
L—Damaged wheel cylinder(s)
M—Improper tire pressure

How to approach overhaul (drum brakes)

CAUTION: DO NOT TAKE CHANCES. If you do not feel confident doing a brake job, or feel that you are not technically able, or do not have specific details (service manual or other data) for the brake system used in your car, leave the job to a professional.

Figure 22. High spots, roughness, scars and other brake-drum defects can be removed by taking a light cut on a brake drum lathe.

Instructions may be derived from a service manual for your car or from manufacturers of brake replacement parts. Two manuals that are particularly good are the *Delco Moraine Drum Brake Service Manual for American Automobiles* (Delco Moraine Division, General Motors, Dayton, Ohio) and *Raybestos Brake Service Guide* (Raybestos Division, Raybestos-Manhattan, Inc., Bridgeport, Connecticut). You can order them by writing the companies' publication departments.

You will need some special tools to do overhaul. They will be specified in the detailed instructions for your braking system (Figure 17).

The following general directions will help you do the best brake job:

1. When you disconnect the brake line at the wheel cylinder, close off the end of the line to keep out dirt by placing tape over the opening. Be careful you don't bend the line.

2. Remove the wheel cylinder and place it on a bench. Remove and discard the rubber boots. Press out pistons, cups and expanders. Discard any old parts that are duplicated by new parts in the wheel-cylinder rebuild kit (Figure 18).

Parts made of metal usually are retained. Those made of rubberized material usually are discarded.

3. Clean wheel-cylinder parts you have retained in fresh brake fluid or alcohol. Inspect them for scratches and corrosion, especially the cylinder bore. Make sure spring expanders aren't corroded or distorted.

4. If the wheel cylinder is stained, polish it with crocus cloth. Revolve the cylinder with your fingers while resting the crocus cloth against the wall (Figure 19). Clean the cylinder in brake fluid or alcohol after polishing.

Caution: Do not slide the crocus cloth lengthwise across the bore. Do not put pressure on the cloth. Do not use emery cloth or sandpaper.

5. If a cylinder is scratched, don't hone it unless instructions specify that the manufacturer suggests doing this. (Figure 20).

6. After polishing the cylinder, insert parts, but before you do, coat them with clean brake fluid which acts as a lubricant.

7. Inspect the brake linings carefully for clues to defects in the brake drum. If the linings of one wheel are worn more than those of the other wheels, it signifies that the drum's surface is rough. Uneven wear from side to side on any one set of linings is caused by a tapered drum. Linings that are worn badly at toe or heel indicate that the drum is out-of-round.

8. If the drums seem to be in good condition, clean them thoroughly. Use a stiff brush to remove hard deposits (Figure 21). Swab the drum's surface with a non-oil base solvent, such as lacquer thinner.

Figure 23 (below). Make sure that the thickness of the metal is checked with a micrometer after the drum is cut. If the metal is too thin, discard the drum. Do not take chances with a questionable brake drum. Your life literally depends on its integrity.

Figure 24 (right). Linings should be matched to drums to assure full lining contact. This is done by grinding the linings to remove high spots.

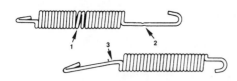

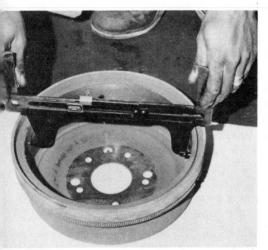

Figure 25 (left). Damaged springs cause problems. Look for (1) sprung areas; (2) chewed areas; (3) bent areas.

Figure 26 (left). Set brake gauge to inside diameter of drum; lock it.
Figure 27 (right). Place gauge on the linings and measure heel-to-toe to see if adjustment is correct. Expand or retract shoes as necessary.

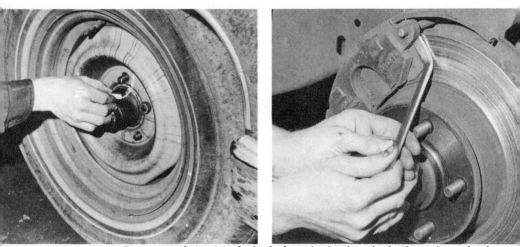

Figure 28 (left). Mark the hub and wheel with chalk so that wheel balance will be maintained.
Figure 29 (right). To check disc trueness, insert a prying tool and move the outer pad away from the disc.

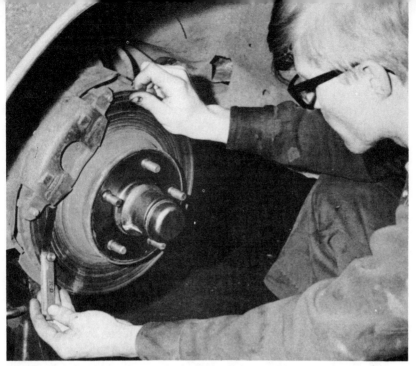

Figure 30. Check the disc for trueness with a feeler gauge. Turn the disc slowly by hand and feel for differences.

If there is grease or oil on the drum, find out where it is coming from and fix the leak.

9. Look the drum over carefully. If it is cracked, get rid of it. Never weld a cracked drum. It won't work, and the weld may give way just when you are in the midst of a panic stop.

10. Most surface defects on brake drums, such as roughness and scoring, and also high spots, can be removed by having the drums turned on a drum-turning lathe (Figure 22). Take the drums to a professional brake shop to have this done, but make certain that the operator does not remove too much metal. Only a thin cut is necessary most times to get rid of roughness and score marks.

After the operator makes the cut, he should check the drum with a brake-drum micrometer to determine if the amount of metal remaining meets manufacturer safety standards (Figure 23). If the drum metal is too thin, the drum can crack when it gets hot. This constitutes a serious safety hazard.

11. A brake job means that new linings (shoes) will be installed. Have the brake shop match each of the new linings to its respective brake drum by grinding the lining to the drum's micrometer reading (Figure 24). This will assure that the linings will make full contact with the drums. Partial contact results in more difficult braking and more rapid lining wear.

12. Examine all springs closely. Replace those that have lost tension or are damaged (Figure 25). Weak springs will cause excessive brake lining wear and scored brake drums.

13. Examine the backing plate for damage, especially for corrosion and dirt on raised shoe pads which can keep brake shoes from sliding freely. Use fine emery cloth to remove minor defects on backing-plate surfaces.

14. When all parts are reinstalled (except drums), the brakes should be properly adjusted. Use a brake-shoe adjusting gauge. Set this tool to the inside diameter of the brake drum and tighten its locking screw (Figure 26).

Now, turn the tool over and fit it over the brake shoes. Expand the shoes by manually turning the adjustment star wheel until the gauge just slides over the linings (Figure 27). Move the gauge over the entire lining surface to assure that there is correct clearance from heel to toe.

15. Bleed the hydraulic system and make sure that the master cylinder is properly filled with the right kind of brake fluid.

How to overhaul disc-brake systems

THE FIRST THING you should realize is that there are basically two variations of disc-brake systems: single piston and opposed piston.

The single-piston system uses one large piston that acts against the inner pad and creates a back pressure to pull the outer pad against the disc surface.

The opposed-piston setup has four pistons—two opposite the other two—that press the opposing pads against the disc.

The procedure is the same, whether you're overhauling a single-piston or an opposed-piston disc brake

Here we describe the repair of a single-piston disc brake. The same procedure, however, applies to repairing the opposed-piston system.

Important: You should have specific service data for the brake used in your car.

The following steps will acquaint you with the procedure involved in doing a complete disc brake job:

1. Before removing the wheel and hub, mark them with chalk (Figure 28). When remounting the wheel, make sure that the marks line up. This will allow you to retain wheel balance. (This is a good tip to keep in mind when repairing drum brakes, too.)

2. Test the trueness of the disc by pulling the outer pad away from the disc (Figure 29). Insert a flat feeler gauge between pad and disc. Use a size gauge that will have a slight drag put on it when it is between the pad and disc.

Turn the disc slowly by hand, feeling for spotty tightness and looseness (Figure 30). The "feel" that you get must be the same around the entire circumference of the disc. If it isn't, then the disc is not true and should be removed and brought to a brake shop for truing. The way that you remove the disc is explained below.

Important: If you cannot make this test, because you can't get the outer pad away from the disc far enough to insert a feeler gauge, take the car to the brake shop to have trueness checked with a dial indicator (Figure 31).

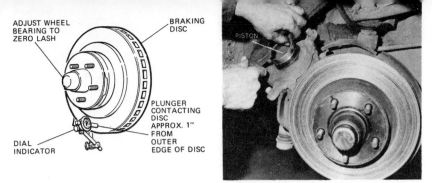

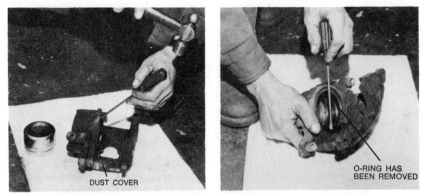

Figure 31 (left). Here's how to check disc trueness with dial indicator.
Figure 32 (right). Remove piston by hand as someone steps on brake.

Figure 33 (left). Remove, discard ring and the dust cover it holds.
Figure 34 (right). Remove O-ring and clean ridge in the cylinder wall.

If seizing is a problem, you'll have to remove the piston and clean out the cylinder

3. Check for seizing by turning the disc by hand (no feeler gauge) after stepping down on the brake pedal to reposition the pad. If turning is heavy (compare it to the opposite wheel), the piston probably has seized and is compressing one of the pads against the disc. To repair the problem, you have to remove the piston and clean out the cylinder.

4. Remove pads as explained before.

5. Remove the piston by having someone in the car activate the brake pedal very slowly. Make sure he doesn't stomp on the pedal. (You will get splattered with brake fluid).

Hydraulic pressure will force the piston to protrude from its cylinder so you can grasp it by hand. Work the piston from the cylinder by hand (Figure 32).

Caution: Do not use pliers or any other tool to remove the piston.

6. Disconnect the brake line from the caliper. Cover the end of the line with tape to keep fluid from being lost.

7. Lay the caliper and piston on a clean covering. Remove the dust cover from the caliper. Most are held in place by metal rims. Crimp the rim, pry the cover off, and discard it (Figure 33).

8. Pull the O-ring from the ridge in the cylinder wall and discard it. Use a wood scraper or tip of a screwdriver to remove all dirt from inside the ridge (Figure 34).

173

Figure 35 (left). Reassemble the caliper, using new parts.
Figure 36 (right). Remove hub dust cap, cotter pin, wheel nut, bearing.

Figure 37 (left). Screw the wheel nut back on loosely and jerk the disc toward you to pop the rear wheel bearing from place.
Figure 38. Note the two cutters—one for inner surface, one for outer.

9. Clean the piston off with crocus cloth, and use crocus cloth to clean the inside of the cylinder after you apply some brake fluid. Brake fluid (or alcohol) placed on the inside of the cylinder acts as a lubricant and aids polishing with crocus cloth.

10. Reassemble the caliper, using new parts from a rebuild kit that contains a new O-ring and dust cover (Figure 35). Use brake fluid as a lubricant when reassembling.

Be sure the O-ring is pressed all the way into the cylinder wall ridge by hand. Press the piston into the cylinder by hand. Use plenty of brake fluid as a lubricant. Put on the dust cover.

11. To remove the disc for turning, remove the hub dust cap, cotter pin and wheel nut (Figure 36). With the wheel nut off, you are able to remove the outer wheel bearing.

Screw the wheel nut back on the spindle loosely and jerk the disc toward you (Figure 37). This action pops the inner wheel bearing from the disc. It will fall on the spindle.

12. Remove the disc.

When having the disc turned be sure that it is cut on both its front and rear surfaces at the same time (Figure 38). If only one side is cut at a time, the disc will not true up, because the cutter will skip.

Be sure that no more metal is removed than the amount specified by the manufacturer. To remove more is hazardous.

Chapter 12

What to do when the power goes out of your power brakes

When a touch of the toe no longer works, the power assist unit may need repair. But it's not likely to be a complicated or difficult undertaking. Only a few things can go wrong; just follow these steps.

THE BRAKE POWER assist unit, which is commonly called the power brake, is simple and reliable. Allow your visions of a highly technical system that performs complex maneuverings to dissipate.

In fact, the assist unit is nothing more than a large can that is divided into two halves by a diaphragm—a large rubbery device that is also referred to as the power piston (Figure 1). One side of the can is the low-pressure side, while the other side is for high pressure. However, pressure on both sides is more or less equal until you apply the brake pedal.

When you press the brake pedal, the side of the assist unit nearest you becomes an area of high pressure while the side of the unit nearest the master cylinder becomes an area of low pressure. The master cylinder is the reservoir in which brake fluid is kept.

The typical domestic passenger car uses a vacuum-suspended brake power assist unit, which lets outside air into the brake pedal side of the unit when you press the brake pedal. Valves open to let the air in.

Meanwhile, on the other side of the diaphragm, a vacuum of sorts is being maintained by the engine through a hose that connects the assist unit to the intake manifold. As the engine runs, air is literally being pulled from the master cylinder side of the power assist unit. What this all means is this:

With the brake pedal not in use, pressure on both sides of the diaphragm is around five to seven pounds per square inch (Figure 2a). This equalization keeps the diaphragm motionless and keeps pressure off the brakes. When the brake pedal is applied and air rushes in to fill the pedal side of the assist unit, pressure on that side rises to approximately 15 pounds per square inch (Figure 2b). This great variance in pressure causes the power piston to move forcefully toward the master-cylinder piston, which in turn shoves fluid from the master cylinder to the brakes. Brakes are thus activated without your having to exert force on the brake pedal. In a car not equipped with a power brake, your foot does all the work.

How to know when there's trouble

IF A POWER-BRAKE unit fails, the effort that must be applied to the brake pedal to stop the car will become that much greater. In a large, heavy car, if the power unit fails entirely, you literally have to stand on the pedal in order to stop.

In a pinch, downshift and let the engine help to slow the car down

This is okay if you are a fullback type. You can do it. But if your lightweight wife is driving the car when the assist unit falters, she may not be able to bring the car to a halt by means of the brake pedal alone. She should also downshift the transmission and let engine braking power help.

Fortunately, the brake power assist unit is highly reliable and is not likely to fail. The cause of a hard brake pedal, therefore, is usually to be found elsewhere (see Chapter 11 on troubleshooting brake problems). However, when a hard pedal is encountered, you have to rule out the power assist before proceeding to the brake system itself.

As you would imagine, loss of vacuum is the major cause of power brake failure. You can test the assist unit from behind the wheel by starting the engine and allowing it to idle for a few seconds. This lets vacuum build up.

Now, shut off the engine and slowly pump the brake pedal several times. You should feel a noticeable increase in the amount of pressure needed to engage the pedal as you apply and release the brakes. If

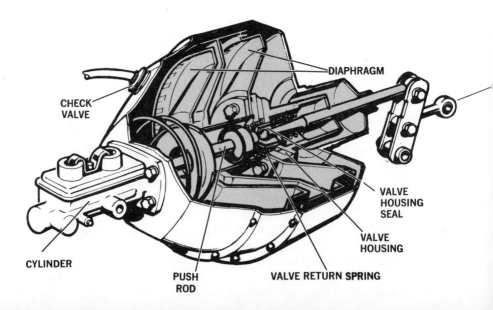

CHECK VALVE

DIAPHRAGM

VALVE HOUSING SEAL

VALVE HOUSING

VALVE RETURN SPRING

CYLINDER

PUSH ROD

there is no change in pressure, there is something wrong either outside or inside the brake power assist unit.

Troubleshooting: Vacuum loss? Hydraulic failure?

THE FIRST THING to check is the vacuum source. If the engine isn't building enough vacuum, the brake power assist unit can't build enough vacuum. In other words, the assist unit itself may be in great shape, but suffering from the failure of another system.

Narrowing down the source of the trouble

The most accurate way of checking vacuum is with a vacuum gauge. Disconnect the hose extending from the power assist unit to the manifold, at the manifold. Attach the vacuum gauge to the manifold. Start the engine and let it idle. The gauge should read from 15 to 21 inches of vacuum. If it doesn't, a malfunction within the engine is causing loss of vacuum.

Now, shut off the engine and reconnect the hose to the manifold. Disconnect the hose from the assist unit. Hook the vacuum gauge to the hose and start the engine. Again, the reading should be 15 to 21 inches of vacuum—in fact, the reading you get here should be the same as the reading you got at the manifold. If the vacuum was adequate at

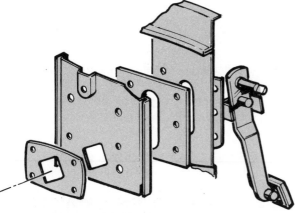

Figure 1 (left). Shown is a typical brake power assist unit. The diaphragm divides the unit into two parts. Brake pedal (above) is shown at far right of exploded diagram.

Figure 2a shows the power assist unit with brake pedal released. An equal partial vacuum exists on both sides of unit. Applying brake pedal (Figure 2b) destroys equalization; atmospheric pressure pushes the diaphragm which pushes rod to the master cylinder.

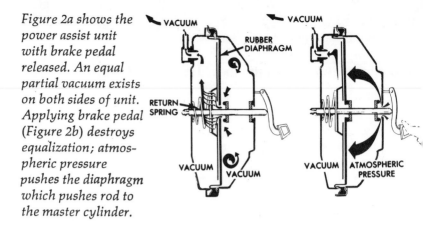

the manifold, but shows low at the hose, then the hose is damaged. Replace it with a new one.

If you don't have a vacuum gauge available, you can get a pretty good idea of the adequacy of vacuum by starting the engine and disconnecting the hose at the power assist unit. Place your thumb tightly over the hose. Your thumb should be pulled to the hose (Figure 3).

Does your hose pass the suction test? If a strong pull isn't felt, inspect the hose closely. Make sure it is straight. Make sure no cuts, cracks, or kinks exist. Replace a bad hose. Also make sure that hose clamps at the engine and at the assist unit are tight and not damaged. A bad clamp can cause a vacuum leak.

Now, disconnect the hose from the intake manifold. With the engine running, press your finger tightly over the vacuum nipple. If you don't feel strong suction, the absence of vacuum is resulting from an engine problem, such as lack of tuneup, a bad intake manifold gasket, or a sticky or burned valve.

Check the check valve. If there is one part of a brake power assist unit that fails the most, it is the vacuum check valve. Fortunately, most

Figure 3. Lack of suction at end of vacuum hose denotes a bad hose, loose clamp, or an engine malfunction.

units have the check valves on the outside where it is easy to get at them (Figure 4).

The vacuum check valve helps create vacuum in the assist unit. Its purpose is to let air inside the assist unit be pulled out of the unit by the "pulling power" of the intake manifold. The check valve is a one-way device; that is, air can get out, but no air can enter the assist unit through the valve. If air does enter, power assist will be lost.

To check the check valve, remove the hose from its nipple and pull the valve from its seat in the assist unit. Blow into the end to which the hose was attached. Then draw out on it.

No matter how hard you blow into it, no air should pass into the valve. On the other hand, you should not have to exert any force on the draw. If the valve demonstrates the least bit of trouble, replace it.

Hydraulic system. Loss of vacuum and subsequent hard braking is not the only problem that the brake pedal of a power brake-equipped car can telegraph. A low pedal indicates a problem with the hydraulic system that may indirectly involve the power assist unit.

How to nail one problem without leaving the driver's seat

To test for the condition, keep the engine off and pump the brake pedal a few times. Now, step down solidly on the pedal and hold your foot steady. If the pedal sinks away under pressure, a hydraulic system leak exists.

To try to find it, remove the vacuum hose from the brake power assist unit and twirl the shank of a screwdriver around inside the hose (Figure 5). The presence of fluid on the shank means that the seals inside the master cylinder have failed, and vacuum is pulling fluid from the master cylinder into and through the power assist unit and into the intake manifold. The master cylinder should be overhauled or replaced, and the power assist unit should be disassembled so its parts can be cleaned with alcohol. If the rubber parts in the assist unit are not cleaned, they will start deteriorating because of the petroleum in the brake fluid. Petroleum causes rubber to disintegrate.

Figure 4 (below). Whenever there is a loss of vacuum, be sure to check the check valve, Figure 5 (below, right). Fluid on shank of screwdriver means master-cylinder seals have failed, leak fluid.

Other reasons for a sinking brake pedal in a car with or without a power assist unit include a leak in a brake line or at a connection, or a leak at a wheel cylinder (see Chapter 11 on troubleshooting brake problems).

Where do you go from here?

IF THE REASON for a "hard" power brake hasn't been found by the methods described, the power assist unit may have an internal failure, and may have to be replaced or overhauled. A ruptured diaphragm, for example, will cause loss of vacuum. However, internal failure of a power assist unit is less likely than the existence of a malfunction in another part of the braking system. So, you should perform an overall brake system check as described in Chapter 11 before tackling the assist unit.

Once you have decided that the cause of hard braking does indeed lie with the assist unit, you have another decision to make. You can either replace or overhaul the unit. Overhauling costs the least. Rebuilding kits cost $7 to $10, while brand-new units cost $50 to $75. However, rebuilding kits are difficult to find, because there isn't much demand for them. Professional mechanics usually don't devote the two hours or so needed to overhaul a unit when they can replace one in 15 minutes.

If you can't get a rebuilding kit, you may be able to locate a used power assist unit for your car from an auto wrecking outfit (use only the unit designed for your car). A used unit should run about $20.

However, suppose you are lucky enough to find a rebuilding kit—how is overhauling done? Sorry, I can't get specific, because there have been over 20 variations of power assist units made. You will need either the service manual for your car or one of the popular general auto-repair manuals, such as *Motor's*, *Chilton's* or *Audel's*. Your public library probably has one or more of these.

Generally, though, to overhaul a brake power assist unit, you will have to proceed as follows:

1. Drain fluid from the master cylinder. In some cars, the master cylinder has bleed valves. In other cars, you have to open the bleed valves on each wheel and pump the brake pedal to discharge fluid.

2. Remove the master cylinder from the power assist unit.

3. Disconnect the vacuum hose and remove the fasteners holding the power unit to the brake-pedal linkage.

4. Remove the power unit from the firewall.

5. Detach any band holding the two sides of the unit together and see if the two halves won't come apart. If not, you have to use a strap wrench to separate the twist locks of one half from the off-set lugs of the other half. Use the strap wrench to tighten the two halves after overhaul is completed.

6. Once the unit is opened, it is overhauled by replacing old parts with those from the rebuilding kit.

Tires, suspension and steering

Chapter 13

How to find, fix, and prevent problems that ruin tires

Often, the cause of tire failure is downright neglect. Or it may be a defect in the suspension or steering system. In any case, here is everything you need to know about tire protection and preservation.

WITHOUT A DOUBT, NEGLECT ruins more tires than anything else. Tire tread that begins to show the effects of underinflation or overinflation, is tire tread that has been squandered—even though steps are taken at that point to rectify the problem. If tires show that they have been operated in an underinflated condition, you have also wasted gasoline. Underinflation can increase fuel consumption by as much as 10 percent.

However, this does not mean that you should overinflate tires. Overinflated tires will wear faster, so what you save on fuel, you lose to wear. There is a happy medium. It is called "correct inflation."

Facts you should know about inflation

LET'S HOPE YOU will never have need for the first two facts we're going to give you:

1. Underinflated tires show more wear on both outside treads than in the center (Figure 1). Tires needing air may also squeal on turns.

2. Overinflated tires show more wear in the center tread than on the outside (Figure 2). Tires containing too much air also produce a "hard" ride and can make the car more difficult to control, because the area of contact between the tread and the road is reduced.

If you practice sensible tire maintenance, you won't see these conditions. Generally, all you have to do is check the air pressure of your tires once a month *with your own personal tire gauge.*

We emphasize a personal gauge because of a disturbing fact made public recently by the National Bureau of Standards. According to a study made by this agency, one of every three air gauges tested at service stations was found to be inaccurate by four or more pounds. Three of five service station air gauges were found inaccurate by two or more pounds.

Check tire pressure only when tires are cold (Figure 3). As tires roll, friction causes heat which increases tire pressure. A hot tire may possess up to six pounds more pressure than it did when it was cold.

This is normal! Never bleed air from hot tires. You will cause them to be underinflated and thus more susceptible to failure. If heat on a tire rises to 250°F, there is a very real possibility of tread separation, which could lead to a serious accident. It is at about 250°F that vulcanization is performed at the factory.

A "cold" tire is not one that merely feels cold. According to the Rubber Manufacturers Association, a cold tire is one that has not been run for at least three hours, and then is driven at a speed of no more than 30 miles per hour to a service station which is no further than one mile away. However, don't sweat it if your service station is more than a mile away—you don't have to equip your home with an air compressor and air hose.

Instead, check tires in your driveway (or wherever, as long as tires are cold) and note how many pounds of air each tire needs. Then simply put in this amount when you reach a service station.

Only rarely should you have to deviate from the tire inflation specification provided in your car owner's manual and probably also on a label that is glued to the inside of the glove-compartment door. The only times that a slight deviation from correct pressure is called for is when you are going to make an extended trip at maximum turnpike speeds, when pulling a trailer, or when carrying a full load of passengers and luggage. Check the owner's manual to determine what the manufacturer considers a "full load" for your car.

Figure 1 (left). Underinflation ruins more tires than any other cause. Watch for wear on both outside treads.
Figure 2 (center). Overinflation can also cause excessive tire wear. Watch for wear in the center of the tread.
Figure 3 (right). Check tire pressure with your own gauge at least once a month, to assure long tire life.

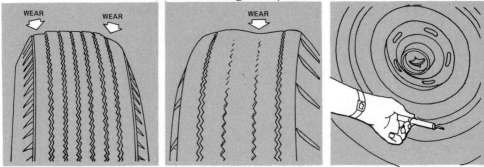

Under these circumstances, add four extra pounds of air to the tires to provide greater protection against heat, but only if the total inflation pressure does not exceed the maximum inflation pressure stamped on tire sidewalls. Never exceed this stamped-on specification. It represents the maximum pressure at which it is safe to operate your tires.

Here are a few other important pointers about inflation:

• **Check pressure** whenever there is a wide swing in climatic temperature. Inflation drops one pound for every 9°F drop in temperature. For example, if your tires are inflated to 24 pounds per square inch (psi) at 70°F and there is a sudden cold snap, with the thermometer falling to 34°F, tires will lose four psi. At 20 psi, they will be under-inflated.

• If you keep your car in a heated garage in winter, check tire pressure when the car is out-of-doors, not in the garage. Tires are going to be in use outside, and they lose pressure when going into cold air from a warm garage.

• Never reduce pressure from normal in the hope of getting better traction in snow and on ice. It doesn't work. On the contrary, reducing air pressure will provide less traction since less rubber will be in contact with the road.

• If your car is equipped with radial tires, keep in mind that looks are deceiving. Radial tires that are properly inflated bulge at the sidewall. This is normal. An attempt to get the bulge out by increasing pressure will result in serious overinflation.

Increase tire life through rotation

THERE ARE THOSE who advocate tire rotation, and there are those who claim it is a waste of time and money. Tire companies and automobile manufacturers are advocates. Manufacturers of front-end alignment and wheel-balancing equipment, in general, argue against rotation, contending that alignment and wheel balancing should be performed frequently instead, to prevent mechanical failures that cause rapid tread wear.

One cannot argue with the fact that front-end alignment and wheel balancing are very important procedures if you wish to remedy a problem that is causing unnecessary tire wear. However, there is too much technical evidence available to allow one to dismiss the value of rotation.

The purpose of rotation is to equalize *normal* tire wear (there is such a thing as normal wear—nothing lasts indefinitely). By equalizing this wear evenly over the entire tread surface, you extend tire life.

Front tires experience normal wear primarily on their outer shoulders, as a result of cornering maneuvers. Rear tires experience normal wear primarily in the center because of the power thrust from the rear axle. (This is assuming a typical rear-end-driven automobile rather than a front-wheel-drive vehicle, such as the Oldsmobile Toronado.)

Rotation equalizes this wear so that no one section wears away faster than an adjacent area. According to the Firestone Tire and Rubber Company, rotating tires every 5,000 miles provides you with 20 percent more mileage from each tire.

If a spare tire is available, it should be included in the rotation plan. According to Pontiac, a spare tire that is not pressed into service can deteriorate from disuse.

Radial tires are rotated from front to rear as seen in Figure 4. Bias and bias-belted tires are rotated in crisscross fashion as seen in Figure 5.

If you use snow tires, they should be considered in your overall rotation scheme; that is, plan rotation so it coincides with the time of the year when snow tires have to be mounted. Follow the recommended rotation method seen in Figure 6.

By the way, if your car is equipped with radial tires having conventional tread, you must equip it with radial snow tires. Never mix radials with any other type of tire. If you use radials on one or more wheels, you should use them on all four wheels. Failure to do so will result in vehicle instability and possible loss of control.

It is wise to provide snow tires with rims of their own, so they don't have to be removed from rims in the Spring and put back on rims in the late Fall. They can be kept on rims of their own during both storage and use. In this way, you will protect tires from the bead damage which becomes a possibility when you break a tire away from a rim. You can probably buy a couple of used rims for your car from an auto-wrecker yard for a few dollars.

Just a few bucks will get you a pair of usable rims for your snow tires

A studded snow tire should always be mounted on the same wheel of the car year after year after year. When storing studded snow tires, mark each tire in chalk with either an "R" for Right or an "L" for Left, depending upon which side of the car the tire was mounted. If studded tires are switched, so that studs rotate in a direction opposite to that

Figure 4 (left). Diagram shows how to rotate radial ply tires, with and without the spare.
Figure 5 (right). Bias and bias-belted tires should be rotated in a criss-cross pattern.

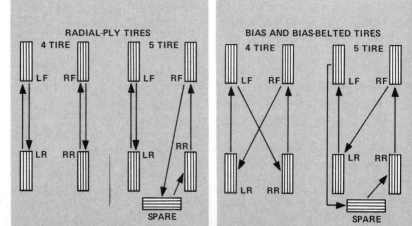

in which they rotated previously, studs will twist, loosen, and fly out of their seats in the tread.

When storing tires, lay them flat, off the tread, and keep them away from electricity-producing machinery. Laying the tire flat keeps flat spots from developing over the tread. Electricity-producing machinery creates ozone. Ozone damages rubber.

The story that tire tread can tell you

ROTATION TIME PROVIDES an ideal opportunity for close examination of tire tread to determine if it is wearing properly. For those who disagree with the concept of rotation, examination of tread (with tires on the car) every six months or so may prove beneficial.

The first thing to look for is tread that is worn to a point where it presents a danger to life. Tires are manufactured with built-in tread-wear indicators. These are solid bands that appear across the tread surface when tires have worn to the point of danger (Figure 7). When tread indicators are evident over two or more adjacent ribs, replace the tire. Tread wear indicators begin showing up when the depth of the tread is only $\frac{1}{16}$ inch.

To detect abnormal tread wear before it goes too far and the tire is ruined, you should equip yourself with an inexpensive tread depth gauge, which you can buy at an automotive supply counter. Use it at the time of rotation (or when conducting your semi-annual inspection) to check the depth of each groove at 12-inch intervals around the circumference of the tire (Figure 8). If two or more adjacent grooves show wear of $\frac{1}{16}$ inch or more than the other grooves, and wear is not being caused by improper inflation (see above), the cause is probably incorrect front-end alignment, or a malfunction in the suspension, steering or braking system (see the appropriate chapter). Furthermore,

Did you know your tires have built-in tread-wear indicators? Check for solid bands across the tread

Figure 6 (left). Follow this rotation when installing two snow tires in place of bias and bias-belted tires. For radials, move left rear tire to left front, and put spare on right front.
Figures 7, 8. Tire-wear bands, tread gauge reveal unsafe tires.

Store fronts for winter

ow tire   Snow tire

if a tire has developed cups or flat spots, suspect a mechanical malfunction in one of these areas.

What driving can tell you about tires

UNFORTUNATELY, BY THE TIME tire tread begins to reveal a malfunction, rubber has been wasted. To prevent this, you should at all times be alert for any change in the way that your car handles. Tires often telegraph trouble.

Suppose you get a continuous or cycling vibration in the steering wheel, floor, or seat of your pants on a smooth highway at a steady speed of about 60 miles an hour or above. The vibration may appear at a certain speed and disappear when that speed is exceeded. Chances are that a wheel assembly (or assemblies) is out of balance (see below for a discussion of wheel balance). However, this type of vibration can also be caused by front-end misalignment, grabbing brakes, worn-out wheel bearings, loose steering-linkage parts, or worn shock absorbers (see the appropriate chapters).

Another way tires telegraph trouble is by thumping, which is felt in the steering wheel, seat, or floor at about 25 miles an hour or slightly above. The cause in many cases is tire irregularity; that is, a high spot on one of the tires. To determine which tire is faulty, inflate all tires to 50 pounds per square inch. Overinflation eliminates a thump caused by tire irregularity.

Drive the car on a smooth pavement. If the thump is still evident, its cause is something else—probably improper balance. But if the thump has disappeared, proceed to find the faulty tire by lowering the air pressure in one tire to normal. Drive the car. If the thump is not evident, lower the air pressure in another tire, and keep repeating the test until you feel the thump, revealing the irregular tire.

An irregular tire can be used for a spare or taken to a tire dealer who usually can grind down the high spot.

Uncover those serious defects that cause blow-outs

AT THE TIME of rotation (or every six months), examine tires for physical damage. Look for cuts in the tread or sidewall that are deep enough to expose ply cords. These indicate that a tire is in danger of blowing out, so get rid of it. Do not let the size of the cut fool you. Small cuts are usually deeper than "big" cuts.

To determine the deepness of a cut, probe the injury carefully with a small screwdriver or your tread-depth gauge. If the tip reaches the cord, get rid of the tire.

A bulge or bump in the sidewall or tread is another reason for discarding a tire. A bulge indicates that the tread or sidewall has separated from the tire body. The tire is a candidate for an imminent blow-out.

Look also for small stones or other foreign bodies wedged in the tread. These can be removed by prying them out carefully with a screwdriver.

What you should know about wheel balancing

WHEEL BALANCING AND TIRES are often mentioned in the same breath. You may have heard over and over again that whenever tires are mounted, they should be balanced. What does it mean? What are the facts about wheel balancing?

Let's start by saying that the term "wheel balancing" is a misnomer. A wheel by itself may be perfectly balanced, but if its associated tire or brake drum (or disc) is out of balance, the wheel too will be thrown out of balance. In other words, instead of using the term "wheel balance," it would be more accurate to speak of "wheel-tire-brake drum (or disc) balance," but for the sake of brevity let's use the more popular term—wheel balance.

Figure 9. Wheels can be balanced with any of several different types of machines, such as this on-the-car balancer. Be sure the machine does dynamic or static balancing, whichever is indicated.

As we have mentioned, if a wheel assembly is out of balance, vibration and tire wear could result. For this reason, a wheel and tire should be balanced whenver you mount the tire on the wheel or replace the tire or wheel with a new one. Furthermore, the brake drum or brake disc, tire, and wheel should be balanced as an assembly when you replace the drum or disc (Figure 9).

A replacement brake drum or disc may not be balanced. However, original-equipment drums and discs are balanced at the factory when a car is assembled.

There are two types of wheel imbalance: static and dynamic. Consequently, there are two types of wheel-balancing equipment: static and dynamic.

When a wheel assembly is statically out of balance, a heavy spot exists at a single point on the assembly. As the assembly rotates, the heavy spot is forced against the pavement with each revolution of the wheel. This creates a pronounced vertical vibration.

If a wheel assembly is dynamically out of balance, the assembly moves from side-to-side, causing a horizontal vibration. The wheel oscillates, and the tire scuffs against the pavement, which creates flat spots over the tire.

Static wheel balancing is done by placing a weight equal in mass to the heavy spot on the wheel opposite the spot (Figure 10). In the case of dynamic balancing, a weight equal in mass to that on the outside of

Figure 10. In static balancing, the heavy spot (A) is balanced by placing a weight (B) on the rim opposite the spot.
Figure 11. In dynamic balancing, the heavy spot (A) is balanced by placing weights on the outside (B) and inside (C) of the rim.

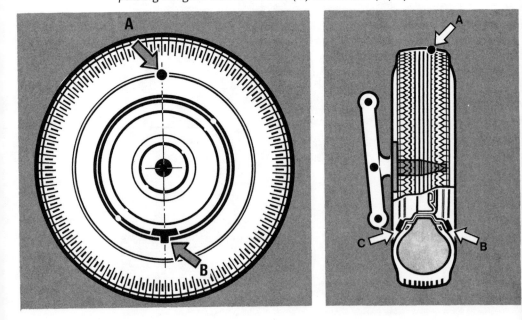

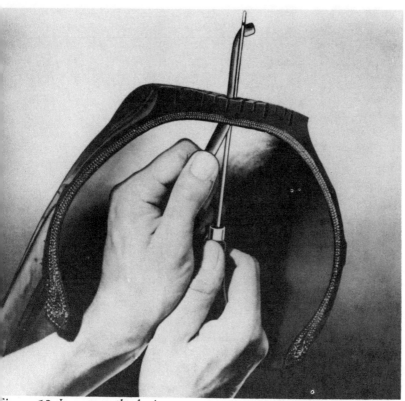

*igure 12. In one method of permanent tire repair, a plug is put in the *ole and reinforced with a patch. The only type of tire repair that *asts indefinitely is one made from the inside out.*

he wheel is placed at the same point on the inside of the wheel Figure 11).

Static imbalance creates vibration mainly at slow speeds, while dynamic-imbalance vibration occurs primarily at highway speeds. So, f you normally drive at higher speeds, you should have wheels balanced dynamically. If you drive mainly around town, static balancing s acceptable. However, if you want to be 100 percent certain that vheel assemblies are balanced perfectly, you should have them balanced both dynamically and statically.

Some important thoughts about fixing flats

THE ONLY REPAIR you should make is to tighten a loose valve core. A loose core lets the tire lose air. When a tire goes flat, inflate the tire and apply soapy water to the valve. Look for bubbles. If they appear, try tightening the valve core.

Speaking of the valve, be sure all valves are equipped with caps. Caps block the entrance of dirt and water into the tire through the valve.

Figure 13. Sometimes you can stop a tire leak by inserting tire sealant from an aerosol can through the tire valve. But this use of puncture sealer is only a temporary measure.

Other than this repair, you should leave the fixing of a flat to a shop that has the necessary tools. Trying to break a bead away from a rim with tire irons, for example, may very likely damage the bead and render an otherwise serviceable tire unusable.

Although you shouldn't make repairs, you should be aware that the only type of repair you should allow someone to make on one of your tires is a permanent repair. A permanent repair is always made from inside the tire out (Figure 12). The tire must come off the rim to have a cold plug and patch, or a chemical and hot vulcanized patch, applied.

Repairs that are made from outside the tire in are temporary at best and will start leaking within a short time. If you have equipped yourself with an aerosol can of tire sealer, remember that this should be used for emergencies only. Use the sealer to stop loss of air until a tire can be permanently repaired (Figure 13). However, never exceed a speed of 50 miles an hour or a distance of 100 miles.

Chapter 14

When your car gets the shakes: vibration and wheel tramp

If your lizzy starts to shimmy or her wheels begin to thump, don't just blame it on aging. These are signs that danger may be just around the corner; you must find and eliminate the source of the trouble right away.

RIGHT OFF, SO WE both speak the same language, let's define vibration and tramp. They are not the same.

Vibration, which also is called front-wheel shimmy, is a continuous shaking sensation you feel in the steering wheel, floor, or seat on a smoothly paved highway. It occurs at one driving speed from 50 to 70 miles per hour, continues as long as you drive at that speed, may disappear when that speed is exceeded, and disappears when speed is reduced.

Front wheel tramp (or thump) is a cyclical thump-thump-thump sensation transmitted through the steering wheel, floor, or seat at about 25 miles per hour.

Some conditions that cause vibration may also cause tramp, but usually what produces one will not produce the other. This chapter examines causes, pinpoints the one affecting your car, and helps you overcome it.

Vibration—a problem with a dangerous root

WHEN YOU FEEL VIBRATION, act. Frequently, the source of vibration is a dangerou condition. Causes of vibration include:
- **Improper tire pressure**
- **Tire bulge**
- **Loose wheel nuts**
- **Worn shock absorbers**
- **Loose steering linkage**
- **Worn or loose front-wheel bearings**
- **Loose motor mount**
- **Drive-shaft problems**
- **Worn ball joints**
- **Unbalanced wheel assemblies**
- **Front end misalignment**

Examine tires and wheels first. Check tire pressure. You may be able to eliminate vibration quickly, easily, and inexpensively. Low pressure and uneven pressure cause vibration.

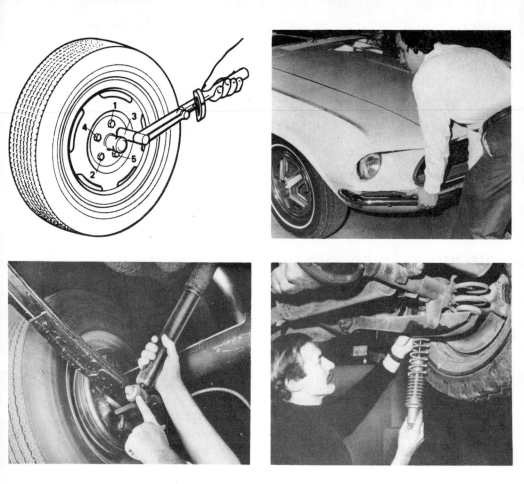

A bulge in a tire's sidewall or tread can also produce vibration, so inspect each tire closely. Get the car on a lift, so that you can give inside sidewalls as close a look as sidewalls that face out.

A bulge in a tire means that the cord is ruptured. The tire can blow at any time. Don't take a chance. Get a new tire.

Service stations and garages generally use pneumatic power wrenches to tighten wheel nuts. That's bad. These tools cause damage that creates vibration.

After the wheel nuts are tightened and loosened a number of times, the wheel's nut holes become enlarged, which keeps the nuts from being tightened properly. The wheel wobbles. Tightening wheel nuts with a pneumatic wrench can also distort brake drums and discs.

Automobile manufacturers urge tightening of wheel nuts to specification by hand with a torque wrench. You can get this specification from the service manual, by writing the service department of the particular manufacturer, or by asking a dealer.

Nuts should be tightened in crisscross fashion to equalize bolt pressure around the wheel (Figure 1). Tighten all nuts to one-half the

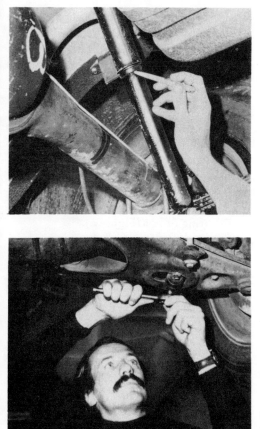

Figure 1 (far left, above). The drawing shows recommended method of tightening wheel nuts. Tighten nuts to the manufacturer's specification. Figure 2 (center, above). A shock absorber that has become weak will often reveal itself when you bounce the car. Figure 3 (left, above). If a shock absorber is leaking hydraulic fluid from this point, replace the shock. Figure 4 (far left, below). Try shaking the shock absorber by hand. If it is loose, tighten the mounting nuts. If that doesn't work, the bottom bushing (finger points to it) may be worn. Figure 5 (left, center). If shock is encased in a coil spring, it and spring must be removed so shock can be tested. Figure 6 (left). Shock absorber enclosed in A-arm must also be removed for testing.

specified torque; then go back and tighten them to the full torque limit.

Shocks from shocks cause vibration

BAD SHOCK ABSORBERS can cause both vibration and tramp. Test for worn shocks by pushing up and down on the bumper at each corner of the car several times, increasing the length of the stroke with each push (Figure 2). Release the bumper at the bottom of a down stroke.

If the up-and-down movement stops quickly, the shock absorber servicing that corner probably is in adequate shape. However, if the car bounces two or more times, the shock should be removed from the car for further examination.

In fact, a weak shock absorber may or may not reveal itself when bounced. A true test of shock-absorber adequacy requires the unfastening of each unit from each of the four corners of the car.

Before you do this, lift the car and inspect each unit for fluid leaking out of the shock onto its case (Figure 3). Leakage means that the seals are damaged. There's no alternative—the shock must be replaced.

At the same time, grasp the shock and try to shake it (Figure 4). Motion indicates a loose shock-absorber mounting. Try tightening top and bottom fasteners, and shake again. If looseness prevails, remove the shock for replacement of the bushing, if possible, or for replacement of the unit itself (see below).

If you want to go all the way and make absolutely certain that shocks are in good shape, loosen their hardware. Shocks that are centered inside coil springs must be removed from the car for testing on a workbench (Figure 5). Only the bottom mountings of most other types can be removed to test the shock on the car. However, if the shock is encased in an A-arm so you can't reach it for testing on the car, it will have to come off—coil spring or not (Figure 6).

How to remove and test shocks

SHOCK ABSORBERS are fastened to the frame on top and on bottom. Clean road dirt and grease from both upper and lower mountings, and treat mounting bolts and nuts with a liberal amount of liquid "nut-

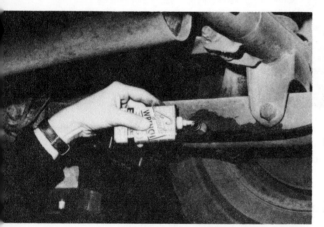

Figure 7 (left). Use liquid "nut-buster" to loosen nuts and bolts. Figure 8 (below, left). Use a jack to take spring pressure off shock. Figure 9 (below). If shock doesn't have to come off car for testing, remove bottom fasteners, move shock in and out, testing resistance. Figure 10 (below, right). The top fastener may be in the wheel well. Figure 11 (below, far right). Strong leverage loosens shock fasteners.

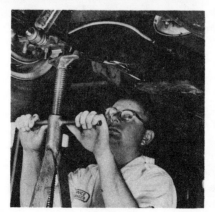

buster" or penetrating oil (Figure 7). Let this soak in for several minutes. The toughest part of removing shocks is loosening fasteners.

If the front or rear of your car is equipped with coil springs, place a jack beneath the lower control arm or on the rear axle near the spring, and jack up so that spring pressure is absorbed by the jack. This will prevent spring tension from releasing itself, causing injury, as the shock is disconnected.

Furthermore, if you have the car on a frame-grip lift so the car's weight is off the wheels, pressure will be placed on shocks, making it impossible to unfasten mounting hardware. Place a floor jack on the spring near the shock and jack up the spring, relieving pressure on the shock (Figure 8).

Remove the bottom fastener and let the shock hang. If the shock is not mounted inside a coil spring, force the shock in and out, and note resistance (Figure 9). There should be an exceptional amount. If the shock moves in and out easily, it should be replaced.

Before testing shocks, it would be wise to test the in-out resistance of a new unit so a comparison with yours can be made.

If shock absorbers are mounted inside coil springs, remove both bottom and top fasteners. If the mounting isn't visible from beneath the car, you can generally reach it through the wheel well (Figure 10).

Remove the shock and spring from the car, take the shock from the spring, and secure the shock in a bench vise. Now, make the in-out resistance test.

A good way to tell if your shocks need replacing—compare their resistance with new ones

If one shock absorber has to be replaced, its mate on the same end of the car should also be replaced to equalize shock-damping action. This is assuming that the mate shock has seen use.

When installing new shock absorbers, carefully follow the manufacturer's installation instructions. Shock fasteners must be tightened as much as possible (Figure 11).

If the shocks are in good condition, but the "shake" test described above indicates a bad bushing (you may also hear a clunking noise as

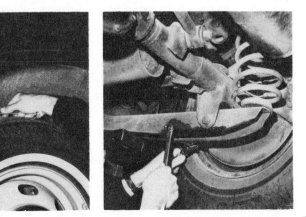

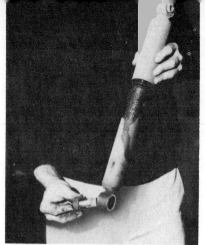
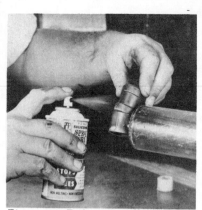

Figure 12. The bushings of some types of shock absorbers can be replaced if the shock is in an otherwise usable condition.

Figure 13. Before installing, spray bushings with plenty of silicone lubricant to make it easier to work them into their eyes.

you drive, if a bushing is bad), you may be able to replace the bushing and save the shock (Figure 12). To determine if this is possible, take the shock absorber to your automotive parts supply store and have the dealer look up the part in his catalog. Usually, the book will tell if the bushing is replaceable.

To replace a bushing, knock the old one from the eye of the shock absorber with a metal drift. Spray the new bushing with a liberal amount of silicone lubricant (Figure 13). Do not use a petroleum product. Petroleum will harm the rubber bushing. Work the bushing into the eye of the shock by hand.

Gremlins in the steering linkage

THE STEERING LINKAGE consists of several interconnected rods that transmit steering maneuvers from the steering wheel to the front wheels by way of the steering column and steering gear (Figure 14). If any part of the steering linkage is bent or loosens because of wear, front-wheel vibration occurs. Other conditions may accompany the vibration, such as loose steering, jerky steering, side-to-side wander of the car (vehicle instability), and rattling from the steering system.

It's easy to check the steering equipment—look for loose and bent parts

Checking the linkage is simple. With the car on a lift, examine each part carefully, looking for bends. A bent part should be replaced.

Firmly grasp and try to shake tie rods, pitman arm, idler arm, and relay rod (Figures 15 & 16). Replace any part that is loose.

The front-wheel bearing story

IN ADDITION TO VIBRATION, signs that front-wheel bearings are failing include wheel tramp, jerky or loose steering, pulling of the car to one side, and vehicle instability. The most serious consequence of front-wheel bearing failure, however, is wheel collapse. Luckily, this usually is preceded by one of the other conditions or by a squealing, clicking, or grinding noise.

The main cause of bearing failure is lack of lubrication resulting from lack of maintenance. When the needles (rollers) of a bearing starve for grease, they become red hot and fuse to the bearing race. The race is the stationary part of the bearing which holds the needles.

The bearing, then, becomes a solid piece of metal that is forced to turn by the rotating motion of the car's wheels. This forcing rotation causes this solid piece of metal to become hot and fuse to the wheel spindle. The spindle is the part to which the wheel is attached.

As the wheel turns, forcing this solid piece of metal that is now fused to the spindle to turn, the solid piece of metal cuts into the spindle and weakens it. In time, the spindle becomes weak enough to snap, causing loss of the wheel.

Just keep your wheels packed and you won't need to make this repair

You can see that any of the symptoms mentioned above demand immediate attention to the front-wheel bearings.

(Rear-wheel bearings seldom fail, because they are continually being lubricated with grease from the rear end, which is that large bell-shaped housing midway between the rear wheels. The rear end is a reservoir of lubricant. However, if you trace a problem to the rear-wheel bearings, you shouldn't hesitate to have the bearings serviced.

Figure 14. This diagram shows a layout of the typical steering system, with emphasis on the steering linkage.

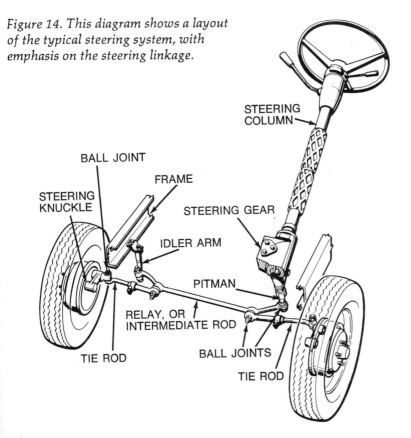

STEERING COLUMN

BALL JOINT

FRAME

STEERING KNUCKLE

STEERING GEAR

IDLER ARM

PITMAN

RELAY, OR INTERMEDIATE ROD

TIE ROD

BALL JOINTS

TIE ROD

Figure 15. Check steering linkage parts, such as tie rods, for play by trying to shake them.

Figure 16. The idler arm can be checked for play by twisting it and adjacent rods.

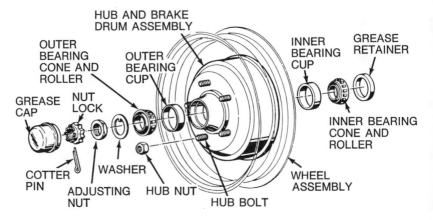

Figure 17. This diagram shows the front wheel assembly for drum brakes.

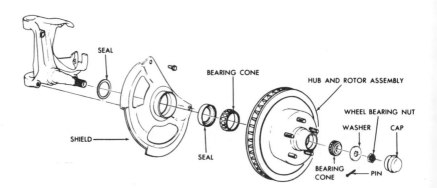

Figure 18. This is the front wheel assembly for disc brakes.

Figure 19. Pry off the grease cup, then remove the cotter pin with a pliers and castellated nut by hand.

Figure 20. Remove the adjusting nut. Lay each part aside on a clean sheet of paper as you remove it.

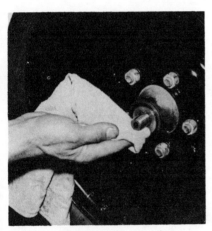
Figure 21. Wipe off areas that might transfer dirt to bearings. Always keep cleanliness in mind.

Figure 22. Pop outer wheel bearing from its seat by pulling the wheel toward you, then pushing it back.

The job requires special tools and should be left to a professional mechanic.)

One way of determining if front-wheel bearings are causing vibration, noise, tramp, and so forth is to feel the hubcaps after the car has been driven. Unless you have been doing much heavy braking, a hot hubcap is an indication of bearing trouble.

Another way of finding out if wheel bearings are failing is to spin each wheel by hand when the car is jacked up. If a clicking, grinding, or squealing noise is evident, don't take chances. Pull the wheel and inspect the bearings.

You don't have to worry about front-wheel bearing failure if you inspect and lubricate bearings periodically. This should be done as suggested by the vehicle's manufacturer. In the absence of effective guidance, wheel bearings should be serviced every 15,000 miles.

Figure 23. Remove the inner wheel bearing by tapping it out with a drift. Cups come out in same way.

Figure 24. A bearing needs plenty of grease. Notice the proper way to hold the bearing.

Don't rush this job. Just proceed carefully, step by step

Figure 25. Seat the inner bearing and grease retainer by giving the seating tool a firm hammer whack.

Figure 26. To keep any grease from being transferred to brake linings, clean brake drums with solvent.

The ABC's of wheel-bearing service (Figures 17 & 18)

EACH FRONT WHEEL has two bearings: an inner bearing and an outer bearing. Each bearing rotates inside a cup that is pressed into the wheel hub. If a bearing or its respective cup is damaged, replace both parts. The two work as a team. Using a new bearing with an old cup, or vice versa, affects performance and could lead to early failure of the new part.

Caution: Be sure that the new parts you purchase are those specified for your make and year of vehicle.

To begin wheel-bearing service, jack up the front of the car (if you can't avail yourself of a lift at a local service station) and chock the rear wheels to prevent accidental roll-back.

Pry off the wheel cover and remove the grease cap by prying it off with a screwdriver or pulling it off with grippers (Figure 19).

If the car is equipped with front disc brakes rather than drum brakes, the brake caliper will probably have to be removed. See chapter 11, dealing with disc brake repair, to find out how to do this.

Pull the cotter pin holding the castellated locknut and discard the cotter pin. Screw off the castellated locknut.

Important: As you remove each part, lay it aside on a *clean* sheet of paper (do not use newspaper—wrapping paper is best) or on a *clean* lint-free rag. When dealing with bearings, the most important word to keep in mind is *cleanliness.* Dirt that accidentally gets on a bearing will cause bearing failure.

Unscrew and remove the adjusting nut (Figure 20).

Using a clean, lint-free rag, wipe dirt and grease from the wheel spindle (Figure 21). Grasp the wheel assembly and snap it toward you about one inch. Then, push it back (Figure 22).

When replacing bearings, don't leave dirt behind. It could cause bearing failure

The outer wheel bearing and a thrust washer will fall onto the spindle. Remove them and lay them aside.

Take the wheel off and lay it face up on a clean cloth. Place a brass drift on the inner race of the inner bearing and gently tap around the circumference of the race until the bearing and grease retainer fall from place onto the rag (Figure 23). Discard the grease retainer. Lay the bearing aside.

Shine a light inside the hub and inspect the inner and outer cups. A pitted, nicked, or scarred cup should be knocked out of the wheel with a brass drift. Install a new cup by tapping it into place with a brass drift. Be sure to replace the bearing which the old cup served.

If cups are in good condition, inspect each bearing by smelling and looking at the grease. If you smell an acrid odor or grease looks black, the bearing has been running hot and probably is damaged. You will be able to tell more when you clean the bearing.

Wash the bearings in a container full of clean kerosene or wheel-bearing cleaning solvent. Work the solvent between the needles with a soft, clean brush. Be thorough.

Important: Handle the bearings properly. Do not wrap your hand around the needles. Dirt and perspiration that can harm surfaces can be transferred to the bearing. Hold the bearing by its race.

Let the bearings dry after they have been washed. If compressed air is available, you can hasten drying by giving the bearing short spurts of air.

When the bearings have dried, dip them into a container of clean lightweight motor oil. This is done to protect the bearings as they are being inspected.

Examine each bearing closely. Discard a bearing that shows physical damage, such as cracks or pitting. Discard a bearing that is rusted or blackened. Blackening indicates that the bearing has been running hot.

A bearing that has a bluish or straw-colored hue need not be thrown away. This coloring is caused by a chemical reaction of metal to grease and is not an indication of bearing damage.

Slowly spin the bearing. If it binds or feels scratchy, replace the bearing. Grit has worked between the needles.

Remember: If you replace a bearing, replace its cup, too.

Whether old bearings are being reused or new bearings are being installed, grease them. Be sure your hands are clean. Use a high-quality high-temperature wheel-bearing grease.

If you don't have a bearing packer, place a glob of grease in the palm of your hand. Work the bearing into it. Make sure that the grease gets between the needles (Figure 24). You cannot overlubricate a bearing, so be thorough. Lay the bearing aside and grease the other one.

In preparation for installation of the bearing, clean the inside of the wheel hub with solvent, let it dry, and apply a light coating of wheel-bearing grease.

Place the inner wheel bearing into the hub by hand. Make sure that the inner wheel bearing goes back into its original place—that is, don't switch inner and outer wheel bearings.

Place a new grease retainer over the inner bearing. Put a grease retainer seating tool on the assembly and give it a healthy whack with a hammer (Figure 25). You need this tool! Make sure of a solid fit by tapping the edge of the grease retainer into place with a brass drift.

Inspect the brake drum or disc for grease. Clean it with a rag that has been dampened in kerosene (Figure 26). Grease must not be allowed to remain on a brake drum or disc. It will be transferred to brake linings and result in brake grab.

Clean off the wheel spindle and place the wheel back on the spindle. Be careful not to bang the wheel against the spindle. Damage may result.

Seat the outer bearing into its cup by hand. Install the thrust washer. Run up the adjusting nut. Wheel bearings of most cars must now be adjusted.

Proper adjustment is very important. If bearings stay too loose, they may be damaged by vibration. If they are overtightened, they will fail from excessive strain.

The best way to adjust wheel bearings is with a torque wrench to manufacturer's specification. This specification may be found in the car's service manual or in other service data available at gasoline stations and garages. You can also call the service department of a dealer who sells your make of car.

The correct way to adjust wheel bearings is to spin the wheel by hand as you tighten the bearings to specification (Figure 27). After the bearings are tightened, spin the wheel to make sure it revolves freely. If it doesn't, back the adjusting nut off and readjust.

Place the castellated lock nut on the spindle and install a new cotter pin. See to it that the legs of the pin are spread wide and are wrapped around the locknut. If the legs are too long, snip them shorter.

Reinstall the brake caliper if you're working on a disc brake. Rein-

Figure 27. To adjust wheel bearings, tighten adjusting nut to specification with torque wrench.

stall the grease cap after cleaning it and coating its inside with wheel-bearing grease.

Attention: your car has motor mounts

COMPARATIVELY FEW DRIVERS give thought to the mountings on which their car's engines rest. (There are usually at least three.) By the time they realize that such components exist, it is often too late.

If a motor mount is loose or defective, an engine won't rest solidly and will vibrate. This is the least that can happen. More serious consequences can result if a motor mount is loose or has failed. The engine can shift and drive the fan through the radiator. Even worse, the engine can shift and cause the throttle to wedge open, leaving you streaming down the highway without being able to stop the vehicle.

This is not a figment of the writer's imagination. Not long ago a New England couple was awarded thousands of dollars in damages by the court after an automobile manufacturer had been found guilty of negligence regarding the motor mounts in their car. The engine of the car had shifted, the throttle had wedged open, and the vehicle had crashed into a barricade.

The sad part of the story is that the couple could not make use of the money. It went to their estate. They had been killed in the accident.

How to test motor mounts. It is very easy to determine if vibration is being caused by a loose motor mount. If the car is equipped with manual transmission, start the engine and allow it to idle. Pull up the emergency brake, put the car in gear, and either you or someone else watch the engine as the clutch is let out. If a motor mount is loose or defective, the engine will give a violent upward jerk as it stalls.

If the car is equipped with an automatic transmission (or, for that matter, with a manual transmission), place a hydraulic or hand jack beneath the oil pan or some such accessible part of the block. Place a

2x4 wood block between the jack and engine, and slowly lift up on the engine.

If a motor mount is loose or defective, the engine will lift up and you will see daylight between the mount and block.

Caution: Be careful how you conduct this test. Don't place excessive force on the oil pan. You could damage it. Anyway, if the engine won't lift with relatively light pressure put on it, the motor mounts probably are in good condition.

If a motor mount displays looseness, try tightening it with a torque wrench to manufacturer specifications (Figure 28). Retest. Motor mounts that won't be tightened or are obviously damaged should be replaced immediately.

Driving out vibration

AS YOU KNOW, most vehicles have a drive line to transmit torque (power) from the power train (engine and transmission) to the rear drive units (differential and rear wheels). The drive line consists essentially of one or more drive shafts (also called propeller shafts) and two or more universal (U) joints (Figure 29). If any part of the drive line is off kilter or damaged, vibration will occur. Furthermore, damaged parts may result in loss of the drive shaft on the highway.

Drive shafts are carefully balanced at the factory. Anything that cakes on the shaft, such as undercoating or even mud, may upset the balance. When this happens, the drive shaft can whip, creating a vibration that can chatter your teeth.

Protect the drive shaft of a car being undercoated by covering the entire shaft with a protective cloth.

There are other things that can throw a drive shaft out of kilter. If the shaft is hit hard enough with a rock, it could be dented. If a U-joint wears out or U-joint flange bolts work loose, the drive-shaft balance can suffer.

The way to check the drive shaft is to lift the car. The kind of professional lift to use, if you can avail yourself of one, is a two-post lift that allows the wheels to hang free and leaves the drive line unobstructed. If a two-post lift is not available, use a hydraulic jack to lift the rear wheels off the ground. Chock the front wheels.

(The instructions in this section apply primarily to rear-wheel-driven cars. Instructions do not necessarily apply to front-wheel-drive vehicles.)

Caution: Never use a bumper jack for this procedure. It is not safe!

Have someone start the engine and put the transmission in gear, meanwhile increasing the engine speed. Watch the drive shaft. You are looking for blurriness (Figure 30).

If the drive shaft is out of balance, the shaft will whip, which will cause it to look blurry around its edges. A shaft that is true revolves smoothly and shows a smooth edge as if it were motionless.

Figure 28. Vibration may indicate loose motor mounts. Tighten them to specification with torque wrench.

Figure 30. When vibration hits your car, examine the drive shaft for out-of-balance.

How to get rid of the blurs

BLURRING MEANS THAT ONE of several problems exist. Here is a logical order in which to troubleshoot the condition:

(1) **Wash the entire drive shaft** down with a cloth that has been saturated with a commercially available cleaning solvent (Figure 31). If undercoating or any other foreign matter is clinging to the shaft, this will make short work of the problem. Conduct the blur test again.

Figure 29. These drawings show two different types of drive shafts.

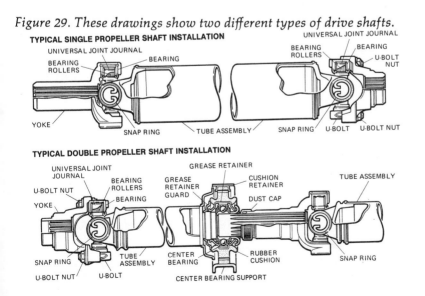

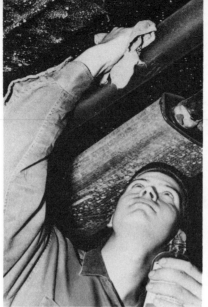

Figure 31. All a drive shaft may need is a cleaning to remove mud or undercoating causing vibration.

Figure 32. Use a torque wrench to tighten U-joint flange bolts to manufacturer's specification.

(2) **Make sure that universal-joint flange bolts aren't loose.** The bolts must be tightened to manufacturer's specification using a torque wrench (Figure 32). Indiscriminate tightening should be avoided. It can lead to trouble since overtightening flange bolts can distort U-joint bearings.

(3) **If your car is equipped with rear leaf springs,** a broken leaf or springs that aren't correctly matched can cause the car to lean to one side. This will throw the drive shaft out of balance. Be sure that the rear of the car is level.

(4) **The drive-shaft angle** between the transmission and differential (rear end) may not be correct. This is more likely to happen with a new car that is fresh from the factory. Drive-shaft alignment between transmission and differential may have been set wrong at the factory.

Figure 33. When working in the area of a universal joint, guide yourself by following this drawing.

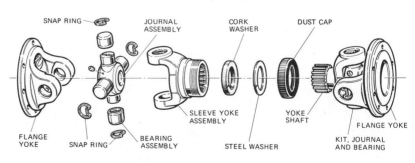

SHORT-COUPLED JOINT

SNAP RING — JOURNAL ASSEMBLY — CORK WASHER — DUST CAP — SLEEVE YOKE ASSEMBLY — YOKE SHAFT — FLANGE YOKE — KIT, JOURNAL AND BEARING — STEEL WASHER — BEARING ASSEMBLY — SNAP RING — FLANGE YOKE

Drive-shaft angularity should be checked with a drive-shaft alignment gauge, which is a professional tool. As a mechanic is checking angularity, determine if the car is level and that it doesn't possess any extra weight other than a full tank of gasoline.

If the drive-shaft angle between the transmission and differential is not as it should be, it can be adjusted. On some models, this is done by installing shims beneath the rear-engine mount, which brings the drive shaft into the specified plane. On other models, the shaft angle is altered by readjusting the differential.

(5) **Examine the drive shaft** very closely for physical damage. If the shaft is bent or dented, it should be replaced.

(6) **Finally, the danger of a worn or damaged universal joint exists.** However, a bad U-joint usually tips itself off by making a clunking sound when the car is being driven at about 10 miles per hour in high gear.

In any case, check on the possibility of a bad U-joint by jacking up the car again and grasping the drive shaft near each joint. Try to rock the shaft back and forth.

Figure 34. To remove drive shaft in most cars, remove U-joint flange bolts at the rear U-joint.

Figure 35. Scribe a mark across the U-joint and flange before removing the drive shaft.

Figure 36. Drop the rear of the drive shaft until it just clears the differential.

Figure 37. Pull the shaft back carefully, pulling it off the splined transmission output shaft.

You should not be able to see or feel play. If there is play, tighten up on the U-joint flange bolts if this hasn't been done already and test again. Now, if there is play, replace the U-joint.

All about universal joints (Figure 33)

SOME CARS POSSESS more joints than others, because some models use so-called split drive shafts. Thus, instead of the most common one-piece drive shaft with two universal joints, your car could possess as many as four U-joints.

The most common type of universal joint is the cross-and-yoke unit, so let's deal with this one here. The procedure for replacing other kinds of U-joints is similar.

To replace a U-joint, drop the drive shaft by lifting the car. The shaft is held by a rear U-joint at the differential. Remove the rear U-joint flange bolts (Figure 34).

The front universal joint is usually part of the drive shaft tube that slides over the splined transmission output shaft. Once the rear U-joint has been unbolted, you can slide the drive shaft from place. But don't do that yet!

Before dropping the drive shaft, make a mark so you can align it properly during reinstallation

First, you should make sure that correct drive-shaft balance will be maintained during reinstallation of the drive shaft. This is done before the drive shaft is dropped by scribing a mark with a file across the rear U-joint flange and its companion flange on the differential (Figure 35). When the shaft is put back into position, lining up the two marks will assure you of proper alignment.

Now, remove the drive shaft (Figures 36 & 37). Bring it over to a workbench and slide supports beneath the shaft so it is held level. Place the end of the suspicious U-joint in a vise, but do not tighten. Use the vise only to hold the drive shaft steady.

Bearing caps must now be removed. With some, it is necessary to use a piece of pipe which has a diameter large enough to encircle the caps. Hit the end of the pipe with a hammer to break the bearing-cap retainer loose and force the retainer and cap from the yoke (Figure 38). Rotate the drive shaft and do the same thing to the bearing cap on the opposite side.

In other cases, you will have to remove the bearing caps by pulling loose a snap-ring retainer with a pair of long-nose pliers (Figure 39). Tap around the circumference of the cap with a hammer until it pops loose (Figure 40).

When bearing caps have been removed, slide the cross assembly from the yoke.

To put a new universal joint into place, install the cross assembly into the shaft yoke, press on the bearing caps, and seat the caps by tapping them into place with a soft-faced hammer.

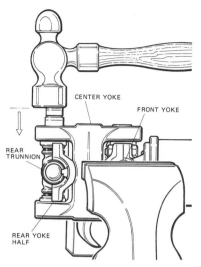

CENTER YOKE

FRONT YOKE

REAR
TRUNNION

REAR YOKE
HALF

Figure 38 (above). With some U-joints, a piece of pipe must be placed over the bearing cap and struck with a hammer to break the retainer loose.
Figure 39 (above, right). Pull loose the bearing cap retainer.
Figure 40. Tap around the bearing cap until it comes loose—this is how the inside of the cap looks.

Bad ball joints can kill you

THE BALL JOINTS we are discussing in particular are front-suspension ball joints. Your car has four—one on the upper control arm and one on the lower control arm on each side of the vehicle (Figure 41).

Many cars also have ball joints at steering-linkage pivot points, such as between tie rods and center link (Figure 14). What applies to front-suspension ball joints insofar as lubrication is concerned also applies to steering-linkage ball joints. However, failure of a front-suspension ball joint is more dangerous and more likely to occur than steering-linkage ball joint failure.

You see, the weight of the vehicle literally rides on suspension ball joints. Although they are very reliable, they can and do wear out. For this reason, they should be checked periodically, because if one does fail (and warning signs of failure are disregarded), the front of your car can collapse when you hit that next bump.

What are the warning signs of imminent ball-joint failure? Vibration is one—that is why ball joints are being discussed in this chapter. Vibration especially when you drive over a bump should make you wary.

Another sign of a ball-joint problem is excessive play in the steering wheel, and vehicle wander and weaving (that is, instability).

Still another warning sign is a crunching or squeaky noise coming from the front of the car that makes you think the car needs a greasing.

A new ball joint is a finely machined, perfectly shaped and sealed cylinder (or socket) in which is contained a finely machined and perfectly shaped ball. Sealed or not, water can seep inside this housing. Water is one main enemy of a ball joint; dirt is another.

Water dilutes grease and washes it out. When this happens, rust starts forming on highly polished surfaces. Rust eats into the seal. This allows more grease to ooze away. Loss of grease causes wear as well as rust, and the ball begins to loosen in the cylinder. Sooner or later one bump too many is going to place all of the weight on the ball joint, and the ball joint is literally going to fall apart (Figure 42).

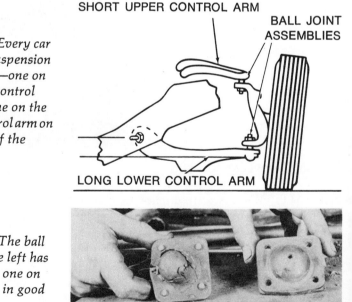

Figure 41. Every car has four suspension ball joints—one on the lower control arm and one on the upper control arm on each side of the front end.

SHORT UPPER CONTROL ARM

BALL JOINT ASSEMBLIES

LONG LOWER CONTROL ARM

Figure 42. The ball joint on the left has failed. The one on the right is in good condition.

When loose is too loose

THE ONE WAY to know if danger exists is to test ball-joint loose-ness—that is, axial play. Axial play is up-and-down movement of the ball joint in its socket.

There has been much controversy concerning what constitutes excessive ball-joint wear. Not long ago, for example, a service bulletin issued by one automobile manufacturer stated:

> ". . . dealers are often confronted by a customer who has been 'sold' new ball joints by an independent garage; yet the removed ball joints are perfectly good in every respect."

Independent garages, for their part, especially front-end shops, are critical of this manufacturer's opinion. One said:

"Loose ball joints are extremely hazardous and have led to serious accidents. I don't want to be the cause of someone's death because I failed to recommend ball-joint replacement."

It boils down to this: replacing ball joints unnecessarily is expensive, but not replacing them when they need replacing is deadly. The way you can be sure that replacement is necessary is by checking ball joint play. The following information will help you do this properly.

Compression versus tension

LOAD ON BALL JOINTS is applied in two ways: compression and tension. A compression-loaded ball joint receives forces that push the stud (ball) hard against the top of the housing. In a tension-loaded ball joint, forces try to pull the stud out of the housing.

To check a ball joint for looseness in the proper manner, you must first determine if it is compression-loaded or tension-loaded; otherwise, the ball joint can't be tested. The load must be taken off the ball joint, and how this is done depends on the suspension system you have in the car.

There are four variables, but three ways in which pressure is relieved. By comparing the following illustrations with the underside of your car, you will be able to determine which of the load-relieving methods you should use.

Figure 43 shows that the coil spring is positioned on top of the lower control arm, and both upper and lower ball joints are tension-loaded. The lower ball joint is the prime load-carrying member—that is, the one that takes practically the whole load and fails first. The other ball joint (in this case, the upper ball joint) is the follower or guiding member. It needs to be checked and replaced, if necessary, only when the prime load-carrying ball joint is removed from the car for replacement.

To test ball-joint looseness, the load must always be taken off the

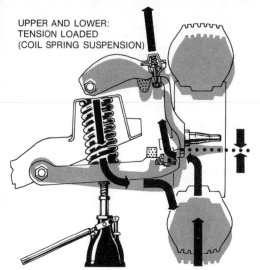

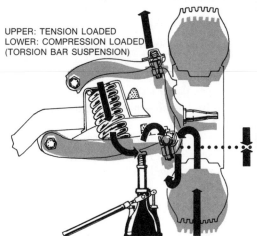

UPPER AND LOWER:
TENSION LOADED
(COIL SPRING SUSPENSION)

UPPER: TENSION LOADED
LOWER: COMPRESSION LOADED
(TORSION BAR SUSPENSION)

Figure 43. Upper and lower ball joints are tension-loaded: place jack beneath lower control arm in line with center of spring.

Figure 44. Upper ball joint is tension-loaded, the lower compression-loaded (coil spring suspension): place jack near wheel.

prime load-carrying member. In Figure 43, as we said, that's the lower ball joint. Thus, raise the wheel by placing the jack beneath the lower control arm as close as possible to the center line of the coil spring.

The second and third variables are seen in Figures 44 and 45. The upper ball joints are tension-loaded, and the lower ball joints are compression-loaded. Both systems are checked for ball-joint looseness in the same way although the one seen in Figure 44 uses coil-spring suspension and the one seen in Figure 45 uses torsion-bar suspension.

In the case of the coil-spring suspension system, the spring is positioned on top of the lower control arm. With torsion-bar suspension, the torsion bar is fixed to the lower control arm. In both cases, the lower ball joint is the prime load-carrying member.

To take the pressure off that lower ball joint, raise the wheel by positioning the jack as close to the wheel as possible.

Figure 46 shows still another system. The coil spring is positioned on top of the upper control arm. The upper ball joint is compression-loaded and is the prime load-carrying member. The lower ball joint is tension-loaded and is the follower member.

Since the coil spring is mounted on the upper control arm, the force of the spring against the control arm must be locked out to unload the upper ball joint. To do this, place a support wedge between the upper control arm and front cross member. Raise the wheel by placing a jack beneath the front cross member.

Axial play: the key to the test

THE WHEEL AND TIRE ASSEMBLY must be jacked up high enough to provide clearance for the car's rebound bumpers. These are rubber shock-absorbing devices mounted to the frame. Pressure on the

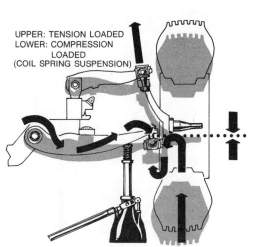

UPPER: TENSION LOADED
LOWER: COMPRESSION
LOADED
(COIL SPRING SUSPENSION)

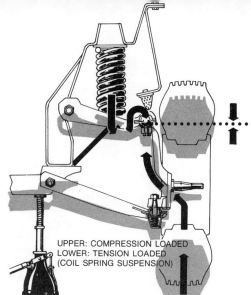

UPPER: COMPRESSION LOADED
LOWER: TENSION LOADED
(COIL SPRING SUSPENSION)

Figure 45. Upper ball joint is tension-loaded, lower compression loaded (torsion-bar suspension): place jack near wheel.

Figure 46. Upper ball joint is compression-loaded, lower tension-loaded: place jack beneath front cross member.

bumpers must be relieved to test the ball joints, because rubber rebound bumpers put a load on ball joints and would therefore be the cause of an inaccurate test result.

Attach a dial indicator so that its "trigger" is in contact with the bottom of the wheel housing. The indicator must be capable of recording thousandths of an inch. You can purchase one at a nominal price from an automotive parts supply store.

"Zero" the dial indicator, and place a pry bar beneath the wheel and tire assembly. Force the assembly upward. Note the amount of axial movement recorded by the dial indicator (Figure 47).

Each car manufacturer specifies for each model the allowable amount of ball-joint axial play. Consult service data. However, if you were to use the limit of .050-inch you would be safe.

In other words, a ball joint showing more than .050-inch axial movement should be replaced!

There is another way of checking ball-joint wear, called radial (side-to-side) movement. It is not accurate, because it doesn't truly reflect ball-joint operation.

Ball joints move axially (up-and-down); not radially (side-to-side). Furthermore, when you check radial movement, it's possible that an inaccurate indication will be attained. If wheel bearings are loose, a wheel would demonstrate radial play whether or not a ball joint was worn.

The "ins" and "outs" of replacements

REPLACING A BALL JOINT is something we won't go into detail about here, because there are many variations and ways of doing the job. Exactly how to do it for your car is outlined in the car's service manual, which you should have.

Figure 48. Grease ball joints until the seals just begin to bulge. Use a hand grease gun.

Figure 47. Dial indicator at rim measures ball joint axial play.

Figure 49. Wipe ball joint plug clean before greasing ball joint.

Figure 50. Remove metal plugs in ball joints with a wrench.

Figure 51. Insert a grease (Zerk) fitting of the proper size.

However, let's emphasize some points about replacement units. They may be bolted on, riveted in, screwed on, pressed on, or installed by using a combination of methods.

Replacement ball joints come in a kit that contains all the necessary parts and maybe installation instructions. Make sure you order the kit specified for the make and model of your car.

When new ball joints have been installed, apply multipurpose chassis grease to them at once with a low-pressure hand grease gun (Figure 48). Never use a high-pressure gun (one exceeding a rating of 10,000 pounds per square inch). A high-pressure gun can burst seals.

Apply grease until the seal just begins to bulge. Never force more grease into a ball joint than it can take—you can burst the seal.

Most ball joints (originals and replacements) have metal plugs screwed into them. These have to be removed and grease (Zerk) fittings installed in order to grease units (Figures 49, 50, 51).

Zerk fittings are available in a variety of shapes and sizes to fit any ball joint. If you can't easily get a grease gun on a straight Zerk fitting, for example, use one having a 45-degree or 90-degree angle.

Greasing of ball joints, especially upper ball joints, is made easier by equipping the grease gun with an extension adapter (Figure 52). Take great care not to inject dirt into the ball joint with grease. Wipe off the fitting and wipe off the tip of the grease gun with a clean cloth. After greasing, reinstall metal plugs firmly.

Final tip: One indication that a ball joint is damaged and may soon fail is grease oozing from the unit. This indicates that a seal has ruptured. Inspect ball joints visually for this sign whenever you are working beneath the car.

Figure 52. Upper ball joints are usually hard to get at unless you fit your grease gun with a flexible extension.

Figure 53. A front-end alignment rack is needed to align front ends. It is not a "backyard job."

Wheel imbalance and front end misalignment = vibration

WHEEL ASSEMBLIES that are not balanced cause vibration. A discussion concerning this malfunction is offered in Chapter 13 on tire maintenance. No sense repeating ourselves; turn to that chapter.

But what about front-end misalignment? Well, first off, you ought to know that unless you are ready to spend $15,000 or so for a front-end alignment rack, there is no way for you to do alignment work.

Front-end (also called *wheel*) alignment is a job you have to leave to a professional who has the tools. However, if you are knowledgeable, you can make sure you'll get the right job for your money.(Figure 53).

Out-of-line wheels reveal their trouble in various ways—here are some tell-tale clues

There are several ways of telling whether your car's wheels are out of line. Vibration (front-end shimmy) is one indication, but so is a tendency of the car to pull to one side on a level road when you take your hands off the steering wheel. A car with a misaligned front end also has a tendency to wander and weave over the road, requiring constant steering.

Other indications of front-end misalignment include tire squeal on turns and failure of the rear wheels to track with the front wheels.

Camber, caster, toe-in, et al

FRONT-END ALIGNMENT refers to the correct relative position of the front wheels to obtain a true, free-rolling movement over the road without scuffing, dragging or slipping. Five angles determine the wheel alignment of a car.

They are camber, caster, toe-in, turning radius (toe-out on turns), and steering-axis inclination.

These angles are purposely designed into a car so that weight will be distributed more or less equally and steering will be facilitated when the car is rolling.

Look at it this way: if the front end of a car were constructed so wheels were perfectly straight at standstill, forces would throw the wheels out of line when the car started rolling, making steering more difficult and causing tires to wear prematurely. By designing standstill angles into the front end, the manufacturer is able to compensate for forces and attain more or less straight wheel alignment when the car is rolling.

When trying to visualize these angles, it may pay to use your hands

These angles are as follows:

(1) **Camber** refers to the outward or inward tilt of a wheel at the top (Figure 54). It is measured in degrees, which represent the amount that the center line of the wheel is tilted from true vertical.

Positive camber is when wheels tilt outward at the top. **Negative camber** is when wheels tilt inward at the top.

Manufacturer front-end alignment specifications denote whether wheels should be set for positive camber or negative camber by the letter P or N, respectively, or by the symbol + or −, respectively. If neither letter nor symbol is present, it means to set wheels for positive camber.

The camber specification often provides a desired setting and limits. For example, it may be given as $+1° \pm\frac{1}{2}°$. This means that any angle from $+\frac{1}{2}°$ to $+1\frac{1}{2}°$ from true vertical is acceptable, but the desired setting is $+1°$.

When camber is set correctly, road contact of tires is brought more nearly under the point of the load. This results in easier steering, because the weight of the car is borne primarily by the inner wheel bearing and spindle. Tire wear is kept at a minimum.

If camber is not set correctly, too much load is placed on ball joints and wheel bearings. This causes the car to pull to one side, and there is excessive wear on one or the other side of the tire tread, depending on whether camber is out of whack negatively or positively.

Tread wear on the inside indicates excessive negative camber. Tread wear on the outside indicates excessive positive camber.

Camber is adjusted by adding or subtracting shims at the upper control arm shaft or by turning eccentric adjusting bolts. It depends on the car. A gauge attached to the wheel tells when specified camber setting has been attained.

(2) **Caster** refers to the backward or forward tilt of the spindle support arm at the top of the wheel (Figure 55). This is a directional control angle that is measured in degrees and indicates the extent to which the center line of the spindle support arm is tilted from true vertical.

Positive caster (P or +) is the backward tilt of the spindle support arm at the top. **Negative caster** (N or −) is the forward tilt of the spindle support arm at the top.

Proper caster causes the front wheels to maintain a straight-ahead position and to return to a straight position from a turn. Caster also helps to offset the effects of the crown built into much of the nation's roadways for drainage.

There may or may not be a provision on the car for adjusting caster. However, it must be checked anyway since faulty caster often indicates damage to the spindle support arm, which then should be considered for replacement.

Too much caster causes a car to pull toward the side having the least amount of caster. It can also cause hard steering, road shock and shimmy. Too little caster causes a car to wander and weave over the road.

(3) **Toe-in** refers to the shorter distance between the front of the front wheels and that distance separating the rear of the front wheels (Figure 56).

Toe-out (don't confuse this with toe-out on turns [turning radius]) refers to the greater distance between the front of the front wheels and the rear of the front wheels.

Toe is the primary front-end alignment angle that affects tire wear. It is measured in inches. The purpose of the adjustment is to compensate for wear in the steering linkage that occurs as a car gets older.

Toe-in and toe-out are measured with a toe gauge. Adjustment is usually made by turning tie-rod adjusting sleeves until the measurement falls within the manufacturer specification.

Rear wheels should also be checked for correct toe adjustment. Excessive toe-in or toe-out of rear wheels indicates the existence of a damaged part in the rear end.

(4) **Steering axis inclination** refers to the inward tilt of the spindle support arm at the top (Figure 57). This is a directional angle that is measured in degrees to indicate how much the spindle support center line is tilted from true vertical.

Proper steering-axis inclination aids steering stability and establishes a pivot point about which wheels can turn easily. A car either has it or it doesn't. If it doesn't, adjustments cannot be made to provide it. In other words, if checking on the alignment rack shows that steering-axis inclination is not to manufacturer's specification, the spindle or spindle support arm is bent or there's too much play in a ball joint. Repairs are needed—not adjustment.

Together, steering-axis inclination and camber form the included

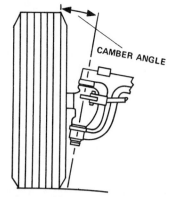

Figure 54. The camber angle is the inward or outward tilt of a wheel, measured in degrees.

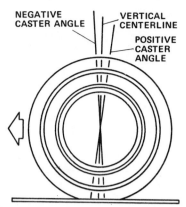

Figure 55. The caster angle is the backward or forward tilt of the spindle support arm.

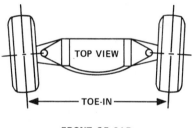

Figure 56. Toe-in is when the front tires are closer together at their front edges.

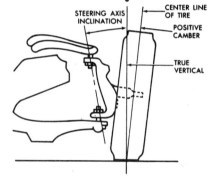

Figure 57. Steering axis inclination refers to the inward tilt of spindle support arm at the top.

angle. If camber is off and cannot be adjusted to specification, you can bet that it's because of a problem causing faulty steering-axis inclination.

(5) **Turning radius** (toe-out on turns) is a tire-wearing angle that is measured in degrees. It refers to the amount that one front wheel turns in relation to the other (Figure 58).

Proper turning radius allows front wheels to roll freely on turns. The angle depends for its correctness, therefore, on other alignment angles.

In other words, if the other alignment angles meet specification, then the turning radius will also meet specification unless the steering arm is bent. If a check on the alignment rack shows that turning radius is not to specification, check for and replace a bent steering arm.

Thumper at work

AT THE BEGINNING of this chapter we mentioned that some of the malfunctions that cause vibration might also cause front-wheel tramp (thump). Front-wheel tramp, as we said, is a cyclical thump-thump-thump sensation transmitted through the steering wheel, floor or seat at about 25 miles per hour.

Causes of tramp include out-of-balance wheel assemblies and bad shock absorbers. These we have discussed.

One major cause of tramp that hasn't been discussed is an eccentric tire—that is, an irregular tire (one that is out-of-round). To correct the condition, you must first find the offending tire.

Inflate all tires to 50 pounds per square inch. If a tire actually is causing tramp, the sensation will disappear.

Now, reduce inflation to normal pressure one tire at a time between road tests to uncover the offending tire. Road tests should be conducted on a smooth pavement.

You can do one of three things with an out-of-round tire:

1. **Continue to use it** if the sensation isn't bothersome.
2. **Use the offending tire as a spare.**
3. **Take the tire back** to the dealer from whom you purchased it for truing. Truing involves grinding down the high spot.

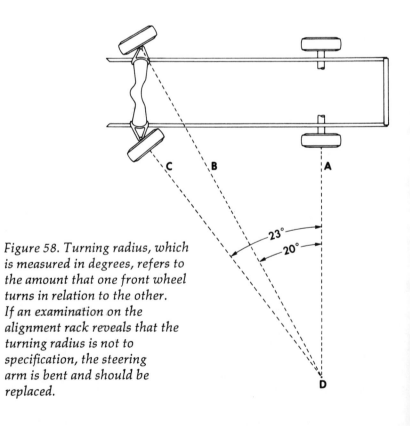

Figure 58. Turning radius, which is measured in degrees, refers to the amount that one front wheel turns in relation to the other. If an examination on the alignment rack reveals that the turning radius is not to specification, the steering arm is bent and should be replaced.

How to put the power back into your power steering

If your power steering is giving you trouble, don't run right away to a mechanic. Here are several simple steps you can take to find and perhaps solve the problem yourself. If these fail, here is what the mechanic should do.

YOU WILL HAVE NO problem knowing if your power steering system is giving trouble. Steering the car suddenly takes muscle power.

Furthermore, noise, binding or shimmy in the steering wheel when you turn the wheel may indicate a problem with the power steering system. It could also mean that a malfunction has developed in another part of the steering system.

Over the years automobile manufacturers have installed two basic kinds of power steering systems in their cars. Both are more or less the same. They have a pump and fluid reservoir, a control valve, and hydraulic lines.

The difference between the two lies in the arrangement of the power piston. One kind has an external power piston, while the other system has the piston inside the steering-gear housing (Figures 1 & 2).

Whether it is externally or internally located, the job of the power piston remains the same: to proportionally assist the driver in steering the car.

By "proportionally" is meant that the more pressure the driver applies to the steering wheel the greater will be the flow of hydraulic fluid through the steering system, and the greater will be the assist provided the driver in steering.

How your car's power steering works

A POWER STEERING system, as I have said, consists essentially of a pump and fluid reservoir, a control valve, and a power piston. The three are connected by hydraulic lines. They work together to make steering easy like this—

When the car's wheels are straight ahead, the control-valve spool is in a neutral position—that is, it is neither to one side nor to the other

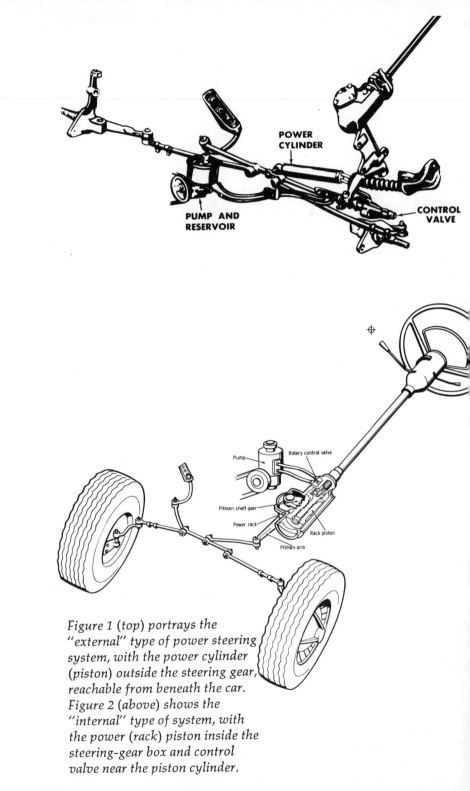

POWER CYLINDER

CONTROL VALVE

PUMP AND RESERVOIR

Pump

Rotary control valve

Pitman shaft gear

Power rack

Rack piston

Pitman arm

Figure 1 (top) portrays the "external" type of power steering system, with the power cylinder (piston) outside the steering gear, reachable from beneath the car. Figure 2 (above) shows the "internal" type of system, with the power (rack) piston inside the steering-gear box and control valve near the piston cylinder.

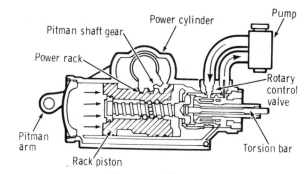

Figure 3. The control valve regulates the flow of hydraulic fluid from and to the pump. This shows the valve of an "internal" system. Hydraulic pressure on the piston assists in turning the steering system's pitman arm by means of the pitman shaft gear, making steering easier.

(Figure 3). A high-tension centering spring keeps the control-valve spool "centered."

As long as the control-valve spool is in the neutral position, hydraulic fluid that is being pumped from the pump and fluid reservoir is equalized throughout the system. The fluid makes a circuitous trip from the reservoir to the power-piston cylinder and back to the pump and fluid reservoir.

Now, when the steering wheel is turned (let's say to the left), a torsion bar begins to twist. This puts enough pressure on the control-valve spool to overcome the force of the centering spring. The control-valve spool moves to the right.

Hydraulic fluid entering the gear housing from the pump under pressure is now able to flow through the hydraulic line that is feeding the right side of the power piston cylinder. Simultaneously, hydraulic fluid on the left side of the power piston is forced back through a hydraulic line to the pump and fluid reservoir.

When you turn the steering wheel, you move aside a control-valve spool. Fluid rushes in to push the power piston in the direction of the turn

Unequal pressure is created on the sides of the power piston, and it is that which provides the assist to steering. The power piston moves to the left, because there is no resistance on this side of the piston.

The same sequence of events takes place when you turn the steering wheel to the right, except that the process is reversed. Hydraulic fluid is pumped to the left side of the power piston, while fluid on the right side returns to the pump and fluid reservoir. You are able to turn the wheels to the right with assistance.

A wise way to approach troubleshooting and repair

YOU CAN EASILY TAKE several steps yourself to try and overcome a problem in the power steering system. They include checking tire pressure, checking the level of hydraulic fluid in the pump and fluid reservoir, and making sure that the fan belt is adjusted properly.

If further testing is necessary, you will probably want to let a service technician do it for you. Several special tools, such as a power-steering pressure gauge, are needed.

Let me emphasize that if you take your car to a mechanic for a power-steering problem you should be fully aware of his ability to do the job. He should follow the sequence that we outline here. Otherwise the repair bill may be out of sight.

Figure 4 (left). Hard steering can result from low tire pressure, so before doing anything else check inflation.
Figure 5. Check power steering drive belt with a belt-tension gauge.

Figure 6 (left). Some cars have a slot in the pump bracket for tightening the power steering drive belt, making prying unnecessary.
Figure 7. Dipstick on cap shows level of power-steering fluid.

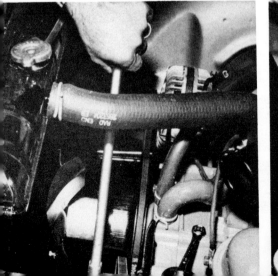
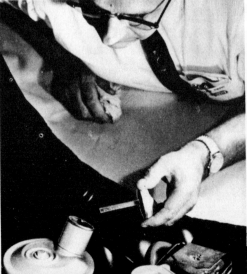

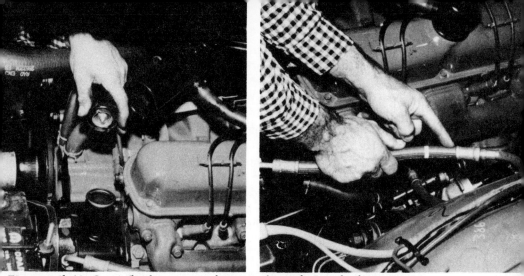

Figure 8 (left). *Some fluid reservoirs have no dipstick. Just look in.*
Figure 9 (right). *Power steering system leaks occur most often when hydraulic fluid lines split or develop faulty connections.*

Following the correct approach is so important that we can't emphasize it enough. Here is what Chrysler Corporation says about service technicians who follow another approach or who don't know the right way to do power-steering repair:

"Because power steering is remarkably trouble-free, many technicians probably haven't bothered to keep up with data or to learn much about troubleshooting their equipment. A lack of understanding often results in 'guesswork fixing' by changing parts instead of making a proper diagnosis. This may not correct the real cause of the trouble . . . and more often than not builds up a customer-jolting bill."

The best way to troubleshoot a power-steering system

DO IT BY THE NUMBERS, as follows:

1. **Check tire pressure** (Figure 4). Make sure tires are inflated to manufacturer specification. Low tire pressure can produce a hard steering condition.

2. **Check drive-belt tension.** A loose belt will slip and result in a lack of power assist, intermittent off-on assist, and/or noise. It is one of the most common reasons for power steering "trouble."

The most accurate way of checking power steering drive belt tension is with a belt-tension gauge (Figure 5). The gauge is fitted to the belt and pressed down. The tension is recorded on a dial.

The tension must be to manufacturer specification. If it isn't, tighten the belt.

Also examine the belt for glaze. A glazed belt will slip. Replace it.

Suppose a noise is coming from around the pump and fluid reservoir. Don't make a snap judgment that the pump is bad and should be replaced. Be sure. Here's how.

Adjust drive-belt tension with the belt-tension gauge and test to see if noise is still present. If noise is still there, pour some water over the belt. If the noise ceases or changes pitch, you can be sure that it is being caused by the belt or by the belt pulley. The pump is not making the noise.

However, even if water doesn't affect the noise, you still should not conclude that the problem is with the pump. Loosen the belt if it operates only the power steering pump. Run the engine.

Now, if there is *no* noise, you have traced the trouble to the pump. It is damaged internally and should be replaced.

If noise continues with the belt loosened, and the power-steering pump not being driven, then the cause of the noise is either the alternator or water pump.

Caution: When the power-steering drive belt is being tightened to specification, make sure that any pry bar which is being used is not placed against the pump and fluid reservoir. Pressure against this component can crush it or cause a seam to break, resulting in a fluid leak. The pry bar is normally placed against the pump bracket (Figure 6).

3. **Check power-steering fluid level.** Low fluid level leads to hard steering, alternate off-on assist, and/or noise.

Some pump and fluid reservoirs have a dipstick that is part of the reservoir cap (Figure 7). If you have this type of setup, drive the car until it reaches operating temperature. Wipe the area around the reservoir cap with a rag, and remove the cap. Check fluid level on the dipstick.

Instead of a repair job, the power steering unit may only need a little fluid

If there is no dipstick attached to the reservoir cap, you have to check the fluid level just by looking down the throat of the reservoir (Figure 8). Start the engine and turn the steering wheel all the way to the right stop, and then all the way to the left stop.

Do this a few times. However, do not keep the wheel against its stop for any length of time, and definitely no longer than five seconds.

Wipe the area around the reservoir cap and remove the cap. If the engine is cold, the fluid level should be to the bottom of the filler neck. If the engine is warm, the fluid level should be halfway up the filler neck.

If the level is too low, fill the fluid reservoir with the hydraulic fluid specified by the manufacturer in the owner's manual. If you have to fill a reservoir almost constantly, there is a leak that should be found.

Clean dirt, oil, and grease from hydraulic lines and from the pump and fluid reservoir. Let the engine idle and turn the steering wheel all the way to the right stop and then all the way to the left stop, but do not keep the wheel against either stop for more than five seconds.

Turning the wheels to the extremes forces hydraulic fluid through the power steering system under great pressure and will cause fluid to leak from a defective part. Examine hydraulic lines and the metal seams of the pump and fluid reservoir.

Fluid leaks occur primarily through split hoses and at hose metal connections (Figure 9). If a hose is leaking, replace it (Figure 10).

Keep connections tight and be sure to cap hydraulic lines when working on the system

Figure 10. In some systems, as with this "external" type, loose connections may cause leaks. Tighten them to see if the leak stops. The hoses seen here connect control valve to power piston cylinder.

Figure 11. Whenever hydraulic lines have to be disconnected to repair the system, cap the lines to prevent loss of hydraulic fluid.

If the leak appears to be coming from the pump and fluid reservoir, seals may be bad or the housing itself may have ruptured. In any event, the unit should be replaced.

4. Trouble at low speeds only? Suppose the power steering system operates satisfactorily at medium and high speeds, but the car is difficult to steer at low speed. The cause of the problem is probably a defective control valve.

The control valve provides full hydraulic pressure at slower speeds when steering is more difficult. At higher speeds, when the forces of acceleration help make steering easier, the control valve reduces the flow of hydraulic fluid.

When steering becomes more difficult at slower speeds, the control valve may be sticking. It may be possible to free it just by revving the engine with the car at a standstill. Do this a few times.

Revving builds up hydraulic pressure and loads up the control valve. High pressure often frees a sticking valve.

If this action fails to achieve success, the valve should be replaced (Figures 11 & 12).

5. Troubleshoot the pump with a pressure test (Figures 13 & 14). Run the engine until the hydraulic fluid reaches 150° to 170°F. No

Figure 12. The control valves of many "internal" type systems are located right on top of the steering gear to permit easy removal.

more—no less. (Cold fluid will provide higher than normal pressure readings, while hot fluid will give readings that are on the low side. For accurate results, the fluid must fall within the temperature range given.)

Check the temperature of fluid by placing a thermometer in the fluid reservoir. With the engine idling, hold the steering wheel against each side stop for a few seconds (no longer than five seconds) until the thermometer reaches the correct fluid temperature.

Caution: When turning wheels from side to side don't keep the car in one spot. After a few turns in one spot, move the car so the position of the tires is changed. Moving the car keeps flat spots from forming in tires as they rub against the ground with the car at a standstill.

Connect a power-steering pressure gauge. Start the engine and allow it to idle. Keep the shut-off valve of the pressure gauge open.

The manufacturer's service manual (or other relevant publication) should be consulted to determine the "low-speed" test specification for the particular power steering system. This specification differs from car to car, but is generally below 100 pounds.

If the pressure gauge shows that pressure is higher than that specified by the manufacturer, you know that there is a restriction in the

Figure 13. A pressure gauge is needed to troubleshoot the pump of a power steering system.

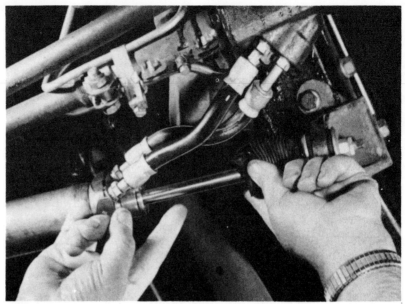

Figure 14. The piston of an "external" type system can be checked for damage by pulling back the protective boot. The piston rod must be highly polished without score marks or nicks.

system. Look in particular for a hose that is kinked or has become clogged.

Increase speed so the engine is idling rapidly and close the shut-off valve of the pressure gauge. This test is done to determine if the power-steering pump is able to develop specified pressure.

With the shut-off valve fully closed, pump pressure should reach the specified reading given by the manufacturer in the manual for the "high-speed, closed-valve" test. This specification is generally from 850 to 1,000 pounds.

If the specified reading is not recorded on the pressure gauge, it means that the pump has gone bad. It should be replaced.

If the reading for the "high-speed, closed-valve" test is according to manufacturer specification, open the shut-off valve on the pressure gauge and run the engine at fast idle. Hold the steering wheel hard against the left-hand stop, and then hard against the right-hand stop.

Take pressure readings with the steering wheel against both stops. These readings should be the same. If they aren't, there is a leak inside the power-steering gear housing. The housing will have to be disassembled, and the faulty seal or seals replaced, or the entire gear box will have to be replaced.

In most instances, service technicians will insist on replacing faulty components. This is because the cost of overhaul is usually equal to or more than the cost of a new part.

Clutch and transmission

Chapter 16

How to keep your car's clutch out of danger's grip

The clutch and manual transmission have been used on cars since the
first one took to the road. (Automatic transmissions, by comparison, have been
around only since 1939.) Yet, for all its history, the clutch remains a mystery.

BASICALLY, THE CLUTCH is used to disconnect the engine from the
manual transmission when gears are shifted. But this is not its only job.

The clutch allows an engine to attain sufficient speed to start and
run on its own power. This speed is on the order of 300 to 600 revolutions per minute.

If an engine were forced to remain coupled to the transmission, it
could never attain this rpm for starting since the load (resistance) imposed by the transmission would be too great.

Furthermore, once an engine begins running, the engine and transmission must be kept decoupled as long as the car stays stationary. If
this were not done, the load imposed by the transmission would cause
the engine to stall.

Your auto's clutch has three very important functions to perform

As the car begins moving, the clutch is used to allow the speed of
the transmission input shaft to increase gradually until it matches
the speed of the engine crankshaft.

How the clutch does its job

FRICTION! THAT IS THE KEY to the way that a clutch works.

A clutch is composed of a pressure plate and a clutch disc (or plate).
The pressure plate is attached to the engine flywheel. The clutch disc,
which drives the clutch shaft, is placed between the flywheel and the
pressure plate (Figure 1).

The clutch shaft, which is also known as the throwout bearing shaft,
is the output shaft of the clutch to the transmission.

Now, the clutch disc makes everything work together. On each side
of it is a layer of highly frictional material. When the clutch is engaged,

coil springs (or a diaphragm spring) clamp the clutch disc firmly between the flywheel and pressure plate.

This causes the entire ensemble to be clamped firmly together, and all rotate together, which permits engine torque as represented by the rotating flywheel to be transmitted through the clutch to the transmission (Figure 2).

When you step down on the clutch pedal to disengage the clutch, a clutch fork moves and applies pressure to the clutch release (throwout) bearing. The rotation of the bearing puts pressure on the clutch release levers. This, in turn, compresses clutch springs and moves the pressure plate to the rear.

The pressure plate and flywheel now rotate independently, and the clutch disc and clutch shaft come to rest.

Clutch types and how they differ

ALL CLUTCHES WORK pretty much on the principles we just described, but there are different types.

Is your car's clutch single-plate or multiple-plate, "wet" or "dry"? For example, there are single-plate clutches—they are the ones described above—which possess one clutch disc between the flywheel and pressure plate.

And there are multiple-plate clutches. They use more than one driven clutch disc between the flywheel and pressure plate.

The major difference between single-plate and multi-plate clutches, other than the number of elements, is a difference in the time required to engage the clutch. Clutches with single-driven members engage and begin motion more rapidly than clutches with multiple-driven members.

Automobiles and light-duty trucks are generally equipped with single-plate clutches, while medium- and heavy-duty trucks are usually equipped with multi-plate clutches.

A clutch may be either "wet" or "dry."

Figure 1. This exploded view of a typical clutch assembly shows that the driven plate assembly, which is the clutch disc, is positioned between the flywheel and the pressure plate.

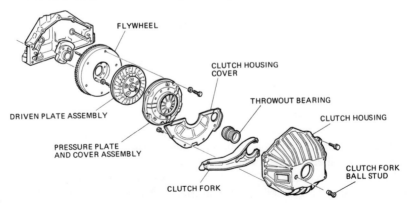

A wet clutch is one that has oil supplied to the clutch for lubrication. A dry clutch is lubricated by the graphite coating of the cast iron or nodular iron of which the pressure plate and flywheel are made. A dry clutch "grabs" faster than a wet clutch.

Dry clutches predominate on cars and light-duty trucks. Wet clutches are used mainly on heavier vehicles. Obviously, on heavier vehicles, the friction on the clutch elements is greater, and more concentrative lubrication is required.

Some clutches have a hydraulic assist. Oil is forced into the clutch housing through a boring in the engine shaft from a master cylinder that is similar to a brake master cylinder. The oil presses against a piston and squeezes together a series of clutch discs which are connected alternately to the rotating driving side of the clutch and the stationary driven side.

When the discs lock, the driven side turns the driving side, and power is delivered to the transmission output shaft and to the gears that are attached to it.

Other hydraulic clutches use a slave cylinder. Oil from a master cylinder activates the cylinder which helps move the clutch fork, taking the strain out of clutching (Figure 3).

Ever heard of a "power clutch"? Many imported cars have one

Clutch problems and what to do about them

A CLUTCH CAN eventually wear out from normal use, but it will be many thousands and thousands of miles if it does. In fact, a clutch may outlive the car.

However, driver abuse is something else again. You can kill a clutch in a few hundred miles by mistreating it.

Riding the clutch pedal is the chief form of abuse. Driving along with your foot resting on the pedal so the pedal is partially depressed keeps the clutch partially engaged. This will cause extreme and rapid wear.

Figure 2. When clutch is engaged, clutch disc grasps flywheel and pressure plate; all turn together.

Figure 3. This Datsun and many other imports employ a hydraulic clutch that works like power brake.

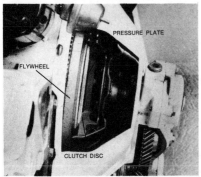

One thing should be in your mind at all times: "I won't rest my foot on the pedal." Furthermore, when stopping for a traffic light on an ascending hill, you shouldn't play with the clutch to keep the car from rolling back. This will cause damage. Instead, depress the clutch pedal right to the floor, so the clutch is disengaged, and hold the car still with your brakes. That is what they are for.

A bad clutch will slip, drag or chatter. It may also cause the car to creep.

A slipping clutch is typified by a lessening of vehicle speed in respect to engine speed. In other words, the car lacks power, especially when climbing a hill. Car speed doesn't keep pace with engine speed.

In its early stage, a slipping clutch may be mistaken for an engine problem. A slipping clutch can cause the engine to lose speed, overheat, and consume more fuel.

To determine if a clutch is slipping, park on level ground, set the parking brake firmly, depress the clutch pedal, and shift the transmission into low (first) gear with the engine idling.

Here's the test for a slipping clutch —which causes loss of power

Step down on the accelerator pedal gradually, and at the same time slowly release the clutch pedal. The engine should stall. If the engine continues to run and the car remains stationary, the clutch is slipping.

A clutch will slip because of a lack of free play, oil or grease on the clutch disc facing, a worn facing, weak clutch springs, or pressure plate or flywheel runout. "Runout" refers to non-concentricity, not operating in a perfect circle.

All causes of a slipping clutch, other than incorrect free play, which is discussed below, require disassembly and repair. This is normally a job for a professional mechanic.

To test for a dragging clutch, allow the engine to idle. Depress the clutch pedal to the floor and shift into any gear. Then, shift into Neutral.

Hold the clutch disengaged and depress the accelerator pedal part way to the floor. Shift into gear. If a grinding noise accompanies the shift, the clutch undoubtedly is dragging.

A dragging clutch may be caused by excessive play which can be corrected by proper adjustment as explained below. Other reasons for the condition are weak or worn springs, a bad bearing, and a warped clutch disc. These problems require a major overhaul.

When a clutch grabs, it engages suddenly, and the car moves abruptly as the clutch pedal is released to a partially engaged position. The vehicle creeps.

The cause of this problem most frequently involves a faulty clutch disc. Overhaul is generally indicated.

How to adjust a clutch

THERE IS ONLY ONE service that a clutch generally requires: a free-play adjustment. Free play refers to the amount of movement in the clutch pedal before the clutch disc actually engages.

As a clutch wears during normal use, the amount of free play is reduced. If this free play is not maintained at a correct adjustment, the clutch may receive damage and could wear more quickly.

One of the most prevalent conditions that lead to a ruined clutch is to forget that free-play adjustment exists.

All automobile manufacturers agree that clutch free play should be checked periodically and an adjustment made, if necessary. However, there are differences of opinion concerning the frequency of service.

For example, Volkswagen, Pontiac, and Fiat recommend clutch adjustment every 6,000 miles. Ford recommends adjustment every 12,000 miles.

You should check your owner's manual or service manual to find out what the manufacturer of your car suggests, but keep in mind that more frequent adjustment will not harm the clutch. It is lack of adjustment which does damage.

Clutches on some cars should be adjusted every 6,000 miles

Clutches from car to car are adjusted differently (Figures 4 & 5). It is therefore not possible here to detail for you each method. You will have to consult the service manual or other service literature for your particular model. However, to give you some idea of how a free-play adjustment is made, we describe how to adjust the clutches of late-model Volkswagens and Ford Pintos.

The clutch of a Volkswagen is checked for free play by placing a ruler along the clutch pedal with one end resting against the toeboard. Note the distance of the pedal from the toeboard.

Now, press the pedal down until pressure is felt. This *free* movement should be between ⅜ and ¾ of an inch. If it is more or less, the clutch cable needs to be adjusted.

Park the car on a level surface and jack up the left side. Remove the left rear wheel. Be sure to place support stands beneath the car for safety purposes.

Figure 4. To adjust Datsun clutch, loosen locknut at clutch fork, adjust pushrod for specified free play.

Figure 5. When you can move clutch fork maximum of ⅛-inch, clutch is adjusted.

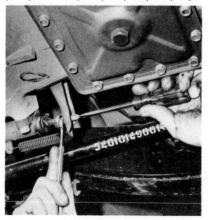

Adjust the clutch by holding the end of a pair of pliers and turning the cable wingnut until pedal free play falls within the manufacturer's adjustment specification. By turning the wingnut counterclockwise, you shorten pedal travel. Turning the wingnut clockwise increases pedal travel (Figure 6).

When the adjustment has been made, leave the wingnut so the wings are horizontal and the lugs in the nut engage recesses in the clutch lever. Work the clutch pedal in and out a few times, and then double-check to make sure that the free play is still within specification.

The clutch of the Ford Pinto is adjusted from beneath the car by loosening the cable locknuts and the adjusting nut at the flywheel housing boss (Figure 7). Pull the cable toward the front of the car until free movement of the release level is eliminated.

Holding the cable in this position, insert a ¼-inch spacer against the flywheel housing boss on the engine side. Tighten the adjusting nut by finger until it comes to rest against the spacer.

Replacing any part of a clutch may be too big a job for many amateurs

Do not disturb the spacer. Tighten the front locknut against the adjusting nut to a 40-to-60 foot pound load. Remove the spacer, and tighten the rear locknut against the flywheel housing boss.

Other clutch facts to think about

SOME AMATEUR MECHANICS are perfectly able to overhaul a clutch, but the task does require a good deal of technical skill, some special tools, and pertinent literature. To replace any part of a clutch or the entire clutch normally requires dropping of the transmission and the removal of other engine components, including the propeller shaft, flywheel housing, and starter motor.

Some manufacturers (not all) recommend that clutch service include lubrication of some parts, especially the clutch linkage. This is a task that anyone can do, so consult service literature in your owner's manual or in the service manual to determine if your clutch needs lubrication.

Lubrication, if indicated, will help prolong the life of the clutch.

Figure 6 (right). Clutch pedal free play in Volkswagen is adjusted by turning clutch cable wingnut.
Figure 7. In a Ford Pinto, locknuts and an adjusting nut at flywheel boss adjust clutch free play.

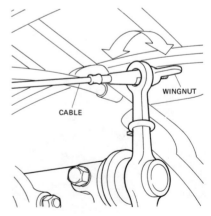

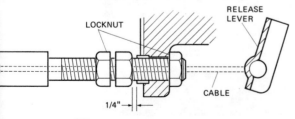

Chapter 17

How to find and maybe fix the bug in your automatic transmission

Most automatic transmission malfunctions are minor enough in nature so the car owner, with a bit of guidance, can iron a problem out himself. Don't despair that it will be a professionally performed job costing hundreds of dollars.

DEAD-CENTER TROUBLESHOOTING of an automatic-transmission problem on your part is very important. When something happens that makes you believe there is automatic-transmission trouble, make sure that you are right. If you misinterpret the symptoms or allow your imagination to play tricks, you could leave yourself wide open to a fleecing by an unscrupulous mechanic.

Never leave troubleshooting to anyone else. Do it yourself. First establish whether there is indeed a problem with your automatic transmission. Then, if you decide that there is, try to locate the trouble and fix it yourself if possible.

The first point that must be made is that you should never be bound by a specific shift-pattern specification. Some car owners have the misguided opinion that an automatic transmission should shift at 15 miles per hour, 20 miles per hour, 30 miles per hour, or some such exact figure. Forget it even if you find a shift pattern specification in a service or owner's manual.

Don't expect your car to shift gears at rigidly determined speeds

The shift pattern of an automatic transmission can vary by as much as 25 miles per hour from one gear to another by the simple act of the driver varying the amount of pressure on the accelerator pedal. In other words, automatic transmissions which are in perfectly sound condition can be made to shift at different speeds just by increasing or decreasing the amount of pressure on the gas pedal.

Furthermore, there is just no way for anyone to establish an exact speed at which an automatic transmission will shift. There are too many variables.

Consider two same-model cars having exactly the same automatic transmission. However, if one has different-size tires and a different rear-axle ratio than the other, the two will shift at different speeds.

There is, though, a general test you can perform to determine if the automatic transmission in your car is shifting properly or whether an abnormality may exist. When driving under typical city-traffic conditions, an automatic transmission that does not upshift into direct drive (high gear) by the time the speedometer reads 25 miles per hour is a transmission that is not acting normally.

However, don't rush to an automatic-transmission repair shop just yet. Some of the do-it-yourself methods provided below may solve the problem.

Noise usually indicates big trouble

Some whine is normal, except when the auto is in high gear

THERE IS NO ARGUING with the fact that a grinding, knocking, scraping or clicking noise coming from an automatic transmission, no matter in what gear or under what circumstances it occurs, indicates a serious problem.

Not as certain, however, is the meaning of a whining noise. Transmission whine is one of the most misleading symptoms, because a certain amount of whine is normal.

The gears of an automatic transmission, you see, are in constant mesh. In first gear and in reverse, therefore, a whine often will be created as gears rotate. The whine may even increase in intensity as the speed of the car increases.

However, if the whine persists in high (Drive) gear, then a malfunction is evident, because in high gear the gears of an automatic transmission do not rotate.

An objectionable shrill coming from a transmission should not be confused with whine. A shrill that emanates from a gearbox at any speed is a sure sign of a malfunction.

Another condition that may be confusing involves the difference between a fluid leak and seepage of fluid. Leaking is evidence of a problem. Seepage is a normal condition.

If you discover drops of automatic transmission fluid on the ground beneath the transmission or if you see fluid actually dripping from the transmission case, that is a leak. On the other hand, an oily film around a bolt or around a gasket joint is normal seepage.

Some leaks can be fixed by the car owner himself. Methods are discussed below.

The role of the neutral safety switch

OBVIOUSLY, IF YOUR CAR won't move forward or backward when the automatic-transmission shift-selector lever is put into gear and the engine is running, the transmission needs attention. However, this is not the case if the engine doesn't start with the transmission selector lever in Neutral or Park (assuming all other mechanical parts of the car bearing on starting are in good condition). Neither is it the case if the engine starts with the shift selector lever in any position.

A part called the neutral safety switch controls starting vis-à-vis the position of the transmission selector. The switch assures that the engine won't start unless the transmission is in Park or Neutral. However, if the switch vibrates loose or malfunctions, erratic starting will ensue.

The engine may not start although the battery and all other parts that bear on snappy starting are in good condition. Or the engine may start with the transmission selector in Drive, Low or even Reverse.

The neutral safety switch is usually located on one side of the transmission (Figure 1). If you cannot locate the one in your car, consult the vehicle's service manual or ask your mechanic to show you where it is.

Make sure that the neutral safety switch is tight in its seat and that all connections are firmly attached. If this fails to restore normal starting, replace the switch.

Taking a hand in automatic-transmission repair

OTHER THAN STARTING problems caused by a faulty neutral safety switch and fluid leakage, discussed below, the way to approach automatic transmission repair is to start with automatic transmission fluid. Improper fluid level is one of the main reasons for malfunctioning.

Begin by consulting the owner's manual for your car regarding the correct procedure to follow in making an automatic-transmission fluid-level check. Usually, the transmission must first be warmed up to normal operating temperature, which takes about 10 miles of driving. The

Figure 1 (left, below). Replace the neutral safety switch if you suspect it is faulty. It must be tight or starting is erratic.
Figure 2 (right). Check the automatic transmission fluid level often.

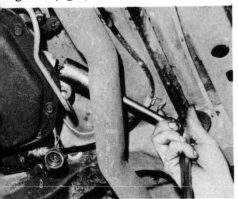
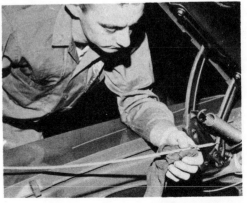

transmission selector level is then normally placed in Park or Neutral with the car parked on a perfectly level surface.

The automatic transmission dipstick, which is usually found at the rear of the engine compartment, is pulled from the dipstick tube *after* wiping dirt from the area (Figure 2). It is very important that you take all precautions to see that dirt does not get on the dipstick and that it does not fall into the dipstick tube.

Dirt transferred to the interior of the transmission by the dipstick can cause internal transmission damage that will cost you much money to have repaired.

Most transmission dipsticks have two index marks on them. The one on top is the "Full" mark. The one lower down is the "Add" mark.

See to it that the transmission fluid level falls on the "Full" mark or between the "Add" and "Full" marks. If the fluid level is too low, a harshness in shifting can result. Another consequence of low fluid level is delayed shifting. Still another result is noise from the transmission.

If the fluid level is extremely low or all fluid has been lost, the transmission will refuse to shift when it is placed in gear. The car won't move.

If the car won't move when placed in gear, you may be out of fluid

Naturally, if fluid level is low, add fluid. Make sure that it is the type of fluid specified by the manufacturer of your car in service data. Fluid designation is spelled out in the service manual and owner's manual. Use no other type!

As important as it is to keep fluid level from getting too low, it is just as important to make sure that fluid level isn't too high. It must not be over the "Full" index mark on the transmission dipstick.

Excessive fluid in the transmission causes aeration. This condition lowers fluid pressure and can lead to slipping or some other erratic shifting problem.

If the transmission contains too much fluid, it must be drained off. This can be done by removing the transmission-case drain plug, if there is one, or by dropping the transmission pan. The procedure is discussed in detail below.

What to do if a fluid check proves fruitless

THE SIMPLE ACT of adding automatic transmission fluid, if the transmission needs fluid, or drawing off excessive fluid may resolve your transmission problem. But suppose fluid level is normal, and a problem of harsh, slipping, delayed, or erratic shifting continues. What do you do now?

Your course of action at this point depends on the transmission in your car. In any event, you should secure some information about that transmission before you proceed.

The service manual for your car contains the information about the automatic transmission that you need. You can also get data if you find the transmission number, which is probably stamped on the transmission case. Send this number to the department of technical information of the car's manufacturer and request operational and service information for the transmission.

Trying to repair your transmission without this information is akin to trying to fly without navigational aids. For instance, some transmissions are equipped with an electric kickdown switch.

This switch can cause all sorts of shift-pattern problems if it goes bad. If you did not know that your transmission had this switch, you might have your transmission torn apart in search of the cause of a problem. That is a very expensive way to solve a problem that a faulty kickdown switch, which costs a couple of dollars to replace, is causing.

If service data tell you that an automatic transmission possesses an electric kickdown switch, a preliminary step would be to disconnect the harness going to this switch and road-test the vehicle. If the problem "disappears," you can fix the transmission by just replacing the switch.

Other transmissions are equipped with a manual kickdown valve, but you wouldn't know this unless you had operational data available. This valve is controlled by linkage on the carburetor.

As with the electric kickdown switch, a malfunctioning kickdown valve can cause an erratic shift pattern. The transmission should be road-tested with the valve blocked out of the system; disconnect the pressure linkage (Figure 3). If the valve is the cause of trouble, the transmission will perform flawlessly. Replace the valve.

Another part that often leads to erratic shifting is the vacuum modulator. Most transmissions, but not all, have one. Service data will tell you if your transmission possesses this part. If it does, replace it when a problem crops up (Figure 4).

Figure 3 (left). When erratic shifting occurs, disconnect kickdown valve linkage at carburetor and road test to see if problem disappears. Figure 4. Replacing the vacuum control may correct erratic shifting.

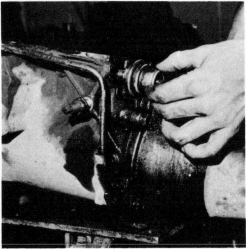

If your transmission does not have a vacuum modulator, it uses fluid pressure. See to it that the fluid line is tight and not leaking.

A faulty vacuum modulator or restricted fluid pressure produces delayed shifting, rough shifting on acceleration, or shudder. If the situation is allowed to continue, transmission clutches may burn.

One final effort before seeking professional help

IF YOU HAVE FAILED to iron out a shifting problem, after performing the steps outlined, your final action should be to drain the transmission fluid and drop the transmission oil pan.

Some transmissions have drain plugs in the pan, but most do not. If you find a drain plug in the pan of your transmission, remove it and allow the fluid to drain into a receptable (Figure 5).

If there is no drain plug, remove all bolts from the transmission pan except two opposing ones. These should be loosened.

Now, pop the pan loose from the transmission case by prying with a putty knife. Be ready to spring out of the way. As soon as the transmission-pan gasket seal is broken, fluid will come flowing out (Figure 6).

A large-enough receptacle to catch fluid should be placed beneath the transmission.

Figure 5 (left, below). Look for a fluid drain plug on transmission. If there, remove it and allow fluid to drain into a receptacle. Figure 6 (right). Fluid is drained from transmissions that don't have drain plugs by loosening the transmission pan.

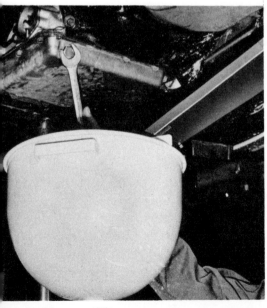
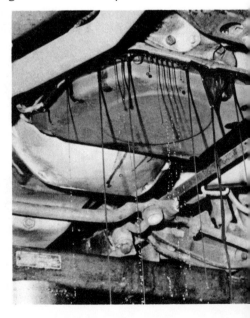

The converter must also be drained (Figure 7). Remove the covering. Most converters have one drain plug, but some (many Ford transmissions, for example) have two drain plugs. Look for them. They may be 180° apart. All drain plugs must be removed from the converter to drain off all the fluid.

When the fluid has drained from the transmission case and converter, remove the two bolts still holding the transmission pan and take the pan off. Now proceed to closely examine the drained fluid and the inside of the pan.

Look for particles first. Any debris, even tiny particles, lying in the pan or suspended in the fluid indicates that some part or parts in the transmission have failed or are in the process of failing.

Examine the color of the fluid with a critical eye. Automatic transmission fluid is red. If the fluid that came from your transmission appears black or orange, a serious defect exists inside the transmission.

Now, smell the fluid. A smell of trouble is an odor resembling varnish.

Particles, faulty color or a bad odor is a sign that your transmission is a candidate for a major overhaul. However, you might be able to avoid or at least postpone this very expensive proposition by "tuning up" the transmission. Service will usually be effective if damage hasn't gone too far.

Figure 7 (left, below). Fluid should also be drained from the converter. Look for more than one drain plug.
Figure 8 (right). On most automatic transmissions, the front band adjustment can be made from outside the unit, without removing pan.

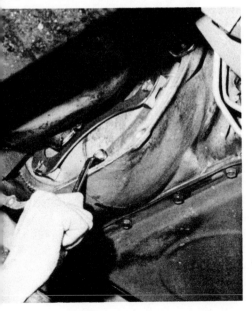
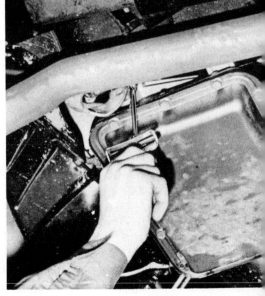

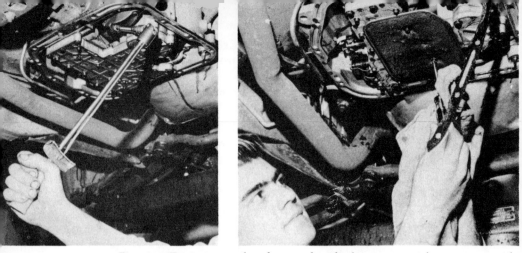

Figure 9. Drop pan and make rear-band adjustment with torque wrench.
Figure 10. Replace the fluid filter and replace the old pan gasket.

Here's how to tune up your transmission

TRANSMISSION SERVICE involves adjusting bands, cleaning the transmission pan, replacing the transmission-fluid filter, and installing fresh fluid.

Service information from the manufacturer is needed to adjust the transmission bands. Band adjustment is made generally by tightening the front- and rear-band adjusting mechanisms with a torque wrench (Figures 8 and 9).

Important: You must have this tool, which should be calibrated in inch-pounds. You cannot guess.

Clean the transmission pan thoroughly. Scrape off old gasket material from the pan and transmission case.

Caution: Do not reuse an old gasket even if it appears to be in good condition. You should use a new gasket to prevent leaks.

Wash the pan with a solvent, such as kerosene. Make sure that all debris, plain dirt, and old fluid are removed. Allow the cleaned pan to air-dry.

The fluid filter is usually held to the transmission body by a couple of screws. As soon as you remove the pan, the filter will become evident.

Unscrew the old filter and throw it away (Figure 10). Replace it with a new filter.

Reattach the transmission pan to the case, making sure that the new gasket is properly installed and does not "crinkle." See to it that transmission-pan bolts are firmly set.

Now, insert a clean funnel into the transmission-fluid dipstick tube and pour in fresh fluid (Figure 11). Use only the type of fluid specified by the manufacturer of your car. Any other may cause damage.

Important: Guard against the introduction of dirt!

When the transmission has been refilled so the fluid level reads be-

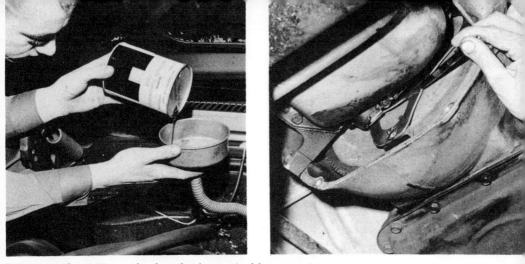

Figure 11 (left). Use only that fluid specified by manufacturer.
Figure 12. Crack in converter drive plate made this transmission click.

tween the "Add" and "Full" marks on the dipstick, check to see that no fluid is leaking from around the pan, drain plug, or pan bolts. The transmission should not be filled to the "Full" mark yet.

Since the transmission is not warmed up, the fluid is not in an expanded state. If you fill the transmission so the fluid level is at the "Full" mark now, you may be overfilling the transmission.

Drive the car until the transmission warms up. Now, check fluid level. You can add more fluid, if necessary, to get the level to the "Full" index mark on the dipstick.

During the road test, you will be able to tell if your effort to forestall a transmission overhaul is successful. If the harsh, slipping, delayed or erratic shifting has cleared up, you can breathe a sigh of relief.

However, if the problem persists, the transmission and converter should be removed from the car and disassembled. All parts should be inspected, and new parts, seals, rings, and gaskets installed.

This should be done by a competent automatic transmission specialist.

Attempting to find the cause of noise

IF A GRINDING NOISE is coming from the transmission, there is no hope. The transmission will have to be disassembled.

If there is a knock, click, or scrape, inspect the torque converter before resorting to transmission overhaul. There is a good possibility that the converter drive plate has loosened or has cracked (Figure 12). This is far less expensive to repair than a transmission.

Excessive whine or buzzing can either be coming from the transmission or from the torque converter. With the car on a lift or securely on jacks, place the transmission into gear and try to determine where the noise is coming from by placing your ear near both parts.

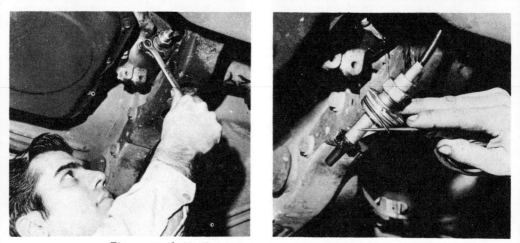

*Figure 13 (left). Every joint is a potential leaking area. The
speedometer gear housing, for example, may have to be removed.
Figure 14. Replace the damaged speedometer adapter O-ring to stop leak.*

If the whine or buzz is coming from the torque converter, that part
will probably have to be repaired or replaced. If the noise is coming
from the transmission, drop the pan and look for particles, which indicate that a part is in the process of failing.

If there are no particles in the pan or in the fluid, then the noise may
be caused by a faulty vacuum modulator.

A word about leaks

**Most leaks can be
fixed by tightening
fittings or
replacing gaskets**

YOU CAN REPAIR many fluid leaks yourself, but first you have to
find the leak (Figures 13 and 14). When you get service information
from the manufacturer, it will probably contain a drawing that points
out designations. Look for leakage at the lever-shaft oil seal, kickdown
wire terminal plug, pressure-gauge plug, vacuum-control unit seal,
oil-cooler fittings, and speedometer adapter O-ring.

Once you find the area of leakage, remove the part and replace the
gasket. This will usually stop the leak. If not, perhaps the part itself
has to be replaced.

Naturally, a loose fitting will also cause a leak. See to this first.

Appearance
and comfort

Chapter 18

How to find and silence noises by expert methods

Sounds coming from body and chassis components are disturbing, irritating, and often hard to track down. Use the professionally proven methods discussed here to finally locate and do away with these racket producers.

THE MAJOR TASK (and frequently the hardest) in getting rid of noise coming from somewhere in your car is finding the source of the sound. Once this is done, tightening a part, or reconnecting or replacing a noise-making component frequently is quick and easy.

Today's auto, compared with the car of a decade ago, has more places where rattles, groans, squeaks, and other noises can be created. It has a more powerful and complex engine, low-slung styling that requires a more severe driveline angle, much ornamental chrome, wider use of under-the-hood options such as power steering and air conditioning, and shock-absorbent bumpers—all of which are liable to loosen and produce noise.

Finding noise begins with a road test

LET'S SAY YOUR CAR develops a noise you can't exactly put your finger on. How do you go about locating it?

A carefully conducted road test done over various types of road surfaces must be your first step. Varying the road conditions often helps to amplify the noise—that is, some road surfaces tend to make a certain noise louder while other types of road surfaces silence or diminish it.

Furthermore, certain types of noises develop only at a particular speed or under specific engine-load conditions.

By determining the driving conditions under which the noise is produced and/or is at its loudest, you create a starting point from which to find the noise.

OFFSET

Figure 1. A nonunitized body is fastened to the frame with bolts that pass through rubber spacers. Rattles will develop if bolts loosen.

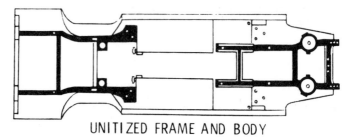

UNITIZED FRAME AND BODY

Figure 2. A unitized body is spot-welded to the frame. Frame and body appear as a single unit. If spot welds break, noise will develop.

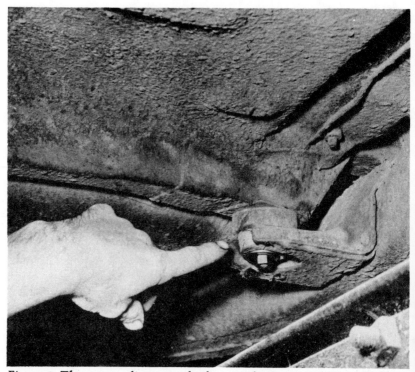

Figure 3. The way to discover whether you have a nonunitized body in your car is to look for body bolts.

(Much of the information provided in the chapters on vibration and wind and water leaks apply to tracking down noise. Some of that information is repeated in this chapter, but it is suggested that you go back over those chapters and pull out applicable data.)

To make it easier to find a noise, try to categorize the noise you are hearing into one of two groups—

(1) A noise that is being produced somewhere in the *body* structure.

(2) A noise that is originating somewhere in the *chassis*.

As the discussion develops in this chapter, you will be able to get a better appreciation of what is body noise and what is chassis noise.

Get to know your car's body design

NOISES PRODUCED by the body structure are caused by loose body bolts or broken spot welds, a loose part, an improper mounting, or wind.

One of the main causes of noise, obviously enough, is the car's body itself. Over the years three types of basic body designs have been employed: nonunitized, unitized, and semiunitized.

• A *nonunitized* body is attached to the car's frame with bolts (Figure 1). As you can imagine, body noise will develop if one or more of these bolts works loose.

• A *unitized* body is welded directly to the car's frame (Figure 2). No bolts are employed, and there is less chance of body noise developing. However, spot welds can part, and when they do the noise that develops is readily discernible.

• A *semiunitized* body is a combination of the other two. Some sections are bolted to the car's frame and other sections are welded. Thus loose bolts and parted spot welds alike are possible.

You can tell which type of body your car has by examining it from

Figure 4 (left). Unitized body, welded to frame, has boxlike nature.
Figure 5 (right). Body bolts of nonunitized and semiunitized bodies should be tightened periodically with a torque wrench.

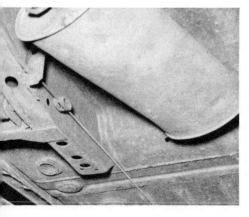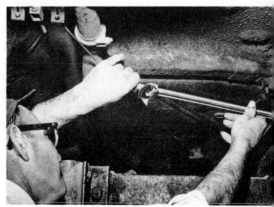

Figure 6. Many rattles in a car can be traced to their source by tapping the vehicle over its entire area with a rubber mallet.

below. A nonunitized body is easy enough to spot. You will see bolts securing the body to the frame (Figure 3).

The underside of a nonunitized body looks like a one-piece box rather than a conventional frame (Figure 4). The front of a semi-unitized body is usually the part welded to the frame, while the remainder of the body is bolted.

You can avoid rattles by periodically tightening bolts and/or restoring spot welds

You should periodically tighten the bolts of nonunitized and semi-unitized bodies (Figure 5). Loose body bolts cause rattles, most often when the car hits bumps.

Tighten the bolts with a torque wrench to the specification given by the manufacturer in the service manual. Generally, this specification is 20 to 30 ft. lbs.

If a spot weld of a unitized or semiunitized body comes loose, you will hear groaning, squeaking, and/or snapping sounds when the car goes over bumps. This is one repair you can't handle yourself. It must be done by a reputable, competent automotive-body repair facility.

In making the repair, the service technician should use a spot welder. He should not use a torch, which causes heat to spread and which in turn causes undercoating to melt and dissipate. This will create a whole new noise problem for you.

Loose parts: the most common noise-maker

ALL VEHICLES, INCLUDING those with unitized bodies, have their share of parts which are attached with bolts. Each bolt represents a potential creator of noise.

That rattle in your door may be a screwdriver dropped by one of the men who made your car

In addition, cars on more than one occasion have come off the assembly line with rattles built into them. Nuts, bolts, screws, tools, and other miscellaneous items of hardware have been inadvertently left in the bottoms of doors.

Buy yourself a rubber mallet. It is an excellent tracer of this type of noise.

Begin at one end of the car and gently strike *each* area, especially along the underside (Figure 6). When you hear a rattle, inspect the immediate area for any parts held by nuts and bolts. Tighten any you find and test again to see if the noise has disappeared.

If you hear a rattle coming from a door, it probably means that there is something loose inside. Remove the trim panel to see what is lying in the well. Probably it is one of those bolts, nuts, etc., and it is sliding and banging.

The trim panel is the decorative (upholstered) surface of the door on the passenger's side.

Windows and doors are noise producers, too

WINDOWS VIBRATE AND RATTLE when window regulators wear out and loosen, or when channel weatherstripping wears out.

To check the condition of a window regulator, tap the surface of each trim panel with the rubber mallet. If this causes a rattle, chances are that window-regulator rivets or bushings are worn. One or more parts of the regulator will have to be replaced.

This is no job for a layman. Consult an experienced automotive-body specialist.

What must be done to determine if noise is being created by loose or worn window-channel weatherstripping is described in the chapter on air and water leaks. Also consult that chapter for other causes of wind noise.

If an entire door seems to be rattling, it probably is not aligned properly. Determine this by checking the gap between the door and fender, and between the door and pillar.

If a gap is wider for the particular door than it is for the door on the opposite side of the car, the hinges of the "widely gapped" door should be realigned. Generally, you do this in the following way:

1. Loosen the hinges (Figure 7).

2. Use a pry bar to move the door, as required, to get it to line up properly (Figure 8). Alignment is correct when the gaps we referred to just now are the same as those of the opposite side door.

3. Retighten the hinge bolts *securely*.

4. Realign the striker plate, which probably has been thrown out of line with the door lock. The correct distance between the striker plate and door lock of most installations is 3/32 to 5/32 inch.

Make this adjustment by loosening the striker-plate bolts, removing the plate, and inserting metal striker-plate shims behind the plate until the correct clearance is obtained (Figures 9 & 10). Striker-plate shims are available from the parts department of a dealer who sells your make of car.

You can check on striker plate-lock alignment by cleaning the jaws of both parts and applying a thin layer of dark grease to the striker. Open and close the door a couple of times. A pattern will impress itself on the grease which can be measured to determine if the striker is correctly positioned.

What to do about chassis and dashboard noises

IT IS NOT UNUSUAL for a body noise to result from a failure in the chassis. For example, loose or worn engine parts, or a misaligned front end or driveshaft can produce sufficient vibration to cause body rattling. You have to find the chassis element that is at fault before you can eliminate the rattle.

This can be done with a portable tachometer. Hook the instrument up and mount it in the car so revolutions per minute can be observed as you drive. If your car is equipped with a "tach" as part of its instrumentation system, you can use that.

Test-drive the car. Drive at the speed at which the noise is created. Notice both the speedometer reading and the revolutions per minute registered by the tach.

Now, shift down to the next gear range and speed up until you reach a rate of speed at which the noise is once again created. If the noise occurs at a lower speed than before, but at the same rpm, this is because of a problem in the engine. If the noise occurs at the same rate of speed, but at a higher rpm, it is caused by a misaligned driveline or wheels.

The following chart sums up for you the various parts of the chassis which can create noise and what must be done to correct it (also consult the chapter on vibration):

When it comes to tracing a noise from the dashboard, I can't be too encouraging. It's tough to find because there are so many components located behind the dash.

Noise Source	Noise Produced	How to Find	Repair
Loose or broken motor mount	Rumbling or shaking sound; vibration	Let engine idle; pull up handbrake; put car in gear. Engine will rock if mount is loose	Tighten or replace mount
Weak shock absorbers or bad shock mounting	Rattles	Test condition of shocks	Replace shocks
Sway bar connection	Groaning as car corners	Check connectors	Replace worn connectors
Loose, bent or misaligned pulleys	Rattling	Check pulleys for noise with stethoscope (Figure 11)	Tighten, realign or replace
Loose or worn mounting bracket for alternator, power steering pump, air conditioner compressor	Squealing or rattling as engine idles	Use stethoscope to find noisy component	Tighten or replace bracket
Steering column coupling	Rattles	Shake steering wheel to recreate noise	Tighten or replace
Exhaust system	Rattles or hammering	Examine for misaligned brackets, broken straps	Tighten or replace

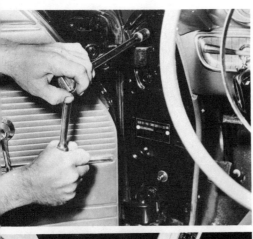

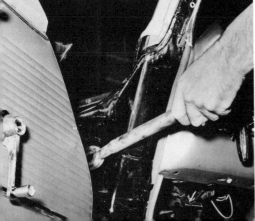

Figure 7 (left, above). When correcting door alignment, first loosen hinge bolts.
Figure 8 (left, below). Use a pry bar to reposition the door. Then make sure that hinge bolts are retightened securely.

You will have to use a trial-and-error procedure. Push, pull and jiggle until you find the offending squeak or rattle.

One noise-maker that is easily controlled, however, is a tool or other loose object you are carrying—perhaps in the trunk. Look for objects like this before tearing into everything else.

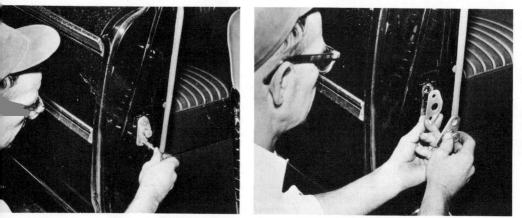

Figure 9 (left). To realign the striker plate with the door lock, first remove the striker plate.
Figure 10. Then place shims behind plate so door will lock firmly.

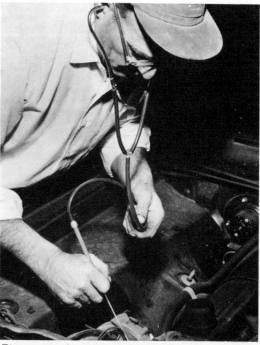

Figure 11. An automotive stethoscope, which you can buy in an auto parts supply store, is a handy diagnostic tool to have in your tool kit.

Chapter 19

How to seal your car's interior from wind and water

You don't have to endure irritating noise and water leaks. This chapter reveals professional methods that will surely help you to restore interior integrity

LET'S TALK ABOUT WIND first: The noise produced by wind swirling around and through a car can be awfully annoying. It occurs in one (or both if you are really unfortunate) of two ways: by air leaking through open cracks and crevices, or by turbulence.

Noise caused by air leaking into or out of the car occurs when weatherstripping around doors and windows wears out, or if weatherstripping wasn't installed properly to begin with or is disrupted.

Noise caused by turbulence refers to the interruption of airflow around the outside of a car as the vehicle travels along the road. It is caused by the shape of the car's body, or some protruding or loose part.

The biggest task you face in correcting a noise condition created by an air leak or by turbulence is to find out why it is happening. The actual repair, if it is possible, is usually a relatively simple matter.

Discover the cause of the leak, and most of your problem is solved

Keep in mind that the noise created by an air leak sounds different from that created by turbulence. An air leak generally produces a hissing or whirring sound, while turbulence usually creates a rushing noise.

You troubleshoot an air leak with the car parked. But you must put a car in motion to troubleshoot a noise produced by turbulence.

Here are surefire ways to find an air leak

AN IMPORTANT POINT to keep in mind when trying to find the cause of an air leak is this: very often, air pressure is greater inside than outside the car. This means that noise created by an air leak will often be created when air leaks *out of* rather than into the vehicle.

The reason for this is that many times you drive along with doors and windows closed, and with air vents open or with the heater or air conditioner turned on. When air pressure inside the car becomes higher than air pressure outside the car, higher in-the-car pressure forces the top edges of door glass outward. If there is an air leak, the air which rushes out will produce an irritating noise.

The type of air leak that produces noise is usually confined to the upper part of the car—that is, from the top to about a foot below the bottom of the windows. If an air leak occurs lower down, it normally causes drafts, and may allow dust to be blown around. But this type of leak seldom produces noise.

Troubleshooting noise created by an air leak should proceed from simple to more esoteric procedures. The following one-two-three outline is the one used by many professional body-shop mechanics. At any point in the procedure, the leak may be uncovered.

1. **Examine all weatherstrippings** closely for worn spots and for tears. If weatherstripping is worn, buy some automotive roll-type caulking compound in an auto parts store. Carefully pull the weatherstripping away from the frame and place a length of caulking beneath it to "shim" the weatherstripping out (Figure 1). Reattach the seal firmly.

There is no way of effectively repairing a length of torn weatherstripping. Replace the entire strip with a new one.

2. **Is weatherstripping loose** in its channel? If a length is loose, pull it from its seat. Coat the frame and the backside of the weatherstripping with rubber cement. Now, press the weatherstripping firmly back into its seat.

3. **Check around each door,** looking for rust spots and for holes in sheet-metal joints. If you find any, remove all rust and seal holes with an automobile body repair compound that you can purchase in an auto store which sells body supplies. Follow instructions in applying the repair compound.

Rust spots and holes in joints may be causing the leaks

Caution: Do *not* seal the holes you find in the bottom of each door. These are drain holes which permit water that gets inside the door to run out, keeping the door from rusting. These holes should be cleaned out periodically with a sharp-pointed tool, such as an ice pick or awl.

Figure 1. Shim weatherstripping by pulling it from its channel and placing roll-type caulking under it. Be sure that it is firmly reattached.

4. **Run your finger and eyes** over door opening surfaces, looking for solder lumps and other uneven spots which may be keeping weatherstripping from making full contact with the door frame (Figure 2). Use a hammer and a metal chisel to chip away solder lumps and other high spots, but be careful not to dig into the door surface with the chisel (Figure 3).

It is very important that weatherstripping have an even surface against which to seat if air leaks are to be avoided.

5. **A road test** at this point may reveal that you have not found the irregularity which is causing the noise problem. The most minor imperfection, which can easily escape detection, can cause an air leak. Therefore, more intense investigation is needed.

Roll up the car's windows and close fresh-air inlets. Make sure that the inside of the vehicle is completely sealed off.

Start the engine and let it idle. Set the heater or air-conditioner controls so that air is coming into the car, and fix the blower at its highest speed.

Now try the pressure test, using your own homemade "stethoscope"

Get out of the car, and check to make sure that all windows and doors are tightly closed. Allow pressure to build up inside the car for several minutes.

Using a length of heater or vacuum hose as a stethoscope, slowly pass one end around the edges of doors and windows (Figure 4). Even the most minor air leak will become audible.

When the area of leakage is uncovered, mark it and turn off the engine. Check the weatherstripping and frame in that area, and make necessary repairs.

Air can leak from outside to the inside, too

ALTHOUGH, AS WE said, air most frequently leaks from the inside of the car to the outside, such is not always the case. Air can leak from the outside into the car if air pressure on the outside is greater or moves at high velocity. This will create noise and also a blowing of dust.

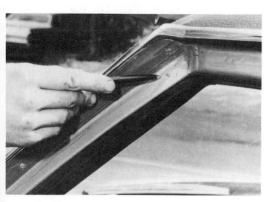

Figure 2. Look for solder lumps. They can be causing air leaks around windows.

Troubleshooting this kind of a leak is relatively simple. First determine if there is a weak seal around the door by placing a strip of heavy paper between the weatherstripping and door frame.

Close the door and pull the strip of paper out (Figure 5).

Important: Test every section of the weatherstripping.

If the paper can be removed easily, and offers no resistance, replace or shim out the weatherstripping. However, if weatherstripping doesn't seem to be loose or worn, suspect that the door is misaligned. This will require that the hinges be tightened, the striker be repositioned, or a similar adjustment be made.

Air can also rush into the car around the windows. Test by closing each window securely and squirting tracing powder or chalk dust along the edges (Figure 6).

Open the door and look for traces of the powder or chalk dust on the inner side of the window. Dust indicates that window weatherstripping has to be shimmed, tightened or replaced, or that the window should be readjusted.

How to get rid of annoying turbulence-caused noise

UNTIL INDUSTRY CAN build a comfortable car that is completely streamlined, some turbulence-caused noise will have to be endured. However, there is a difference between excessive and bearable noise.

To find the cause of noise, you will have to conduct a road test in an open, low-traffic area that permits you to cruise at high speed and pull safely off the road to make adjustments. Equipment you need includes a roll of masking tape and strips of automobile caulking, which you can purchase in an auto-parts store that sells body supplies.

In this road test, you mask off the possible causes of leaks and check results immediately

Before beginning the test, close all doors and windows tightly, make certain that the blower and heater or air-conditioner controls are off, and see to it that fresh-air vents are closed.

Now, cruise at the speed at which noise is annoying. Be sure that the noise is really outside the vehicle. If it is inside the car, then it is not being caused by turbulence, but by an undetected air leak. Notice the speed at which noise is created.

Once you have definitely established the character of the noise, pull off the road and cover parts of the vehicle's body that are likely to create turbulence noise. Here's what I mean—

Start with a radio-whip antenna. Retract it and drive the car to see if noise has lessened. Be sure to hit the speed at which noise is at its worst.

If noise has lessened, you know that the cause of the problem is the antenna.

Chrome moulding strips are also likely suspects. Noise is often created when wind whips beneath a strip of moulding and "rushes" through the hollow.

Cover one strip at a time with masking tape. Then, proceed with the

Figure 3. Remove solder and other high spot imperfections with chisel, hammer.

Figure 4. Seal the car and use a hose as a stethoscope to detect air leaks.

Figure 5. If wrapping paper can be pulled from doors without resistance, weatherstripping seal is weak.

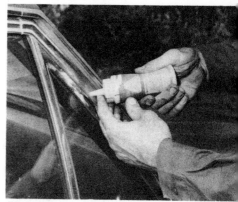

Figure 6. To check window seals, use marking chalk that comes in squeeze containers. None should go through.

Figure 7. Look for puckers in rubber weatherstripping, especially in corners. Apply heat and smooth out the rubber.

Figure 8. Do not remove windshield molding strips with any but the special tool made for the job. Glass could crack.

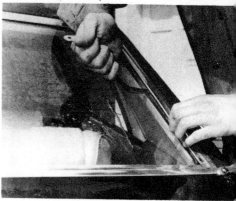

road test. Again, make sure you drive at the rate of speed at which noise is produced.

If the noise disappears, you have identified the problem. Remove the moulding strip and fill the hollow space in back of it with auto-body caulking compound. Reattach the strip firmly to the body. By doing this you have eliminated the hollow through which wind was rushing.

Another exterior part that frequently causes noise is rubber weather-stripping around the outside of vent windows, especially that weather-sealing material in the lower front corner. This section frequently becomes distorted and pulls away from the frame.

Professional body repair men call this a pucker. Puckers are usually caused by passengers exerting undue force on the vent window when closing it (Figure 7).

To get rid of a pucker, soften the rubber with heat. You can use a propane torch. When the material becomes pliable, smooth it out with a putty knife, working the rubber material into shape. You may have to apply heat several times before the entire pucker is fully straightened out.

Another source of noise created by turbulence is roof railing. Again, tape one section at a time between road tests until the noise disappears.

If a roof rail has rusted or pulled away from the main body of the car, it should be repaired to eliminate the noise.

How to keep from getting wet feet

THE TOUGHEST PART of fixing a water leak into a car is finding the source of the leak. Don't be deceived. The entry point of water into the vehicle's interior often does not coincide with the source of the leak.

Let me give you an example of what I mean. Suppose you find water in the luggage compartment. Your first thought is that the trunk lid has sprung a leak through its gasket, and well it might have. But it is just as possible that water is entering the body around the top of the rear window, is running down through channels, and is leaking into the luggage compartment through a crack in the cowl section below the back window.

The windshield and rear window are prime sources of water leaks

In tracing a water leak into the car, it pays to keep in mind that most water leaks come in through openings around the windshield and backlite, as the rear window is called. Water in the front of the car should lead you right to the windshield. Water in the rear of the passenger compartment or in the trunk should lead you to the backlite.

To test the windshield or backlite, tape a nozzleless garden hose to the roof of the car so that water coming from the hose will flow over the particular glass. Place a tin can right ahead of the spout so water coming from the hose will overspread the entire expanse of glass.

Turn on the hose, making sure that the entire backlite or windshield gets doused with water. Get inside the car, and watch and wait.

Patience, now. A leak may not reveal itself for a long time. As long as 30 minutes may be needed.

Every so often get out of the car and rock it from one side to the other. This will permit water which collects in a seam, but doesn't start leaking until the car turns a corner, to become untrapped.

About stopping that windshield or backlite leak

IF WATER IS LEAKING into the car from around the windshield or backlite, the glass should be resealed with windshield sealer.

Caution: Do not apply sealer over moulding strips. This usually will not solve the problem and can cause the glass to crack when moulding strips are finally removed. Windshields are expensive, costing well over $100.

To seal a windshield or backlite properly, the moulding strips have to come off. You will need a windshield moulding trim removal tool, which may be purchased at a store that sells auto-body repair equipment or at an automotive glass shop.

Slide the tool under the chrome strip (that is, between the glass and strip) until it hits a moulding clip. Carefully twist the tool until the strips pops loose from the clip.

As you strike each clip, mark its location with chalk. This will facilitate replacement.

Caution: Do not attempt to remove mouldings with any other tool except the right one (Figure 8). Using a screwdriver or pry bar will crack the glass.

When trim strips have been removed, take one of the moulding clips to an auto-supply store or a glass shop. Used clips cannot be reused—they will have been twisted out of shape. You will need new ones, and they are available in various sizes and shapes. That is the reason for bringing a sample with you.

Emplace clips in the same spots in which old clips had been placed. Now, apply a generous bead of auto-windshield sealer as directed on the tube. Make sure you hit the entire edge of the glass.

And be generous. If you leave a gap, you will leave a spot through which water can leak.

Now, place the moulding strips back over glass edges and pop them back on to the clips.

Other areas where water leaks

IF WATER SHOWS UP on the floor in front, the windshield may not necessarily be at fault. Other areas that may be leaking include A-posts (that is, windshield pillars), windshield-wiper bosses, hood drip grooves, holes in the upper firewall area, drip rails over doors, and fender joints.

Hit each of these spots and others that look suspicious with a high-pressure stream of water from a hose as a helper inside the car keeps his eyes open.

Incidentally, doors and side windows rarely leak, but you might as well check these, too—just in case.

The way to find a source of leakage into the luggage compartment is to put someone in the trunk with a flashlight and close the lid. Spray each back area with a hose for several minutes at a time. If your partner in the trunk raps on the lid, it means to open up—water is starting to leak or he needs a breather.

Obviously, one of the main ways for water to get inside a trunk is through a damaged trunk lid gasket. Scrape off the old gasket with a putty knife, clean it and the surface to which it sticks by washing them down with mineral spirits, and apply weatherstripping adhesive as directed. Replace the gasket firmly.

If the gasket has shrunk or is mangled, do not use it. Get a new one.

When to call in a professional

IF YOU ARE NOT SUCCESSFUL in uncovering the source of a leak, you should seek the services of a professional automotive glass shop or body-repair facility. Water that gets inside the vehicle and is allowed to remain can rust the body. Then, the expense of repair becomes prohibitive.

Many professionals use electronic detection equipment to find the source of both water and air leaks. The equipment consists of two components.

One part is a signal generator that is placed inside the closed car. The other component is a detecting unit that is passed along the outside of the car close to the body and its openings.

When the detecting unit reaches an area of leakage, it picks up and makes audible the tone signal being sent by the generator inside the car.

Chapter 20

How to repair auto-body damage in a professional manner

Straightening dents and repairing rotted areas may seem like insurmountable tasks that should be left to a professional auto body shop. No such thing. Using the tools and materials described here, you will be able to do this work yourself.

THE FIRST TOOL you will need is called a slide hammer. Most automotive parts dealers and auto-body supply stores carry it.

To repair dents, the first thing to do is to punch holes in the dent an inch or so apart (Figure 1). You can use an awl or you can drill holes with an ordinary household electric drill.

Screw the slide hammer into one of the holes (Figure 2). The tool has a threaded tip.

Now, slam the sliding arm back against the hammer's handle. This will straighten the dent, usually with one blow. Then go on to the next hole.

Incidentally, if the dent is a shallow one—say, a maximum of two inches in diameter and ¼-inch deep—you don't really have to pull it out if you don't have a slide hammer.

Grinding, patching and sanding

WITH THE DENT straightened out, you have to prepare the area for painting. Start by removing all paint so bright bare metal shows.

This can be done easily enough with a grinding disc that you attach to a household electric drill. Be sure that you grind an area which is three to four inches *beyond* the dent (Figures 3 & 4).

You now have to mix the repair material, which is a plastic body filler to which is added a hardener. You can purchase the filler in gallon and quart sizes. The material has an indefinite shelf life as long as the lid of its container is kept tight and it is not mixed with the hardener.

The hardener comes in a tooth-paste-type tube and is in cream form. It is very important that the plastic filler and hardener be mixed

With just a few tools and supplies, you're in business. Some of the tools you probably have already

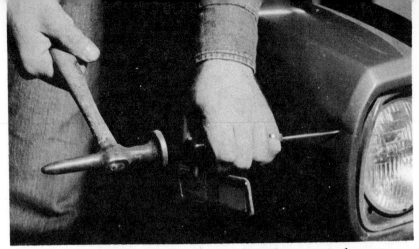

Figure 1. Place holes in the center of the dent about one inch apart.

Holes are made an
inch apart in the
dented area, then
a threaded tool is
inserted and the
metal is pulled
out inch by inch

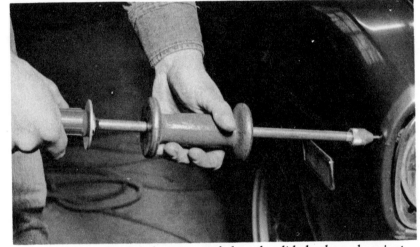

Figure 2. Insert the slide hammer and slam the slide backward against the hammer's handle. This will straighten the dent, usually in one blow.

Figure 3. Grind away paint until the bare metal surface is clean and bright. Extend the area beyond the original damage.

Figure 4. When the work area looks like this, you can start patching.

Figure 5. Add the cream hardener to the plastic filler and mix them. Tool at left is used for mixing. At right is the plastic applicator.

properly. Carefully follow the instructions on the container.

The mixing process is made easier by the fact that the filler is white or gray and the cream hardener is in a color. You are thus able to see when the two are properly blended (Figure 5).

You don't have to mix too much. For most dents, an amount of filler equal to the size of a golf ball and a strip of hardener about ½-inch long is sufficient. Mix the two together on a clean flat piece of cardboard or metal.

After the hardener and plastic filler are mixed, you have from 5 to 15 minutes before the material becomes unworkable. The exact time depends on the temperature. The hotter the day, the quicker the filler/hardener will set up.

Figure 6. Apply the auto body plastic filler in light coats. Build it up to about ⅛ to ¼-inch thick.

Figure 7. The Surform is used to shape the repaired area and to remove excess filler.

Figure 8. Do not hold sandpaper by hand when sanding the repair compound. Use a sanding block, or you may create a dip.

Figure 9. When featheredging, you can hand-hold the sandpaper. When you are finished, the entire surface should feel even.

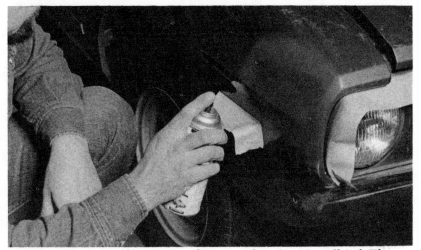

Figure 10. Never apply paint to a bare metal surface. It will fail. The area should first be primed, as is being done here.

You should avoid making repairs if the car's body is cool (under 60°) or damp. If too cool, the repair compound will take an extra-long time to harden. If applied to a damp surface, the filler will develop pinholes.

The ideal conditions under which to work are with the metal dry and at 65° to 75°.

Apply the body-repair compound with a compound plastic applicator. Applicators come three to a package, each a different size.

When applying the body filler to a surface, do so in light coats until the filler is built up to a height of ⅛ to ¼ inch above the surface (Figure 6). If you have ever spackled gypsum wallboard, you know what I mean. Use the same technique. Don't lay on globs of material. Instead mold it on one light coat after another.

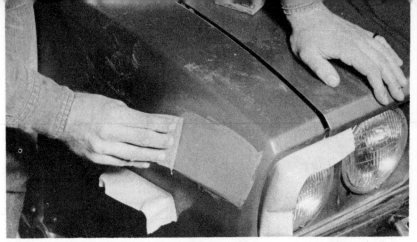

Be careful not to let the filler set too long. When it reaches the right hardness, proceed

Figure 11. Finish the repair by applying glazing putty, sanding, and applying another coat of primer. Surface is now ready for painting.

Try not to get the filler on the car's paint. It won't stick well and could crumble eventually.

Allow the repair compound to set up, but don't interpret this to mean that you should allow it to get solid. You do not want it hard.

You can test to see if the filler is ready for the next repair step by trying to scratch it with your fingernail. If you can put a scratch into it without having it come up in a glob, it is ready. This usually takes about 15 to 20 minutes.

Mold and shape the repaired area

USING A TOOL called a Surform, mold the filler into shape while removing excess material (Figure 7). Surform is manufactured by Stanley Tools and can be purchased in hardware stores. It resembles a blade to which the Surform blade is attached. Once you buy the handle, you can purchase replacement blades.

Surform blades come in a flat shape for treating flat surfaces, in half-round for contoured surfaces, and in rat-tail for working on tight curves.

Shave off about 80 to 90 percent of the built-up filler material. Then let the repair set until it gets good and hard. This takes at least 30 minutes.

Outfit a sanding block with a piece of 40-grit sandpaper. Sand the area. Follow this sanding step with another using 100-grit sandpaper attached to the sanding block. Sand until the area is relatively smooth. The purpose is not to make it absolutely smooth, but to sand until the repair material is brought down to the level of the car's surface.

Caution: When sanding the plastic filler, do not sand while holding the sandpaper in your hand. Always use a sanding block (Figure 8). If you don't, you are liable to remove too much material in a spot and end up with a dip.

You now need a piece of 220-grit wet-or-dry sandpaper for feather-edging the paint around the repaired area. Keep the sandpaper wet and sand from the paint into the repaired area until you have a completely smooth surface. You should not be able to feel any difference in the two surfaces when running your hand over them.

Hand-hold the sandpaper when featheredging (Figure 9).

Time to use spray primer

IF YOU ARE WORKING near body trim or lights, mask them off with masking tape and newspaper. Apply a light coat of primer (Figure 10).

Primer is available in spray cans. Apply it using the same techniques we describe below for applying spray paint. If any of the primer over-sprays onto paint, wipe it off.

Allow the primer to dry. This generally takes about 15 minutes. Now, apply a light coat of automobile-body glazing putty. This material fills sandpaper scratch marks and other imperfections. It is the material that actually smooths the area so paint can be applied (Figure 11). Follow application instructions provided on the container.

Glazing putty is available in tubes, quart cans and gallon cans.

Allow the work area to dry for at least one hour. Now, using a piece of 320 wet-or-dry sandpaper that is wet and attached to the sanding block, lightly sand the entire patch. Apply another coat of primer.

Priming, glazing, and sanding ready the surface for the final painting

It is now time to paint

PAINTING IS NOT DIFFICULT, but it does take some finesse. First of all, to be safe, mask off the good paint around the repaired area to protect it from overspray.

Figure 12 (left). This gives you an idea of what the vehicle's identification plate looks like. It usually is attached to the firewall or a door pillar, and gives the code number of the body color.

Figure 13 (right). The top of the paint can serves to identify the paint. It shows the color as well as the make of car, model, and the paint stock number.

Figure 14. Practice spraying on a tin can. Apply
light coats and hold can 10-12 inches from surface.

Figure 15. Use a fairly rapid motion, move continuously, and apply one
light coat after another, waiting between coats for a few seconds.

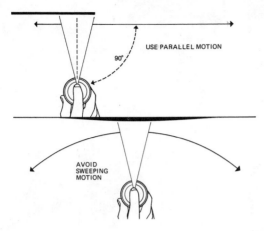

USE PARALLEL MOTION

90°

AVOID
SWEEPING
MOTION

Figure 16. This diagram shows the difference be-
tween parallel and sweeping motions.

Now, get the proper color. This is done by checking the vehicle's identification plate, which is normally attached to the firewall or door pillar (Figure 12). On it you will see the designation "body color," "paint color," or some such.

Bring this code to your supplier. He will consult his reference book and cross match the code to the paint's stock number. The cap on the can he gives you will show the color as well as the make of car, model and paint stock number (Figure 13).

Although there usually is no problem in matching ordinary colors with a spray can of paint, it may be difficult to get an exact match if your car is painted with metallic paint. Paint used on imported cars is also hard to match.

The reason for this is that the equipment used at the factory, such as electrostatic paint guns, is highly specialized. Not even professional auto-body repairmen have it.

If you find it difficult to match your paint color with a spray-can product, you can try to do the job with a "compressed air" supply and paint bought directly from auto-paint dealers which is made by auto-paint manufacturers. The paint comes in quart and gallon sizes.

The "compressed air" supply I'm referring to comes in a kit and is available at most auto-parts stores for a couple of dollars. It consists of an aerosol supply to which is attached a glass or plastic container into which paint is poured. One such kit is called Preval.

If this is your first attempt at spraying paint, it would be worthwhile to practice on a tin can or other scrap-metal surface until you get the feel of it (Figure 14). If this is not your first experience, allow me to refresh your memory with several hints that can make the difference between a professional-looking and a so-so job:

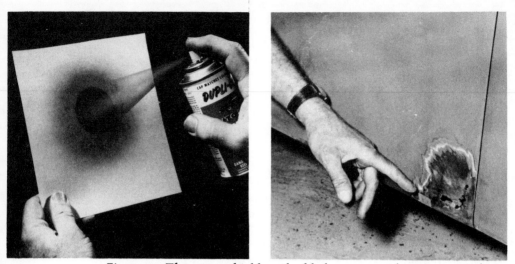

Figure 17. The spray-shield method helps you avoid overspray and permits you to feather-paint properly.

Figure 18. Body rot is a serious problem, but it can be repaired. The method you choose may depend upon how long you intend to keep car.

• Keep the can moving all the time (Figure 15). Stopping will cause the paint to run and sag.

• Move your hand fairly rapidly. If you use too slow a motion, the paint will run and sag.

• Use a parallel motion. Avoid a sweeping movement. Paint goes on in uniform layers when the distance between the spray head and the surface is kept the same throughout. This distance is maintained by using a parallel motion—that is, moving the paint can parallel to the surface that is being painted (Figure 16).

When paint is applied with a sweeping motion, the paint film becomes heavy at the center of the arc and thin at each end.

• When touching up small areas, as you do when painting auto-body scratches and most dents, aim the can's nozzle through a hole in a piece of cardboard that you hold 10 to 12 inches from the surface (Figure 17). This allows the edges of the spray to feather properly so paint blends into the surrounding area rather than concentrating itself at a single point.

• Keep the coats light. Heavy coats run and sag. Apply a thin coat and wait 30 to 60 seconds before applying another.

• Shake the can thoroughly (at least for one minute) before you spray. Shake it occasionally while spraying.

• Read and follow the instructions on the paint can.

After the paint has been applied properly, let it dry for at least one week. Then, rub it out with a wet rag on which you place a little auto rubbing compound.

Rub very lightly. Rubbing compound is highly abrasive. Try to get the new paint to blend with the old.

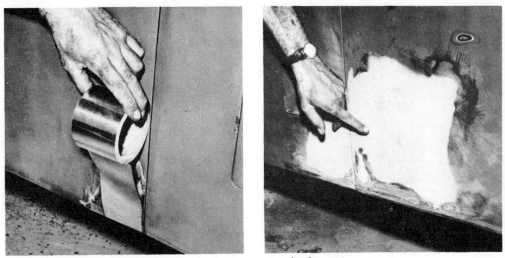

Figure 19. The least expensive method of repairing body rot is to
cover it with aluminum tape. This will stay good about six months.
Figure 20. No matter what method you use, the repair is finished with
plastic filler as outlined in section dealing with repair of dents.

The way to get rid of body rot

ACTUALLY, THERE ARE three ways to handle a body-rot problem
(Figure 18). Two of the methods are inexpensive, but they are temporary. The third method is more costly, but it is permanent.

The least expensive and easiest way of doing the job is with
aluminum tape, which comes in four-inch-wide strips (Figure 19).
Grind the area down to bare metal and cover it with tape, making sure
that the tape extends at least one inch beyond the damage. Pay special
attention to the edges of the tape. See to it that they adhere.

Use a piece of 100-grit sandpaper to roughen up the tape. Then continue making the repair in the manner described above for repairing
dents.

This method will last about six months. Then the repaired area will
begin to bubble out.

A longer-lasting, but still temporary, repair can be made with a piece
of sheet metal that is the same gauge as the metal used for the body of
the car (in most cases, 20- or 22-gauge). Make sure that the sheet metal
will extend one inch beyond the rotted area.

Grind the damaged spot and attach the sheet metal to the car body
with a pop rivet tool, which you can buy in a hardware store.

Roughen up the sheet metal with a grinding disc and proceed with
the repair as described above. Make certain to pay close attention when
applying filler between the edge of the sheet metal and the car's body.
Feather the filler into the body so you won't be able to see the contour
when paint is applied.

Since you are attaching one piece of metal to another, this repair won't last indefinitely. Eventually the condensation and dust that get behind the repair will cause it to break down. It should last, however, for about two years.

The permanent way to get rid of body rot is by welding or brazing sheet metal right to the car's body. If you had a body shop make the entire repair for you, it would cost you about double the way I'm going to suggest—that is, have the body shop do the welding for you, but you take over and finish the job using the procedures outlined above (Figure 20).

Chapter 21

A clean car "rides" better; easy ways to beat dirt

For some reason, an immaculate automobile seems to feel more comfortable on a drive than one that is dirty. Cleaning up a car calls for servicing the engine, the exterior, and interior.

THERE ARE SCORES of commercial products that make car cleaning much easier than in previous years. Still and all, they must be used properly or the outcome will be less than satisfactory.

Let's start by explaining how to clean the engine and engine compartment. The main cleaning agent you should use is engine degreaser, which is available in spray cans. However, before applying the cleaner you should take several preparatory steps.

Before doing anything else, do this to insure safety: Disconnect the battery cables and keep them disconnected for the duration of the job (Figure 1).

There is the possibility that when you are working beneath the hood a metal object will drop accidentally and hit the battery posts. If the cables are attached, a short circuit could result that would damage fuses, alternator diodes, and electrical components.

In addition, a short may create sparks that could ignite the flammable engine degreaser and also the hydrogen gas given off by the battery.

Caution: To further guarantee your safety, do not smoke.

Start the cleaning operation by sprucing up the battery. Follow these steps:

1. Clean dirt and electrolyte salts (corrosion) from battery cable terminals with a battery-cleaning tool that you can buy in an automotive parts supply store. This tool possesses a wire brush that makes fast work of foreign matter covering terminals.

2. Apply strips of masking tape to the top of each battery vent cap. These caps have small holes in them through which pressure escapes.

Figure 1 (left). Disconnect battery cables before degreasing engine.
Figure 2 (right). After cleaning the battery with a baking-soda
solution to neutralize acid, wash it down thoroughly with water.

The purpose of blocking them off is to keep the cleaning agent, which neutralizes acid, from getting inside the battery and weakening the electrolyte solution.

3. Mix some baking soda or ammonia in water. Wash the battery down, using a scrub brush. Rinse thoroughly with fresh water, and keep repeating the scrubbing and rinsing until a fresh application of cleaning solution no longer fizzes when it is applied (Figure 2). This means that acid salts on the battery have been neutralized.

Turn your attention from the battery to the carburetor. Remove the carburetor air cleaner and take it apart. Place the filter element aside (if it is clogged with dirt, replace it) and wash down all metal parts with water.

If the metal air-cleaner parts are coated with an oily film and water proves ineffective, they can be cleaned with engine degreaser.

Caution: As with any commercial product you use, always read the How-to-use instructions before you spray away.

With carburetor air-cleaner parts clean, it is now the carburetor's turn. Use an old toothbrush and some clean kerosene or carburetor cleaner to clean dirt from the carburetor's body, linkages, choke plate, and the carburetor throat (Figure 3). Be thorough.

After the carburetor has been cleaned, cover the carburetor so that none of the engine degreaser or water flush will get inside. Use a piece of cling-type household plastic food wrap (Figure 4).

More steps in preparation for degreasing

DEPENDING UPON THE NUMBER of cylinders that your engine possesses, prepare four, six, or eight clip-type clothespins on which you should write consecutive numbers on each from one to four, one to six, or one to eight. Also prepare an additional clothespin marked "C" for the coil-to-distributor cable.

Disconnect all cables from the distributor and spark plugs by grasping the boots, twisting, and pulling. Do not pull on the cables themselves. You will damage them.

As you disconnect each cable, clip the appropriately numbered clothespin to it so you will be able to match the cable to its respective spark plug later on (Figure 5). Clip the clothespin marked "C" to the distributor-to-coil cable.

To make sure that each cable will also be connected to its correct tower in the distributor when you replace cables after cleaning, cover each of the towers with a piece of masking tape on which you have written the number that corresponds to the number on the clothespin (Figure 6).

As you remove each cable, wipe it clean with a cloth. Also wipe the distributor cap off.

Now cover the distributor cap and coil with plastic food wrap to avoid getting degreaser on them during the cleaning operation (Figure 7).

If your car is equipped with an underhood insulation pad, unclip it. It can be washed in detergent and water.

If the pad is very dirty, discard it and either buy a new one or do without it.

As a final step prior to actual degreasing, clean debris from the radiator core with a soft-bristle brush.

Figure 3. Spray carburetor cleaner or apply kerosene to the carburetor. Remove dirt, using an old toothbrush.

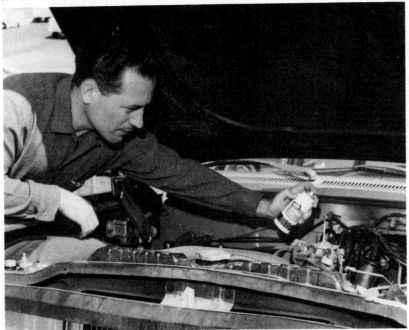

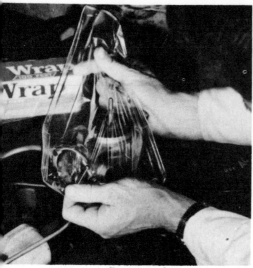

Figure 4 (left). Cover the carburetor with plastic food wrap so engine degreaser and water can't get down the carburetor throat.

Figure 5. As you remove cables, mark each with numbered clothespin.

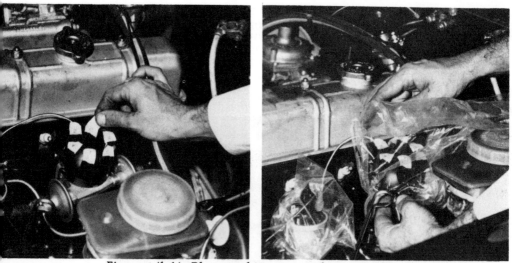

Figure 6 (left). Place masking tape with appropriate numbers over each of distributor cap towers. Numbers correspond to those on cables.

Figure 7. Protect distributor and coil with plastic food wrap.

It is now time to treat the engine

EXAMINE THE ENGINE. Is dirt caked on? If so, scrape off as much as you can with a putty knife (Figure 8). Only surface dirt should be left for the degreaser to handle.

Again, let me emphasize that you should read the instructions on the can of degreaser carefully. In most cases, these instructions will tell you that you should have warmed up the engine before taking the

Figure 8. Before applying engine degreaser, scrape off caked dirt with a putty knife. This eases the job of engine degreaser.

first preparatory step of disconnecting the battery.

With the engine warm, apply degreaser to all parts of the engine and engine compartment, except those that are covered and those that you are specifically told not to degrease (see instructions on the can of degreaser) (Figure 9). Parts which are generally not treated include the alternator, hoses, and the plastic windshield washer reservoir.

Parts other than the engine block that are usually treated with degreaser include the radiator, underside of the hood, fender splash shields and firewall.

Be sure to note which parts of the engine are not to be treated with engine degreaser

Figure 9. Spray degreaser on a warm engine and allow it to eat at the dirt for about 15 minutes. But first read instructions on the can.

When you have completed applying degreaser, allow it to work on the dirt for about 15 minutes. At this time, wash down the entire engine and compartment with a forceful stream of water from a garden hose (Figure 10).

Examine parts. If some dirt and grime remain, apply degreaser to those spots and repeat the operation.

When the engine is sparkling, reconnect all wires, reinstall the carburetor air cleaner, and reattach battery cables tightly. Start the engine and allow the heat that it gives off to dry out the compartment.

Some drivers prefer to finish their engine-cleaning operation by painting those areas that were originally painted, but which have had paint burned away or worn off. If you decide to do this, make sure that the paint you buy is specifically intended for this purpose. Engine compartment paint must be heat-resistant.

Apply paint only to those areas that should be painted. Keep it away from all electrical connections, wiring, and rubber parts.

Turn your attention to the underside and body

ALTHOUGH THE MODERN car body and automotive paint are tougher than those that preceded them, they are by no means immune to conditions that can cause rust and a breakdown of paint film. Some of the factors that adversely affect a car's body and eat away at paint include road salt, industrial waste in the air, mud and grime that build up beneath the vehicle, and salt air if the car is used and parked near the sea.

Washing not only makes a car look better. It helps keep it healthy

There are several things you should do to protect your car from these deleterious agents. You can, for example, wash the underbody clean periodically. You need a high-pressure stream of water from a hose.

Flush clean such areas as the underside of the engine block, transmission case, driveshaft, differential, exhaust-system components, and frame and suspension.

Pay particular attention to mud and foreign matter that collects in fender wells and on the underside of bumpers (Figure 11). These areas are susceptible to rusting from salt that is mixed with mud and dirt which become trapped.

The best way to protect the finish of a car is by washing it often. Washing removes surface dirt before the dirt has a chance to eat into the finish.

Wash a car with the car parked in the shade. The metal should be cool. If the metal is hot or the sun is beating on the finish during washing, streaking will occur.

Here are several tips that will allow you to do the best possible washing job:

• Use a mild liquid soap or a commercial car-washing agent that is available at an automotive parts supply counter. Do not use a strong or caustic detergent.

- Play a high stream of water along the edges of metal trim mouldings to force out trapped dirt.

- Examine the car's body before applying car-wash solution. Is it covered with dust? If so, first wash off the dust with cold water from a hose.

- Wash one section of the car at a time—the roof, for example, hood, trunk lid, fender. Start at the top of the car and work down so that runoff doesn't flow over a cleaned area.

- Apply the cleaning agent with soft, clean cloths, sponge or car-wash mitten that you can buy in an auto-parts store.

- When one section has been treated with car-wash cleaner, rinse it immediately with fresh water from a hose. Do not "soap down" more than one section at a time. Streaking may result as the soaped section dries while it waits to be rinsed. Don't soap down the whole car before rinsing—streaking of the finish may result

- Tough spots, such as tar, bird droppings or bug spatters, will not wash off unless they are softened. Do not try to rub them off. You may damage the paint. You can soften these hard-to-remove stains by using a commercially available tar and spot remover. Or you can try softening them by saturating a rag with cooking oil and covering the spot until it lifts off.

- When the entire body has been washed and is clean (repeat the "soaping" if necessary), rinse it down thoroughly and dry it at once with soft cloths. The best drying applicator is an automotive-body chamois, which is available in auto-parts stores.

Figure 10 (left). Wash down all "degreased" parts thoroughly with a high-pressure spray from a hose.
Figure 11 (right). Clean out fender (wheel) wells with a high-pressure spray, to remove accumulation of corrosive salts and dirt.

Facts about treating the finish

AUTO-BODY POLISH and auto-body wax are not one and the same. Polish removes oxidized particles of paint pigment from the surface and brings up the paint so the surface shines.

Wax, on the other hand, puts a protective coating over the paint so its brilliance is maintained and the paint is protected from damaging agents that can cause deterioration.

A dull finish should be serviced. But should it be polished or waxed? The way to tell is to examine raindrops that fall on the car. If they bead when they land, there is sufficient wax on the finish to provide protection; polish the surface to restore luster. If raindrops spread out when they hit, wax the body.

Modern polishes make the task of polishing relatively easy. They are available in liquid form, presoftened pastes (or cream), and sprays. Follow directions on the container of the polish you select.

Generally, the car should first be washed and allowed to dry completely. Use a clean soft cloth to apply the polish.

Do one section or panel at a time, employing a circular, overlapping motion to spread the polish. Apply pressure on the cloth as you rub so that the film caused by oxidized paint will be removed.

Let the polish dry thoroughly. You will know when it has dried sufficiently; it attains a hazy appearance.

Now remove the coating with clean, soft rags. Be sure that you change the polishing rag frequently. A clean rag must be presented to the surface.

Hard automotive paste wax provides the surface of a car with maximum protection. Before applying this protection, however, you should wash and polish the car.

To use a paste wax, soak a clean cloth in water and wring it out as completely as possible. Rub it into the wax and then rub the wax over the car's body vigorously. Use a circular, overlapping motion, and work on one small section at a time.

Plenty of clean cloths, changed frequently, make for better results in waxing

Let the wax dry thoroughly. It, too, will attain a hazy appearance. Now, wipe it off with clean, soft cloths or a chamois. Buff the finish to a high luster.

Use only a clean rag to remove wax. When a rag becomes caked, discard it.

In recent years, vinyl tops have become popular. They require frequent cleaning, because once they become really dirty restoration becomes more difficult.

Start by washing off all surface dirt while scrubbing with a soft-bristle brush.

Caution: Never use a wire brush on a vinyl roof. You will rip right into it.

To clean the top, use one of the different vinyl-top cleaning agents carried by auto-parts supply stores. Also available are restoring agents in colors to match the top (or in a neutral shade) that restore luster to the vinyl.

Cleaning white sidewall tires is another way to help maintain your car's "like-new" appearance. Use only a commercial agent made for the purpose, obtainable in auto-parts supply stores.

Do not use gasoline or kerosene. They will cause tires to deteriorate. Remember: a petroleum product eats into rubber.

Time to tackle the interior

IF YOU CLEAN the interior frequently, there usually will not be a need for drastic action. Simply dust and vacuum it before it has a chance to get too dirty.

A pail of warm sudsy water, containing a mild soap or detergent, may be all the upholstery cleaner you will need

But should upholstery turn dull and grimy, mix up a pail of sudsy warm-water solution using neutral soap or liquid detergent. To be safe concerning the soap to use, just keep in mind that you should not use soap on the inside of the car that you wouldn't use on your skin.

Apply suds sparingly to the upholstery with cheesecloth pads or terry cloth. Rub gently. Then rinse by wiping the material with clear water.

Open the car's doors and windows to let the upholstery dry.

Should the sudsy mixture fail to clean the material to your liking, you can purchase a stronger cleaner from an automotive parts supply store or service station. However, make sure that the kind of cleaner you buy is suited to the upholstery in the car.

Practically every car now uses some sort of synthetic material for its upholstery—nylon, orlon, rayon, vinyl or viscose. Natural fabrics are rarely used. A cleaner intended for a natural fabric will leave a synthetic with a dull finish.

After cleaning upholstery, you will want to brighten up the "chrome" trim in the interior, but watch it. Trim is not usually chrome, but plastic made to resemble metal. Rubbing with chrome polish, auto polish or any abrasive cleaner will cause the trim pieces to lose their brightness.

To clean bright work, simply wipe it off with a damp cloth or sponge. Then buff with a soft, dry cloth.

Use a vacuum cleaner to get dirt off the floor carpeting. Now turn your attention to the car's glass, inside and out. Ordinary dirt can be removed with a household window cleaner.

Stubborn spots on glass, such as bug spatters, can be cleaned off by mixing one part of a household detergent to four parts of rubbing alcohol and five parts of lukewarm water. Rub the spot vigorously, and rinse with clear water. Dry with paper towels.

A problem often arises when the car is equipped with vinyl upholstery. It gives off a vapor that forms a stubborn film on the inside of the glass. Tobacco smoke does the same thing.

Do not treat glass film with water or commercial window cleaner You will smear the film.

Instead, dilute one part of white vinegar in one part of water and wash the glass. The film will disappear, but keep the car's doors and windows open for a while to get rid of the odor.

As a final step in cleaning your car, don't forget to clean out the luggage compartment. You may have a maintenance problem as well as a cleanliness problem.

If you haul bags of dirt, concrete, salt, peat moss or anything else in the trunk, it may have spilled and gotten beneath the trunk mat. Here it may be absorbing moisture that can cause metal to rot.

Remove the trunk mat from the compartment and vacuum the trunk thoroughly, paying particular attention to edges and rims (Figure 12).

Overcoming the problem of stained upholstery

THE BEST TIME to treat a stain is as soon as it happens. However, even stains that have set may be treated effectively most of the time.

You will find upholstery-stain removers sold by automotive parts supply stores. Some of these may be volatile and toxic, so you should read and follow the instructions printed on the container.

Commercial stain removers will remove most stubborn stains, but they must be used with care

In working with an upholstery cleaner, keep the car's doors open. Do not breathe the fumes. One way to dissipate the fumes is to have an electric fan blowing across the work area so that the fumes are carried away from you (Figure 13).

Figure 12. Remove the trunk mat and vacuum up all debris and dirt that can absorb moisture and cause rusting.

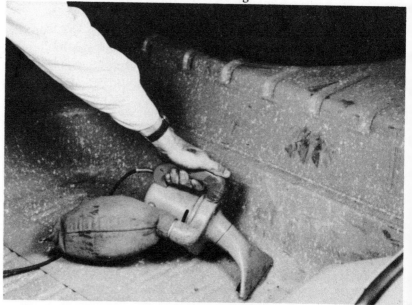

When working with an upholstery cleaner, keep in mind that the cleaner does the work. It should be applied with as little pressure as possible.

Moisten a clean pad with the cleaner and rub gently, using a circular motion. Do not scrub.

Before applying an upholstery stain remover to a spot, it would be a good idea to try it on a small hidden area to see if the fabric will discolor.

Caution: Do not use gasoline, naphtha, acetone or similar solvent, detergents or bleaches on automobile upholstery. They have a tendency to discolor fabric.

The following is a rundown of how to treat some agents that cause upholstery stains:

Here's a handy list of common stains and effective ways to treat them

- **Blood**—Rub gently with a clean cloth that has been saturated in cold water. If this doesn't remove the stain, apply some household ammonia to the spot with a rag, wait for two or three minutes, and follow with a cold-water wash. If the stain proves stubborn, make a thick paste from corn starch and cold water, and apply it to the stain. Let it set until it is dry. Then pick it off and brush away the particles. Repeat the application if necessary.
- **Non-chocolate candy**—Soak a cloth with very hot water and rub the stain.
- **Chocolate**—Soak a cloth with lukewarm water. Follow with a light rubbing with upholstery stain remover.
- **Chewing gum**—If the gum is still soft, place an ice cube on it un-

Figure 13. If your cleaning agent gives off toxic fumes, use an electric fan to blow the fumes away from you.

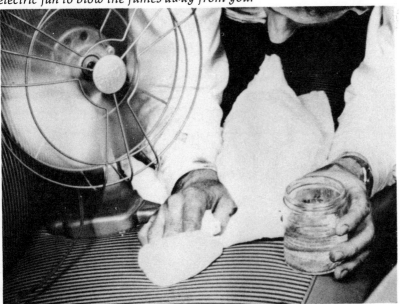

til it hardens. Scrape off as much as you can with a dull knife or putty knife. Moisten whatever remains with upholstery stain remover and use the knife to scrape off particles.

• **Grease and oil**—Scrape away as much as possible with a dull knife or putty knife. Rub gently with a clean cloth that has been saturated with upholstery stain remover. See to it that your rubbing motions are toward the center of the stain. This action keeps the stain from spreading.

• **Ice cream**—Scrape off excess with a dull knife and rub the stain using a clean cloth that has been dipped in very hot water. If the stain is stubborn, rub the spot with a cloth that has been dipped in warm soap suds. Follow this by rubbing with a clean cloth that has been moistened with cold water. Finally, treat lightly with upholstery stain remover.

• **Lipstick**—Scrape off excess with a dull knife or a putty knife. Follow this by treating with upholstery stain remover. Lipstick is a very difficult stain to treat, since lipsticks vary in chemical content. Do the best you can.

• **Nausea**—Sponge the area with a clean cloth that has been saturated in cold water. Wash the area with neutral soap suds mixed in warm water. If the stain remains, rub lightly with a cloth that has been dipped in upholstery stain remover.

• **Shoe polish**—Water-soluble polish is easily removed by brushing it vigorously. Paste or wax polish can be removed with an application of upholstery stain remover.

• **Tar**—Take up as much as possible with a dull knife or putty knife. Treat with upholstery stain remover. Let it dry. Scrape off excess with a knife again. Repeat the procedure as necessary.

Chapter 22

What you should know about air conditioner repair

There are a few things you can do yourself to get an inoperative air conditioner working again. But it's also important to know when to turn the job over to a professional, and what methods he uses.

EXCEPT FOR THE RADIO, the air conditioner is the one accessory that is sold most widely to car buyers. Millions of vehicles now on the road, and millions more to come, possess or will possess air conditioners.

Because of this, it is surprising to me that comparatively few car owners know how a unit works, how to take care of it, what can go wrong with it, and what to do when something does go wrong. Too many car owners mentally build complexity into a system that is not complex.

The principle governing the operation of automobile air conditioners is the same from one car to another. In fact, automobile air conditioners work on the same principle as the air conditioner in your home.

Air conditioners operate on the law of nature which requires heat always to move from a warm area to a cold area. Keep this in mind as we discuss how an auto air conditioner works.

Keep in mind these five major units of the system: condenser, receiver-dryer, expansion valve, evaporator, and compressor

How an air conditioner draws off heat

AN AUTOMOBILE AIR CONDITIONER consists of five major units: condenser, receiver-dryer, expansion valve, evaporator, and compressor.

They are connected to each other by hoses. The cooling agent, which is called refrigerant or Freon, flows through these hoses. Barring an accident that results in a leak, the same refrigerant is used over and over again.

An air conditioner *draws off* heat. It does not blow cold air into the car. The blower you turn on is used to circulate the air in the vehicle. It does not generate coldness.

To understand how refrigerant draws off heat and humidity, and what happens to these undesirable elements, let's start the refrigerant's cycle at the condenser (Figure 1). The condenser receives heated refrigerant.

Liquid refrigerant has a relatively high boiling point. As it absorbs heat from the car, this boiling point is exceeded. The liquid refrigerant begins boiling and transforms itself into a vapor.

It is this heat-laden *vaporized* refrigerant that the condenser receives. The condenser's job is to extract the heat from the refrigerant. It does this because the condenser coils through which the vaporized refrigerant circulates are exposed to the atmosphere.

The cool air circulating around the condenser coils transforms the vaporized refrigerant flowing through the coils back into a liquid state, because the refrigerant is brought below its boiling point. In other words, vaporized refrigerant enters the condenser, but liquid refrigerant leaves the condenser.

As it flows out of the condenser, the liquid refrigerant enters a cylindrical unit called the receiver-dryer. The receiver-dryer is merely a way station where refrigerant is kept until it is needed. The unit also acts to filter impurities from the refrigerant.

"Need" is determined by the action of the expansion valve, which serves as a regulator controlling the amount of refrigerant that flows into the evaporator at any one time. When you set the air-conditioner controls on the dashboard of your car, you are actually establishing the amount of liquid refrigerant that will flow from the receiver-dryer through the expansion valve and into the evaporator.

The evaporator is the unit which actually does the cooling. It is a "low-pressure" area. Heat will flow to it.

The evaporator is adjacent to the car's passenger compartment. The hot, humid air in the car is thus able to "flow" toward the cooler refrigerant passing through the coils of the evaporator. The liquid refrigerant absorbs the heat and humidity, and the air in the car cools.

'Round and 'round the refrigerant goes—soaking up heat, "boiling" it off, then condensing and cooling

As it absorbs heat and humidity, the refrigerant's boiling point is once again exceeded, and the refrigerant vaporizes. Vaporized refrigerant is drawn from the evaporator through a suction line to the compressor.

The compressor, which is nothing more than a pump, is the heart of the system. Without it nothing works, because it draws vaporized refrigerant from the evaporator and pumps it to the condenser where refrigerant reverts to a liquid state. Then, the compressor pumps the refrigerant to the evaporator, and the cycle continues.

Units are placed for top effectiveness

ALL COMPONENTS OF a home room air conditioning system are contained in a single cabinet. However, in your car, the components

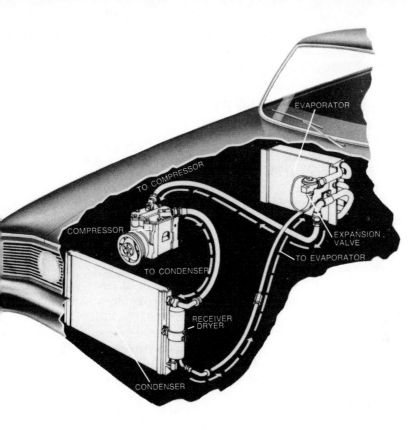

*Figure 1. This drawing will help you to understand the flow of
refrigerant through a car's air-conditioning system and will also help
you in locating components.*

have to be separated to take advantage of other automotive units so the
air conditioner can do the best possible job.

The compressor, for example, is a belt-driven unit. The driving force
of the car's crankshaft must be utilized to operate it.

Thus, the compressor is mounted in the front of the engine so its
pulley lines up with the crankshaft pulley. The two are connected to
each other by a heavy belt.

The condenser has to be placed where it can get the greatest blast
of cool outside air. If it were placed at the rear of the engine compartment, it would instead be subjected to the hot air thrown off by
the engine. The vaporized refrigerant flowing through its coils might
not be brought below the boiling point so it can revert to a liquid state.

The condenser, therefore, is placed up in front of the car—in fact,
in front of the radiator. Here it receives the full blast of cool air
as you drive along.

The evaporator has to be positioned where it can best come into
contact with the hot, humid air inside the car. Therefore, it is generally
installed in the firewall that separates the passenger compartment from
the engine compartment.

Note: Air conditioners that are put into cars after cars leave the factory—so-called "add-on units"—may have the evaporator mounted beneath the dashboard right inside the car.

Troubleshooting tips for the shade-tree mechanic

THE TWO MOST COMMON problems affecting automotive air conditioners are failure of the unit to cool sufficiently and failure of the system to operate at all. When either failure occurs, the first thing you should do is check the condition of the fuse or fuses.

Hopefully, at least one of the fuses protecting the air conditioner circuit will be located in the car's main fuse panel. But even if it is, there is often a second fuse that is difficult to find (Figure 2).

You could try to locate the fuse by looking for a fuse holder in the engine compartment, generally around the compressor. However, the only way to actually determine the location of fuses protecting the air-conditioner circuit is by consulting a wiring schematic for the circuit.

Before you have trouble, be sure you know where the fuses are located

If you have the car's service manual, you will probably find the schematic diagram for the air-conditioner circuit in it. If you don't have a manual, examine the nomenclature plate on the compressor to determine the manufacturer of the system. You can write for a schematic.

When you do locate all the fuses, replace them with new ones although they may look okay. You cannot always detect a bad fuse simply by examining it.

Here are some other troubleshooting procedures you may want to perform before consulting a professional serviceman:

• Consult the owner's manual to make sure that you are setting the controls properly. Many times the cause of insufficient cooling can be traced to an incorrect air-conditioner control setting.

• Examine the drive belt that runs the compressor. If the belt is loose or glazed and slipping, the compressor will not work at maximum efficiency, which would reduce the flow of refrigerant and, consequently, the degree of cooling.

Start the car's engine and turn on the air conditioner. Look at the belt. If it is slipping, the pulley will not rotate, or it will rotate and stop.

Tighten the belt as much as possible. If it fails to stop the slippage, replace the belt.

• Check the compressor's magnetic clutch. The magnetic clutch couples the pulley to the "pumping" parts of the compressor so that refrigerant can be pumped through the system when more cooling is called for. The clutch is the inner section of the compressor pulley.

Turn on the car's engine and set the air conditioner to maximum cooling. Look at the magnetic clutch (Figure 3). If it is not rotating, the compressor should be disassembled, and the clutch examined and repaired.

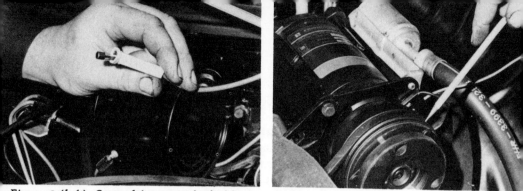

Figure 2 (left). Second fuse may be hidden in a holder near engine.
Figure 3. The magnetic clutch is found on front end of compressor.

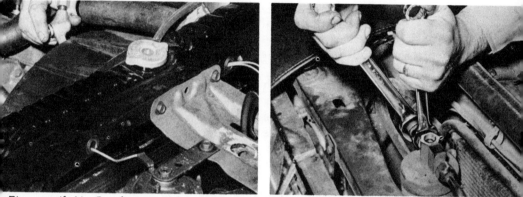

Figure 4 (left). Condensor is ahead of radiator. Air-clean both.
Figure 5 (right). Replace a clogged receiver-dryer unit.

• Inspect the condenser core. If the core is plugged with insects, leaves, and other debris, cooling will be reduced. The condenser core should be cleaned out by blowing compressed air through it (Figure 4). Lacking compressor air, you can do the job by using a soft-bristled brush.

• Determine if the receiver-dryer unit is clogged. Operate the air conditioner at maximum cooling for five minutes. Then feel the receiver-dryer outlet with your hand.

If the outlet feels cool, the receiver-dryer unit is clogged, which is resulting in a restriction in the flow of refrigerant. Cooling will be insufficient.

Replace the receiver-dryer (Figure 5). To do this, the system will have to be discharged as explained below.

• Look for air leaks. Inspect in particular the engine side of the firewall. Any opening through which wires, hoses, or cables pass is an opening through which hot air from the engine compartment can leak into the passenger compartment. This reduces the effectiveness of the air conditioner.

You can seal these openings with automotive caulking compound, which is commonly referred to as dum-dum. You can buy some at automotive parts supply stores.

The nitty-gritty of air-conditioner service

WHEN ALL OF THE above services have been performed, but the air conditioner still does not cool as it should, you can more or less conclude that the cause of the trouble is not enough refrigerant. You can check by cleaning the sight glass on the receiver-dryer unit, running the engine at fast idle, and setting the air-conditioner controls for maximum cooling (Figure 6).

The appearance of "bubbles" in the sight glass confirms that the system is probably undercharged. However, a lack of bubbles doesn't always mean that the situation is normal. Sometimes it is very difficult to see through the sight glass. Besides, a lack of bubbles can also indicate loss of refrigerant, in which case there would be no cooling.

Loss of refrigerant, either partially or completely, often means that the system has developed a leak. The leak must be found and fixed before a fresh charge of refrigerant is pumped into the system. Otherwise it too will be lost.

Leaks are detected with a propane-torch leak detector. This piece of equipment, along with a manifold gauge set and vacuum evacuator pump, will be needed from here on out (Figure 7).

Since this equipment is fairly expensive, you will probably consult a professional serviceman to do the rest of the job for you. However, an understanding of what he should do may be useful to you.

How to approach air-conditioner repair

THE FIRST THING that should be done is to check for refrigerant leaks by placing the leak detector's sniffer hose near all lines and fittings (Figure 8). The torch should be lit and its valve adjusted to provide a relatively small flame.

The sniffer hose should be passed slowly from point to point. How-

Figure 6 (left). One way of determining if the system is undercharged is by peering through the sight glass of the receiver-dryer.
Figure 7. Left device meters out refrigerant. Other is leak detector.

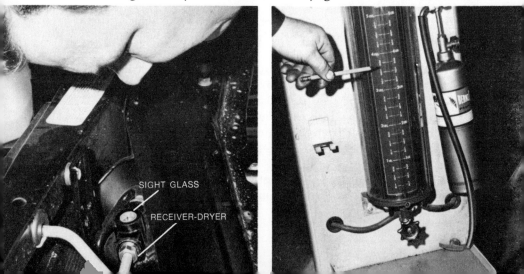

SIGHT GLASS

RECEIVER-DRYER

Figure 8 (left). *The propane torch leak detector is used to find places where refrigerant is leaking from the system.*
Figure 9. *Before connecting manifold gauge set, unscrew valve caps.*

Figure 10 (left). *Discharge refrigerant from air-conditioning system by opening high and low-pressure valves of manifold gauge set.*
Figure 11. *Vacuum pump clears impurities from the system.*

ever, the open end of the hose should be kept *below* each point being tested, because refrigerant is heavier than air and drops.

When refrigerant isn't present, the flame of the leak detector will be almost colorless. Any change to green or bluish-green indicates a refrigerant leak. If the leaks shows up near a threaded connector, tighten the connector. The leak may be due to nothing more serious than a loose fitting.

Caution: Do not breathe the fumes given off by the flame of the leak detector in the presence of refrigerant. These fumes are toxic phosgene gas, which is commonly known as mustard gas of World War 1 fame.

If a connector or hose is leaking (or if the receiver-dryer has to be replaced or some other component repair made), the air conditioner system has to be discharged. The following explains the procedure that should be employed:

1. Connect the manifold gauge set so the inlet-suction (low-pressure) gauge is attached to the low-pressure service valve, and the outlet (high-pressure) gauge is attached to the high-pressure service valve (Figure 9).

Figure 12 (left). This shows one way of recharging system, using cans of refrigerant.

Figure 13. Proper refrigerant charge and test pressure may be shown on plate on compressor.

2. Extend the exhaust lines from the gauge away from the area where work is being performed. If work is being done inside a garage, the exhaust line should be extended to the outside. However, it is best to do this job out-of-doors.

Caution: Stay away from the spot where refrigerant will be discharged, and wear goggles to keep any accidental spray of refrigerant from getting into your eyes. Refrigerant can blind you.

3. Slowly open the valves of the manifold gauge set so refrigerant discharges slowly through the exhaust line (Figure 10). See to it that the refrigerant doesn't leave the system in a rush since it can force oil from the compressor with it. When the needles of the gauge show zero, the system is cleared of refrigerant.

4. After making whatever repairs have to be made, and before recharging the system with refrigerant, vacuum the system. Vacuuming removes moisture and air, which are detrimental to refrigerant.

Leave the manifold gauge set in place and connect the gauge's exhaust line to the vacuum pump.

Open all valves of the gauge set and start the pump. Let the pump operate for at least 15 minutes (Figure 11). The inlet suction gauge needle should drop below zero, indicating the existence of an almost perfect vacuum inside the air conditioner system.

5. When vacuuming has been completed, recharge the system with refrigerant. This is usually done by connecting the manifold-gauge charging hose to the discharge valve of a can of refrigerant. The can is placed in water which has been heated to about 125°F. This is done so refrigerant will be forced in vapor form from the can into the system (Figure 12).

6. The engine is run at a specified rpm, which may be indicated on the nomenclature plate on the compressor, and the air conditioner is turned on. The inlet suction valve is opened until the suction gauge registers a specified reading. This reading, too, may be indicated on the nomenclature plate (Figure 13).

7. Refrigerant is added to the system until all foaming disappears from the sight glass of the receiver-dryer unit and system pressure coincides with the specification given on the nomenclature plate. Then, just to provide a safety factor, an additional one-half pound of refrigerant is added.

Lubrication
and safety

Chapter 23

The lowdown on lubricants and lubrication

The life of your car can be extended many tens of thousands of miles if you provide it with the lubricants it needs when it needs them. The information here will serve as a helpful guide to good greasing.

BEFORE YOU CAN BEGIN to lubricate your car, you will need the lubrication chart printed in the car's service manual. Lubrication requirements change from year to year. You cannot be certain that you are giving your car the lubrication it needs if you don't have this information.

The lubrication section of a service manual informs you where to place jacks to lift the car safely. It also points out every item and fitting that requires lubrication. It spells out when each should be lubricated and what lubricants to use.

The best buy in "optional equipment" you can order for your car: a $5 service manual

Service manuals aren't expensive. Most automobile companies charge about $5 for one. You can order the manual for your car by sending to the technical publications department of your car's manufacturer. Be sure to specify the year and model of car when ordering.

The many tasks of engine oil

REPLACING ENGINE OIL periodically with a high-quality product is the most elementary of all automotive maintenance chores. Yet not too many people realize that engine oil performs many tasks in the engine other than lubrication. Consider this list, and you can begin to appreciate the versatility of a *good quality* engine oil:

1. In lubricating your engine, it offers minimum resistance, but maximum protection, so that starting is not impeded. It also circulates promptly throughout the engine so no part is left unprotected.

2. It provides a viscous film between moving parts to reduce metal-surface friction and wear.

3. It protects all surfaces it comes in contact with against rust and corrosion.

4. It contains chemical detergents that help clean the inside of an engine.

5. It "assists" a car's cooling system, because it helps keep the engine cool.

6. It is the medium by which hydraulic valve lifters work. Oil is the "hydraulic" component on which lifters ride.

7. It helps seal spaces around piston rings, thereby preventing combustion leaks.

But what is a "good quality" engine oil? This is difficult to explain, because engine oil continually is being improved. What might have been a "good quality" oil for a 1967 automobile, let's say, may not be "good quality" oil for a 1974 model.

How to select the best oil for your car

THE FIRST THING to do is consult your owner's manual. It will tell you just what oil to use in your car's engine.

This recommendation, of course, assumes that your car is in good condition and is not burning oil. Suppose, though, that it is an oil burner, and you don't intend keeping it much longer. It would be throwing money away to use a good-quality oil. Just buy the most oil you can get for the money and keep pouring it in.

Once you have established in your mind which oil the manufacturer recommends, get into the habit of reading the information on oil containers. Everything you need to know is right there (Figure 1).

Information on the oil container will tell you, for example, if the oil inside meets the automobile manufacturer's warranty requirements. The warranty given by most manufacturers specifies that if engine failure occurs during the warranty period, the malfunction will be repaired at no cost to you *if* you have provided the engine with the maintenance required by the manufacturer.

One of the requirements specified by the manufacturer is that you use the proper oil, so look on the can of engine oil for a statement to the effect that the product inside meets or exceeds automobile manufacturer warranty requirements. This statement, which is worded differently from oil can to oil can (but the meaning cannot be misinterpreted), indicates that the oil meets automobile manufacturer specifications and can remain in the engine for the period of time recommended by the manufacturer on the lubrication chart (Figure 2).

If the can of oil bears no such statement and your car is under warranty, the oil does not meet the manufacturer's requirements and should not be used. If it is used, you will void the warranty and may be stuck for a big repair bill if something goes wrong within the warranty period.

You might become confused if you encounter two different cans of the same brand of oil that differ in price by 10¢ or 15¢ per quart; yet both of them carry the statement that the product meets automobile manufacturer requirements. You will find upon examining both con-

VEEDOL HD+ MOTOR OIL PROVIDES POSITIVE LUBRICATION AND SUPERIOR PROTECTION AGAINST OIL OXIDATION, CORROSIVE WEAR AND ENGINE DEPOSITS IN MOST SEVERE ENGINE SERVICE. SURPASSES CAR MANUFACTURERS' WARRANTY PERIOD REQUIREMENTS AND MILITARY SPECIFICATIONS.

Figure 1 (above). Always read the information given on an oil can. The important part of the statement on this can is that the oil "surpasses car manufacturers' warranty period requirements."
Figure 2 (left). On some cans, like this one, the warranty statement stands out. It assures you that the product inside is of high quality.

tainers that one product is a multiviscosity grade, while the other is single viscosity (Figure 3).

Viscosity (or weight) refers to the resistance to flow of the oil. Viscosity varies with temperature.

A single viscosity (single weight) oil is oil that flows easily and provides protection over a relatively short temperature range. For instance, an SAE 20W-20 engine oil should only be used between 32°F and 70°F.

Figure 3. The top of the can usually is reserved for viscosity data. Some oils are of single viscosity, and others are multiviscosity.

If the temperature drops below freezing, SAE 20W-20 oil should be replaced with SAE 10W oil, which flows more readily in cold weather. If the temperature goes above 70°F, SAE 20W-20 oil should be replaced with SAE 30 oil, because the SAE 20W-20 will become too thin and won't provide ample lubrication.

By comparison, a multiviscosity engine oil is one that "changes" its viscosity as the temperature changes. Thus, fluidity and protection are provided over a wider temperature range.

An SAE 10W-40 engine oil, for example, will serve a car in weather from 0°F to 100°F. The difference in price between the two cans of oil mentioned above is the extra price you must pay for the convenience of this variability.

What all those symbols on the oil can mean

LET'S BEGIN WITH the two just mentioned—SAE and W.

SAE stands for the Society of Automotive Engineers. This designation appears on oil cans because the SAE devised the numerical system used for designating viscosity.

W in SAE 10W and SAE 20W-20 stands for Winter. It means that the oil is intended for use in winter. In the case of SAE 20W-20, which can be used in cold weather and in warm weather, 20W means the oil can be used in winter, and the 20 designation means it can be used in warm weather (up to 70°F).

Other symbols you will find on an oil can, either separately or in combination with each other, are SE, SD and SC. They spell out in what cars the oil should be used.

SE designates an oil intended for use in cars built from 1971 onward. At present, SE oil provides maximum protection against the high temperature, wear, rust and corrosion that the modern engine is subject to. However, keep in mind that new oils are constantly being developed that are better than the older oils, and engines of the future will probably require them.

In fact, as this chapter was being prepared a new synthetic oil had been announced (but not yet marketed) to provide advantages which far surpass those of a high-quality SE oil. These advantages include—

• A change period of 25,000 miles or one year, whichever comes first. SE oil is supposed to be changed after being in use for no longer than 6,000 miles or six months (less in some cases), whichever comes first.

• A film strength that is eight to 10 times as great as natural engine oil.

• The ability to operate 50 percent cooler under high temperatures than natural engine oil.

• A pour point of −60°F, which makes this oil undeniably more suited for cold-weather use.

• A biodegradable product. A major problem has arisen vis-à-vis the environment as to how to dispose of used engine oil. This product does not add to the problem.

The symbol SD signifies an engine oil that fulfills the requirements of 1968 through 1970 cars. The symbol SC signifies an engine oil that fulfills the requirements of pre-1968 cars.

How to install your own lubrication facility

THE BASIC PIECE of equipment you will need to grease your car is an all-purpose hand grease gun that develops 10,000 pounds of force. The best type to get is the kind that accepts cartridges of grease.

A cartridge-type grease gun is more convenient to use than the type of grease gun into which you have to pack grease by hand. With the cartridge-type gun you simply slip a cartridge of grease into the gun as you would slip a tube of caulking into a caulking gun (Figure 4). You avoid the mess of hand filling, and grease will never have to be cleaned from the inside of the gun.

Be sure that you get a flexible extension adapter for your grease gun. This piece of equipment is about 18 inches long and is used to reach places that the gun by itself can't get to easily, such as upper ball joints (Figure 5).

You should also have a trigger-type oil can in your tool kit. Engine oil is used to lubricate points that require penetrating oil, such as door-hinge pins (Figure 6).

Another piece of equipment that you may need eventually is a suction gun to add lubricant to the differential and manual transmission (Figure 7). However, these components may not require the addi-

Figure 4 (left). Using cartridges of grease instead of loading a gun by hand is much more convenient and far less messy.
Figure 5. Extension adapter lets you reach less accessible areas.

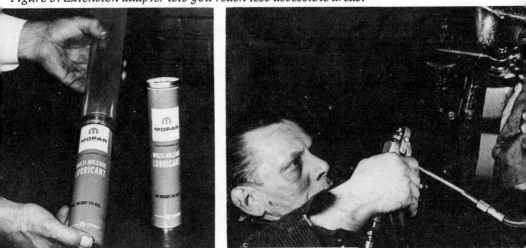

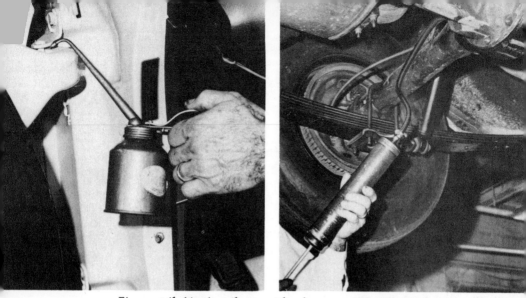

Figure 6 (left). An oil can with a long curved spout makes it easy to lubricate hard-to-reach spots with penetrating oil (SAE 20 engine oil). Figure 7. Suction gun lubricates differential, manual transmission.

tion of lubricant for thousands upon thousands of miles, if ever, so don't rush out to buy a suction gun yet. Wait until you need it.

Incidentally, the suction gun is also used to draw lubricant out of a differential or manual transmission when it has to be flushed.

You may need grease (Zerk) fittings. These screw into ball joints that have to be lubricated. The grease gun is attached to the fitting and grease is pumped through the hole in the fitting into the joint.

Check suspension and steering linkage joints that require lubrication. If they are fitted with metal or rubber plugs rather than grease fittings, buy fittings. The plugs are removed and the fittings are put in their place (Figures 8, 9, 10, & 11).

Fittings come in various sizes and shapes. Your automotive parts supply dealer can assist you in determining which size is needed in your case, and the shape of fittings that will make it easiest for you to attach the grease gun.

Crawling beneath a car to grease it can be awkward. If you have the area, you might want to dig a grease pit. Just make sure that the sides of the pit are reinforced so it won't crumble under the weight of the car.

If a grease pit is not practical, ask your automotive parts supply dealer about the "do-it-yourselfer" ramps that allow you to get the car high enough off the ground to permit you to work beneath it comfortably.

What you should stock in your lubricant inventory

HERE ARE SOME of the lubricants you will need to carry to do a complete "grease job."

Figure 8 (left). If ball joints are fitted with metal or rubber plugs (here they are rubber), wipe dirt from area before removing plug.
Figure 9. Metal plugs are unscrewed, reused. Pry off rubber plugs.

• **Multipurpose chassis grease** lubricates the front suspension and steering linkage.

• **Multipurpose gear lubricant** replenishes the supply in standard differentials and manual transmissions.

• **Positive-traction differential lubricant.** This is needed only if you have a positive-traction rear end in the car. It is a special lubricant that must be used to prevent damage. You should never use multipurpose gear lube in a positive-traction differential.

• **Power-steering fluid** goes into the power-steering fluid reservoir.

• **Automatic transmission fluid** lubricates the automatic transmission.

Figure 10. Install the grease fitting. A straight fitting is used here, but in your case you may need a fitting that is shaped at an angle.

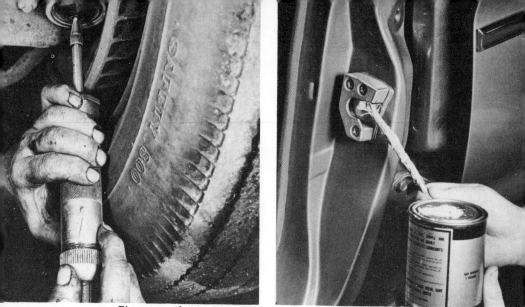

Figure 11 (left). Attach the grease gun and apply the grease.
Figure 12 (right). All-purpose white grease goes ~~on door latch~~.

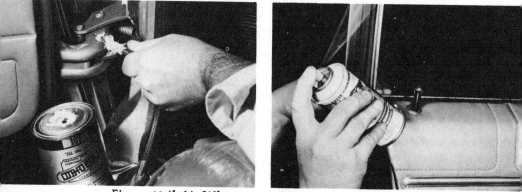

Figure 13 (left). White grease helps metal parts to slide easier.
Figure 14. Silicone spray keeps weatherstripping from drying out.

• **All-purpose white grease** lubricates metal body points that slide or rub against other body points. Latches, hinges and catches fall into this category (Figures 12 & 13).

• **Engine oil** is used to lubricate points requiring penetration. As we have said, hinge pins fall into this category.

• **Silicone spray lubricant** is used on rubberized-type parts that may begin to squeal or bind when dry, such as the channels of windows and insulation around doors (Figure 14).

• **Graphite spray lubricant** keeps door locks working freely (Figure 15).

• **Manifold-heat control-value lubricant.** This applied periodically will keep the manifold-heat control valve in working order.

Make sure that all lubricants you purchase are of the highest quality!

Chapter 24

Give your car the safety check that you deserve

Every so often you should give your car a walk-around inspection to make certain that safety-related components are functioning and not about to fail. It's easy and protects the lives of you and your passengers.

START WITH LIGHTS. Turn on the lights and check for burned-out headlamps, parking lights, taillights, and front and rear side marker lights if the car has them.

Have someone step on the brake pedal while you check to see if the stoplights are working. Be sure, too, that the license-plate light glows.

Now, place the transmission into Reverse gear to determine if the backup lamps are working.

If a headlamp has to be replaced, take off the bezel, unscrew the lamp's retaining screws, and pull out the sealed beam. Detach the lamp from the connector, and install a new unit (Figure 1).

Headlamps that are part of a dual-lighting system are designated Type 1 (low beam) and Type 2 (high beam). Headlamps that combine low and high beams in a single unit are designated No. 6012 or Type 2, Single Unit. Use these designations when buying new units.

How to align headlamps in your own garage

YOU CAN make your own headlamp-adjusting facility by drawing a pattern on a wall or garage door like that seen in Figure 2. Place the car on a level surface 25 feet from the pattern.

Adjust the low beam first (Figure 2). Then check the high-beam adjustment pattern. (Figure 3).

The lights of most late-model cars can be brought into adjustment by turning the headlamp adjusting screws that are accessible through the bezels, or by turning the adjustment knobs behind the lamps that are reached from under the hood (Figure 4).

Figure 1. To replace sealed-beam head-lamp just pull it off the three-connector plug and slip a new beam into place.

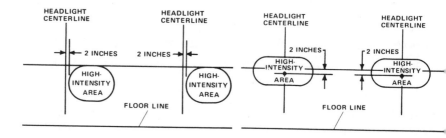

Figure 2. To align headlights, first draw this pattern on wall or garage door. Place car 25 feet away. Turn on lights, adjust low beams. Figure 3 (right). Use this pattern to check high-beam adjustment.

If neither adjustment screws nor knobs are offered, the adjustment screws are beneath the bezels. The bezels have to be removed to reach them.

Burned-out parking lights are replaced by removing the lenses if they are equipped with screws (Figures 5 & 6). If the lenses do not have screws, then the parking-light bulbs are reached from beneath the bumper.

A burned-out front side marker light is reached from under the fender or by removing its lens if it is held by screws. Burned-out rear side marker lights and taillight bulbs are changed from inside the trunk or by removing lenses if they are held by screws.

The final lights to check are the turn signals and the hazard warning flashers. If any signal fails to pass your inspection, replace the bulb first. Chances are that the filament has burned out.

However, if a new bulb fails to rectify the problem, replace the flasher. Flashers are generally located somewhere beneath the dashboard (Figure 7). You will have to check the car's service manual for the exact location or go hunting.

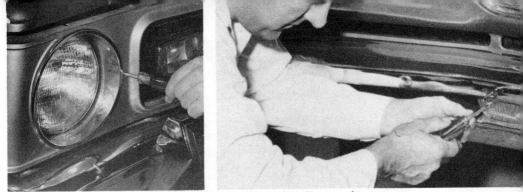

Figure 4 (left). Screwdriver inserted near side of headlamp adjusts this headlamp for horizontal plane. Adjust vertically at the top.
Figure 5 (right). To replace parking lights, remove screws on lens.

To drive, you have to be able to see

INSPECT ALL VISIBILITY EQUIPMENT. This includes glass, windshield wipers and washers, and defrosters.

Just a glance at the front and rear windshields, and at side windows is all that is necessary to determine if the glass is cracked, discolored or cloudy. Replace any window or windshield that hampers vision.

Keep windows and windshields clean. Make sure, too, that rearview mirrors are clear and clean, and are tight in their mountings.

Now, check windshield wipers and washers. Windshield wiper blades must be "alive"—not cracked and dried out, and they should not streak the windshield (Figure 8). Replace bad blades.

Do windshield wipers work when you turn them on? If not, the cause is probably a bad switch. However, a windshield wiper motor can malfunction, so don't overlook this possibility.

Check to see that the windshield-washer reservoir is full (Figure 9). If you need to replenish the supply, use two parts of water to one part of washer fluid when the temperature is above 32°F. When the temperature is below 32°F, use a ratio of 1 : 1.

Figure 6 (left). Remove parking light bulbs by giving them a twist.
Figure 7 (right). Turn-signal flasher units in most cars can be found beneath the dash. In some cars, they are on engine side of firewall.

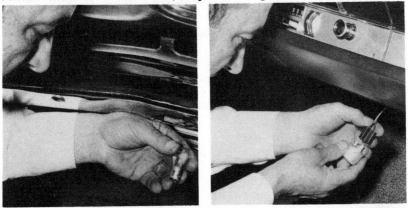

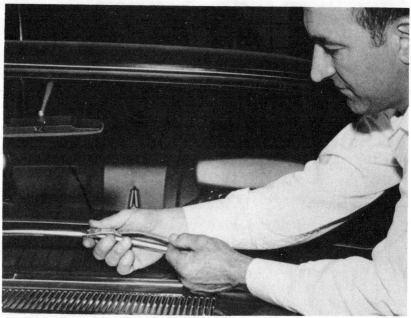

Figure 8. Make sure that windshield wiper blades are in good condition. Also check wiper arms. They should not be bent.

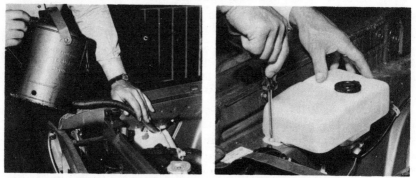

Figure 9 (left). Keep the windshield-washer reservoir filled.
Figure 10 (right). To clean out the windshield-washer reservoir, unscrew the container and pour fluid into clean container for reuse.

Figure 11 (left). Clean filter strainer in container with a brush.
Figure 12 (right). Many times a defroster doesn't work properly because its hose has become detached or damaged.

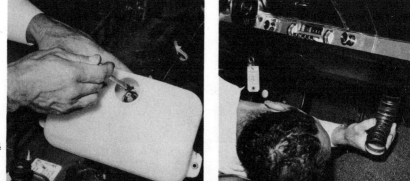

Windshield-washer fluid is available from service stations and automotive parts supply dealers.

Operate the washers. If the fluid just dribbles out instead of squirting out strongly, clean out the tube outlets carefully with a piece of wire. If this fails to get you a jet spray, remove the windshield-washer reservoir, pour its contents into a clean container (it can be reused), and clean off the strainer screen in the bottom of the reservoir or on the end of the delivery hose (Figures 10 & 11).

Make sure the defrosters work. If they don't, check hoses to see that they are connected properly and aren't split or torn (Figure 12).

They have to hear you

BLOW THE HORN. That is all you have to do to see if it is working. If the horn isn't working, pull off the connector at the horn and connect a test light to ground. Probe the connector while an assistant behind the wheel pushes the horn button (Figure 13).

If the test light glows, the horn itself has gone bad and should be replaced. If the test light fails to light, the problem is a faulty horn relay or the horn switch.

Disconnect the connector at the horn relay and probe it with the test

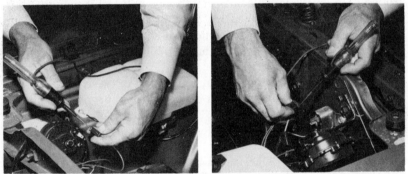

Figure 13 (left). Remove connector from horn, probe with test light. Figure 14 (right). Then check out the relay. This procedure will pinpoint the cause of the problem at horn, relay, or horn switch.

Figure 15 (left). Put sealer, clamp over leaking exhaust-system joint. Figure 16 (right). A safety inspection should always include an examination of wheel bearings, steering linkage, tires and brakes.

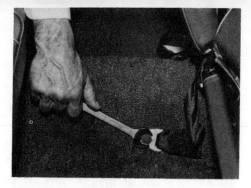

Figure 17. Safety belts won't hold you steady in an emergency if anchor bolts are loose. Tighten them.

light as your assistant presses the horn button (Figure 14). If the test light glows, the relay has gone bad and should be replaced. But if the test light does not glow, the horn ring should be pulled off and the steering wheel opened to get at the horn switch.

Get out and get under

YOUR SAFETY INSPECTION should now take you beneath the car to inspect the exhaust system for holes and rusting. Start the engine and examine the entire system for puffs of exhaust that indicate a leak. This quick inspection should take your eyes from the exhaust manifold-exhaust-pipe joint connection all the way back to the tailpipe.

Now, if no exhaust is evident, don't let it go at that. Put your hand around each joint. If it is leaking mildly you will feel it puffing.

You can try and seal a leaking joint by loosening the clamp and coating the joint with joint-connection sealer, which you can buy at an automotive parts supply store (Figure 15). Slide the clamp back on the joint and tighten it firmly.

Caution: Do not overtighten. You will distort or crush the pipe.

Turn off the engine and tap each exhaust-system part, especially the muffler, with the end of a wrench. The metal should "ring." If it gives a dull thud, it means that the system is failing and will soon have to be replaced.

Now raise the front wheels. Make sure they are solidly supported. Chock the rear wheels. Grasp each front wheel and shake.

If either wheel seems loose, wheel bearings may be loose or worn. Check the bearings as we discussed in chapter 14.

Inspect the steering linkage for looseness by grabbing each component in turn and shaking. This includes the idler arm, pitman arm, and tie-rod ends.

If there is any movement, the stability of the car is affected. Replace worn parts. Also check the condition of shock absorbers as we discussed in chapter 14.

Lower the car and test its brakes (see chapter 11) and tires (see chapter 13). Finally, examine safety belts. Make sure that buckles hold by giving each a quick firm pull when they are coupled.

Inspect each belt for broken or frayed fiber strands. This is the first sign that a belt is weakening. Replace it.

Give each belt a hard pull as you examine its anchor. If an anchor bolt is loose, tighten it (Figure 17).

Chapter 25

What to do when your exhaust system fails

The main job of the exhaust system is to carry away noxious carbon monoxide (CO). A system that is leaking cannot do its job, and, without your suspecting it, may be endangering you and your passengers.

IT IS VERY IMPORTANT for drivers to remember that when a part of a car's exhaust system fails it often does so without giving warning. A faulty system does not always make noise. Poisonous CO may be leaking from an exhaust system part without your knowledge, and the gas may be seeping into the car through holes and gaps in the body.

The only way to make absolutely certain that carbon monoxide is not endangering passengers is to conduct a visual examination of the system every six months. A typical exhaust system consists of several parts (Figure 1). Starting where carbon monoxide leaves the engine and proceeding toward the rear of the vehicle, those parts are as follows:

- **Exhaust pipe** (also called the header). The exhaust pipe is attached to the engine's exhaust manifold of six-cylinder in-line engines. In a V-8 engine with a single exhaust system, the exhaust pipe is in the form of a crossover. Exhaust gases are funneled from both banks of cylinders through two branches of the exhaust pipe into a common single pipe.

 In a V-8 engine with a dual exhaust system, two exhaust pipes are normally attached directly to the exhaust manifolds.

- **Exhaust extension.** An extension pipe may be used between the exhaust pipe and muffler. It is simply an extension of the exhaust pipe.

- **Muffler.** The muffler is the heart of the exhaust system. Its primary task is to muffle exhaust roar. It does this by funneling exhaust through a series of chambers which are separated by baffle plates and perforated tubes.

- **Resonator.** A resonator is nothing more than a small muffler which is designed to reduce the noise level of exhaust gases even further (Figure 2). Not every car is equipped with a resonator. In fact, only vehicles with large engines have them. A resonator may be positioned ahead of or behind the muffler.

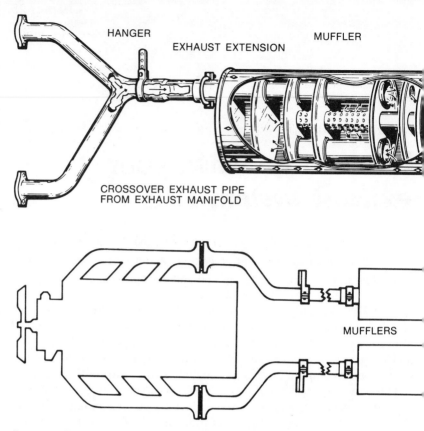

HANGER

MUFFLER

EXHAUST EXTENSION

CROSSOVER EXHAUST PIPE
FROM EXHAUST MANIFOLD

MUFFLERS

Figure 2. Resonators are small mufflers that further reduce exhaust-system noise. Here is a typical dual-exhaust system.

Figure 3. Finding and tightening loose hangers before they allow other parts to become damaged will save you money.

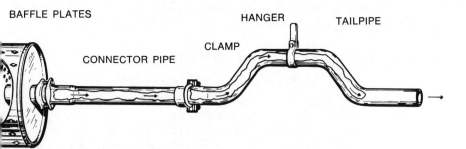

BAFFLE PLATES   HANGER   TAILPIPE

CLAMP

CONNECTOR PIPE

Figure 1. This drawing shows the usual parts of a typical single-exhaust system. Crossover exhaust pipe is used for V-8 engine.

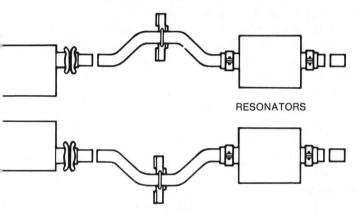

RESONATORS

• **Connector pipe.** Vehicles that have two-piece tailpipes and single mufflers will have a connector pipe. It is a pipe that allows the tailpipe to branch.

• **Tailpipe.** The tailpipe is the last part in the exhaust system. It is attached directly to the muffler, resonator or connector pipe, depending upon the style of the system. It allows exhaust gases to flow away from the car.

• **Hangers.** These parts hold other exhaust system parts securely to the undercarriage of the vehicle. They are usually made of a combination of metal and rubber, or metal and fabric. Hangers must be flexible to permit exhaust system parts to "give" with vehicle vibration, and to allow room for expansion and contraction which take place as parts alternately get hot and cool off. If hangers were not flexible, pipes and muffler would be damaged.

You have to be aware that hangers can break. When they do, parts flop around and can be damaged by banging against other parts of the vehicle or by dragging along the ground. A strange sound from beneath the car is a warning that a hanger may have snapped or has loosened sufficiently to let a part drag. Don't wait. Check the condition as soon as possible. You may save yourself the cost of having to buy a new part (Figure 3).

• **Clamps.** These parts, too, are critical components. They are positioned and tightened around other parts to seal the joints between them through which exhaust causes would otherwise escape.

How to inspect an exhaust system (Figure 4).

The muffler fails faster than any other part of the exhaust system, so this is the place to begin your inspection. Look for some form of damage, such as a hole or a split seam.

Interestingly enough, a muffler often fails from the *inside* out. Acid and vapors accumulate inside the chamber and rot it out. This is not to say that external factors cannot cause muffler failure. Road splash which possesses ice-melting salt spread on roads in winter is a major reason for muffler damage. The muffler is also subjected to hard knocks from flying rocks, high curbs, and steep driveways.

After examining the muffler closely for holes and seam damage, run your hand over the surface. If rust flakes off, you may not have to replace the part yet, but probably it will fail you soon. Rust is an indication that acid, vapors and road salt are eating metal away.

Take a wrench from your tool box and tap the muffler with it. A sound component will emit a ringing sound. If the part is defective and about to fail, it will issue a dull thud. In fact, if the component is on the verge of failure, you may pop a hole in it with the wrench.

After completing the muffler inspection, inspect the exhaust pipe flange-to-exhaust manifold connection. This can usually be done from inside the engine compartment.

Look for a white powdery substance around this joint. Deposits mean that the gasket sealing this joint has gone bad or that bolts holding the exhaust pipe to the manifold have loosened. Whatever the case, exhaust gases are escaping.

Try tightening bolts. If they are tight, then you should replace the gasket by disconnecting the exhaust pipe from the exhaust manifold (Figure 5). After inserting a new gasket, make sure that bolts are tightened as securely as possible.

Even if white deposits are not present, there is a possibility that exhaust gas is leaking from this joint. A sure way of telling is to start

Figure 4. This drawing shows several different types of exhaust-system failures to look for.

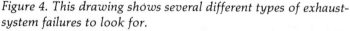
EXHAUST PIPE
FAILURE
CONNECTOR FLANGE
FAILURE

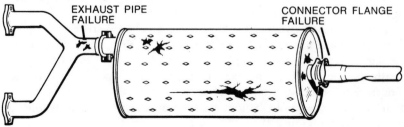

Figure 5. Before placing a new gasket on the exhaust pipe flange where it meets the exhaust manifold flange, clean both surfaces.

the engine and place your ear close to the connection. If you hear a popping noise, exhaust is leaking. Replace the gasket and/or tighten bolts.

Proceeding from the engine end of the exhaust system back to the rear of the car, closely inspect the surfaces of the exhaust pipe and exhaust extension, resonators if they are used, connector pipe, and tailpipe. A hole or crack in any part means that you should discard the part and replace it with a new one.

As you did when testing the muffler, run your hand over each part to see if rust flakes off. Also test parts by tapping them with a wrench.

Inspect hangers to make sure that they aren't on the verge of loosening or breaking.

Start the engine and look for puffs of exhaust smoke from parts and from around clamps. If a part is leaking, get rid of it. If exhaust is puffing from around a clamp, loosen the clamp and slide it off the joint. Spread exhaust-system sealing compound liberally around the joint.

Caution: Make certain that parts are cold before doing this.

Reposition the clamp over the joint and tighten securely, but take care not to overtighten. Coming down hard on a clamp could crush the pipe beneath.

Allow the sealing compound to set. Start the engine again and see if the joint is still puffing. If it is, get a new clamp. However, make certain that the rims of the parts beneath the clamp are in good condition. If they aren't, then the parts may have to be replaced.

The final test of the exhaust system is to check for a restriction. Restrictions can result when a baffle in the muffler loosens; when the ex-

Figure 6. Replacing an exhaust system is hard work. But it can usually be done in about four hours using ordinary workshop tools.

haust extension, tailpipe, or some other pipe collapses; when a tailpipe becomes plugged with foreign matter; or if the manifold heat control valve sticks in the closed position.

A restricted exhaust system leads to higher gasoline consumption, loss of engine power, and stalling. The way to determine if the exhaust system is restricted is to test vacuum at the intake manifold with a vacuum gauge.

With the gauge connected, accelerate and release the throttle rapidly. The gauge's needle should climb to about 24 inches as you accelerate and fall back to a normal 17 to 21 inches as you lift your foot off the accelerator. If this doesn't occur, look for a restriction.

Check the tailpipe first. Run a pry bar up it to ream out any foreign matter and to see if it has collapsed. If it has, you may be able to straighten the pipe with the pry bar.

Test the manifold heat control valve. If it is stuck, try loosening it by tapping with a hammer and lubricating liberally with manifold heat control lubricant.

Tap the muffler gently. If a baffle has come loose, you may hear it rattling. The muffler will have to be replaced if it is causing the restriction.

Should you make repairs yourself?

There is only one way to repair an exhaust system that is in bad shape and leaking. You have to replace faulty parts. The job is not an easy one, because it takes time and effort. However, it is not compli-

Figure 7. A hacksaw makes short work of an old exhaust system that you are going to replace in its entirety.

cated and doing it yourself can save you a lot of money (Figure 6).

If you decide to do the job (I suggest you check around first and determine how much repair shops want to charge), plan the procedure carefully before buying parts. Check off what you definitely need. For example, are parts reuseable? Are hangers in good condition? Don't buy what you don't need.

Caution: Work on the exhaust system with the engine *cold.* Exhaust-system parts get very hot when the engine is warm and can cause serious burns.

If the whole exhaust system has to be replaced, you don't have to be overly careful in removing parts. Use a hacksaw to disengage parts (Figure 7). If only one part of the system has to be replaced, you will have to work carefully to remove the part without damaging adjacent parts.

A difficult part of the job is removing bolts that are frozen. Apply liberal amounts of penetrating oil. If this doesn't work, you will have to use heat. A propane torch is relatively inexpensive and available in hardware stores. It should do the job.

As you install new parts, do not tighten connections. Wait until all components have been put into place. This means that you may have to support muffler and pipes as you work. Blocks of wood can serve as props.

Pipes are generally tapered so they slide into adjacent parts. Be sure to seat them all the way before putting clamps around them.

After you finish the work, drive the car several days. Then be sure that you retighten clamps and hangers. New parts have to set themselves to the heat conditions generated in the exhaust system. This often causes clamps and hangers to loosen as parts expand and contract.

Should you decide not to replace the exhaust system yourself, shop around for the best deal. Exhaust-system repair is a highly competitive business and prices for the same job frequently fluctuate significantly.

Protecting yourself from CO poisoning

One way to protect yourself and the occupants of your car from carbon monoxide poisoning is to seal off the passenger compartment from the exhaust system—just in case the system begins leaking. Examine the underside of the car's body and the engine firewall for holes. Look in the trunk, too. Throw back the rug.

If you see any rusted areas and holes, plug them with automotive body sealer, which is called dum-dum. If an area is rusted very badly and can't be sealed with dum-dum because the cavity is extensive, have a piece of galvanized metal welded over it.

Another way of protecting you and your passengers from CO is to recognize the warning signs of CO poisoning. They are headache or a throbbing in the head, roaring in the ears, nausea, rapid heartbeat, blurred vision, drowsiness, and confusion.

If you or someone else experiences any of these, stop the car at once and get into the open air. Breathe deeply. When you or the other person has recovered, open all the windows in the car and drive to a medical facility.

Let this serve as a warning that something is wrong with the exhaust system. Find and fix the problem before using the car.